Praise for *The World Is a Kitchen*

"A vicarious delight for the virtual tourist, as well as an inspiration for the most seasoned culinary voyager, this beautifully eclectic volume provides the richest vacation experience possible from the comfort of your armchair or your own kitchen."
—Mollie Katzen, author of *Moosewood Cookbook*

"A brilliant concept! A splendidly evocative book celebrating the culinary adventurer in each of us while constructing a magical international matrix of our mutual interests in food, cooking, and unique gastronomic creations. The essays are vibrant and vicariously seductive—the indigenous flavors and recipes lure us in deeply, deliciously, and even a little decadently. You are presented a multitude of home kitchens, restaurants, and cooking schools. You experience the mysterious alchemy of imaginative culinary concoctions; you share in the joy of fine food and creative cuisine and in the love that permeates every page. Could this be a key ingredient for world peace and harmony? If so—*mangia* and *buon gusto!*"
—David Yeadon, author of *The Way of the Wanderer: Discover Your True Self Through Travel*

"Seasoned with recipes and resources, this engaging collection of travel tales proves that food is a doorway into engaging and understanding other cultures. These stories offer an enticing sense of place as they explore the sense of taste worldwide."
—Rolf Potts, author of *Vagabonding: An Uncommon Guide to the Art of Long-Term Travel*

"Those who are passionate about food are in for a delicious treat dished up by Travelers' Tales in the form of this collection of culinary experiences. These appealing, first-hand adventures told by fellow culinary travelers stirred up fond recollections of several of my own experiences trying to capture the essence of a country through its cuisine. Doubtlessly many travelers who read this impressive book are apt to wonder how they ever poked around a country before, so clueless about its food and hence the cultural insight it provides."
—Joan Peterson, author of Eat Smart Culinary Travel Guides

"Generous, funny, wise and unpretentious—a mouth-watering assortment of culinary adventures from Mendocino to Vietnam, Senegal to the Basque Country."
—Andrew Todhunter, author of *A Meal Observed*

"Whatever your taste in reading, a feast awaits in this buffet of personal anecdotes."
—Andrea Rademan, International Food, Wine & Travel Writers Association, editor of *New Asian Cuisine*

The *World* Is a
KITCHeN

Cooking Your Way Through Culture
Stories, Recipes, Resources

Edited by
MICHELE ANNA JORDAN
AND SUSAN BRADY

Travelers' Tales
Palo Alto

Travelers' Tales and Travelers' Tales Guides are trademarks of Travelers' Tales, Inc.
853 Alma Street, Palo Alto, California 94301.

Art Direction: Stefan Gutermuth
Interior Design and page layout: Melanie Haage
Cover Photograph: Copyright © photocuisine / Corbis
Research/Editorial Assistant: Emilia Thiuri

Distributed by: Publishers Group West, 1700 Fourth Street, Berkeley, California 94710.

LIBRARY OF CONGRESS CATALOGING-IN-PUBLICATION DATA
The world is a kitchen : cooking your way through culture stories,
recipes, references / edited by Michele Anna Jordan and Susan Brady.
        p.   cm.
Includes bibliographical references and index.
ISBN-13: 978-1-932361-40-7 (pbk. : alk. paper)
ISBN-10: 1-932361-40-5 (alk. paper)
1. Cookery, International. 2. Tourism. 3. Food habits.
I. Jordan, Michele Anna. II. Brady, Susan, 1958-
TX725.A1W674 2006
641.59--dc22   2006017564

First Edition
Printed in the United States
10 9 8 7 6 5 4 3 2 1

Food is our common ground, a universal experience.

—JAMES BEARD

Table of Contents

Part Two — EUROPE

Part Three — AFRICA/MIDDLE EAST

Part Four — ASIA

Part Five — SOUTHEAST ASIA / OCEANA

Preface

by Michele Anna Jordan

There is no flavor called moon
although I feel as if I can taste it
cool, soft and powdery.
Tea-cookie, translucent jellybean, host.
Swallow her down
nibble by nibble
until you too glow.
Soon, people will stop
to lick your hands
and ask for the recipe.
——Lizzie Hannon, "A Night in My Kitchen"

Whether we travel to eat or eat to travel, when something tastes good we want more: We ask for seconds and sometimes thirds, we lick each other's fingers, we ask for the recipe. We carry the treasure home, in our hands and in our hearts, where we hope to recreate the magic.

I was lucky to have been born with an adventurous palate. My first memory of food on the road was the sweet ripe watermelon I ate on my fourth birthday in Tulsa, Oklahoma. A few days later, on the *California Zephyr* from Chicago to Oakland, I ate what I consider my formative meal, the one that that transformed me bite by bite from a passive into an active eater, one eager to discover and savor all the enticing flavors the world offers.

I was in the dining car, asleep in my mother's lap, when her complaints about rare prime rib awakened me. She'd ordered well done and did not know what to do.

I sat up, tasted the juicy red meat and then devoured the entire slab.

When we got home, I wanted more and I learned how to get it. I began to tell my mother how to cook—yes, I was a cheeky little thing—and I used smell and taste to find my way back to flavors I had discovered here and there, at my grandmother's house, in a friend's kitchen, in the neighborhood Chinese restaurant, in that silver dining car with the tuxedo-clad waiters. Soon, I could convince my mother to take me to San Francisco for Dungeness crab, to a farm stand on the outskirts of town that had the best tasting watermelon and juiciest plums, to an out-of-the-way deli for smoked salmon, smoked oysters, and good Italian salami. On my eighth birthday, I received my first cookbook.

Married at just sixteen, I defied all predictions that my husband would starve at the hands of his child bride. I cooked my way through *The White House Cookbook* by Rene Verdon, the Kennedys' chef, and figured out where to buy ingredients like fresh rosemary that were then all but impossible to find in suburban America. I learned my way around unfamiliar streets and aisles, guided by hunger and curiosity, invaluable tools for any culinary traveler.

With my first venture abroad, an accidental trip to India—I was on my way to Canada when a new acquaintance was so certain that I should go to India that he bought me a round-trip ticket to Bombay—I began to discover how intimately hospitality and the pleasures of the table are entwined in other cultures. A visitor, any visitor, was received with open arms and an abundant table filled with the best foods the family could afford. There was always rice, *dal*, sliced cucumbers and tomatoes, meat (usually goat) curry, vegetable curry, a dizzying array of condiments, including *raitas*, fresh and cooked chutneys, raisins, toasted nuts, coconut, and platters of huge papaya for dessert.

Soon, I was making *chapatis* in a rustic country kitchen with a tiny little woman named Mansari, a long silver braid stretching all the way down her back. As little birds flew in and out of the barred windows, we patted the dough into perfect rounds and cooked them on a hot grill until their aromas filled the air. Mansari sang one Beatles song after another, tunes she learned from young visitors. We spent each afternoon this way, wrapped in the rhythm of the patting and the melody of the songs as we sipped sweet *chai* and savored each other's company.

I was dazzled by the colors, aromas, and flavors of India but it took some time before my hosts—other than Mansari, who knew instinctively that we were eager to learn anything she wanted to teach us—would take my curiosity seriously. Yet by expressing my interest slowly and somewhat indirectly, often the best way to get what you want in a foreign land, I was able to get the cook who worked for the family with whom I was staying to understand my sincerity. Before long, she invited me into her kitchen and let me help as she toasted spices and roots, ground them into fine pastes and powders and stirred them into rich stews. All these years later I can return to that moment in a kitchen on the outskirts of Ahmednager, revisit the aromas and textures and bring them to my own table.

The world opened to me while I was in India and it has never closed. And always, it is the foods of any land that most entice me. I had never thought of what I do as culinary travel because to travel for any other purpose, to not immediately look for the best local trattoria in Genova, say, or the most delicious food stands in Kuala Lumpur's night market, is simply unthinkable. Within an hour of arriving in Paris for the first time, my bags were stashed in the tiny seventh floor walk-up where I was staying and I was happily ensconced in a bustling local bistro over a mound of steak tartare and a hot ramekin of *brandade de morue*. Before noon the next day, I had a recipe for that *brandade* tucked into my suitcase. I am, obviously, one of those lucky people who lives to eat.

It was inevitable, I think, that traveling for culinary adventures coalesce into the popular pursuit it is today. As Americans, we have become, in general, more adventurous when it comes to food. That there is now a chain of fast-food restaurants called Chipotle, after that delicious fiery smoked chile of Mexico, tells it all. As recently as the 1990s, it was almost impossible to find chipotles outside of Mexican communities. Just a generation ago it was difficult to find olive oil and today we travel to Italy to see the olives harvested and to search for the most flavorful oils.

Americans still have a reputation among hotel managers around the world for wanting our own food when we travel, a preference we share with Japanese tourists, but increasingly we are venturing away from bacon, eggs, and cereal for breakfast and Big Macs for lunch and dinner and discovering the joys of *jook*, *tagines*, and *tapas*.

Cooking has become the universal language, an international tongue that allows us to communicate, to resolve every cultural challenge, be it language, custom or belief, and even overcome personal inhibitions like shyness and insecurity. We take a bite, smile, and raise our eyes to see the same response in our companions. *May I have some more, please?*

And you know what comes next: *How did you make it?*

We lick each other's fingers and ask for the recipe.

Introduction

by Susan Brady

*T*he *World Is a Kitchen* was five years in the making, but the concept was formulated, quite unknowingly, fourteen years ago before culinary tourism had become the popular pursuit it is today. I was hired by a nascent travel publishing company—Travelers' Tales—to help produce its first book, but not having traveled much in my life, I seemed an odd choice for the job. My skills, however, complemented those of my two world-wandering bosses, and working on our first book, *Travelers' Tales Thailand,* helped bring alive an unfamiliar country for me. But something was missing. Having never been to Asia was an obstacle, until I found *the* article. Written by Kemp Minifie in *Gourmet*, it was about a cooking school in Bangkok. She wrote that "one of the most vivid pleasures of travel to Thailand is the cuisine" and proceeded to seduce with preparation of dish after dish, eloquently describing smells, sights, sounds, tastes. I had found my connection. I went out and bought my first Thai cookbook, *The Taste of Thailand* by Vatcharin Bhumichitr, which has some wonderful stories as well as recipes. I read about unusual produce and regional foods, and started testing dishes. I felt like an alchemist in the kitchen with all these new ingredients and spices, the mixing, the preparation. The end product was bright, vivid, and full of flavors that tantalized my tastebuds. I was hooked.

To celebrate the publication of that first book, I cooked a huge Thai meal. And subsequent books received the same treatment. India, Spain, Nepal, France, Mexico, Italy…the list goes on. I was able to better understand and to connect to a country and its culture through the indigenous food. And, there was, of course, the side benefit of getting to eat really wonderful things, not just in celebration, but this type of cooking entered my everyday life. My children grew up eating curries and moles and cassoulets, with only the occasional meatloaf thrown in.

In the last five years I have begun to travel, and no matter whether it is to Erie, Pennsylvania, or Taipei, Taiwan, my focus on every trip is the food. Sometimes I am fortunate enough to go to a cooking school, like I did at the Oriental Cooking School in Bangkok, the Boathouse Cooking School in Phuket, and the New Orleans Cooking Experience in Louisiana. Oftentimes I focused on country specialties, like chocolate in Belgium and the Chinese- and Japanese-influenced regional cuisines throughout Taiwan. When a destination did not have a remarkable cuisine, I sought out unusual restaurants or stores, like La Buona Tavola in Seattle, which specializes in truffle-based foodstuffs and small vineyard Italian wines. Everywhere I went, I found common ground when food was the focus of conversation. Street food vendors gladly showed me how things were cooked, waiters went into lengthy descriptions of ingredients of a particular dish, spice sellers were happy to enlighten me as to how to use the *mahlab* fourteen different ways. Food brings out the best in people, and while people in many cultures may be shy or unused to sharing themselves, they have no qualms rambling on about the regional specialties, their mother's famous dish, or even inviting you home for a meal. And some of the best teachers are in the home, as this book illustrates.

I now consider myself a culinary traveler, seeing the world through its food. I have found out that I was not alone in this endeavor. According to recent articles in *Business Week, The Seattle Times,* and MSNBC, the trend toward culinary travel is increasing. *Cooking Light* has expounded the virtues of culinary vacations and Margo True, the Executive Editor of *Saveur,* traveled and learned firsthand what "no TV cook or book could tell her," while making strudel in Vienna and rolling *yufka* in Turkey. And I can attest to hands-on learning. It is something that alerts all the senses: seeing and touching the exotic ingredients, hearing them sizzle and pop in a pan, smelling the fragrant aromas, tasting the unique flavors. When you use all five senses, your memory recall is better and duplicating recipes at home is easier than checking out a cookbook from the library and having a go blindly. Stepping into another kitchen can be intimidating, but oh so worthwhile.

Taking the next step can be difficult. But more and more people are traveling these days and finding that the world is a friendly place. Given the proliferation of cooking shows and rise in popularity of food and cooking magazines, there's little doubt that curiosity toward foreign cuisine is at an all-time high. Culinary travel gives us the opportunity to create bridges between people and cultures, and allows us glimpses into worlds previously unseen. And what marvelous worlds they are.

We have tried to combine first-person experiences of cooking in a foreign land, delicious recipes for you to recreate, and a resource section covering books, magazines, cooking schools, and culinary tours.

In the five sections of this book you will find connections and a direction for your next adventure. Will it be in Cyprus? Thailand? Ghana? France? New Orleans? Will you, like Eileen Hodges Sonnad, learn that it is a privilege to serve food to those you love, if it is done with love, in "First, the Mustard Seeds"? When planning that next trip, our Resource Section can help guide you to find the right tour, class, or school to fit your needs. Or maybe you will enter someone's home through serendipity, like Celeste Brash does in "Mama Rose's Coconut Bread" and find that where a language barrier exists, words become irrelevant as time is passed, working towards the same goal, and a bond can be created that is like none other. Like Augusto Andres, you will come to realize that the *how* is not as important as the *why* while "In the Kitchen with Yuyo." It could be that you will test a recipe, such as the *mafe* in the story "A Scandal in Senegal," and will decide that Africa is the place to go. No matter where it is that this book leads you, we agree with Helen Gallagher, who in "Flavor by the Spoonful," finds that food is the soul of good travel.

The stories included in this collection serve to show just a small portion of culinary experiences abroad to help steer you in a direction that will make you, and your stomach, happy. Along with these great real-life experiences the Resource section will help you take the next step and venture out into the world of culinary travel.

PART ONE

THE AMERICAS

AUGUSTO ANDRES

In the Kitchen with Yuyo

The author experiences a rare moment of alchemy.

It is a mild afternoon in Morelia and warm streams of sunlight filter in from the open-air courtyard of the house, brightening Yuyo's kitchen. Although I've been in this room many times, I've never really taken a good look around and a part of me is disappointed by what's not here. I admit to having some romantic notions of the Mexican kitchen. I picture beautifully decorated clay pots bubbling over with savory *pozoles,* an oversized copper kettle simmering *frijoles de la olla,* a sturdy hand-fired *comal* roasting deep-red *chiles anchos.* On the countertop of blue-and-white tiles from Puebla, I see an aged *molcajete,* the secrets of previous generations ground into the well-worn basalt *tejote.*

But Yuyo's kitchen is stocked instead with all the conveniences of a modern Mexican household: a pressure cooker for the beans, a high-powered blender for perfectly pureed salsas, a cast-iron skillet for frying *quesadillas.* Yuyo shows off her new nonstick cookware. It makes sense that she'd find ways to make cooking less of a chore, especially since she heads a household of eight boys and four girls. Throw in sons- and daughters-in-law and grandchildren and some days there are more than twenty mouths to feed. But I brush aside my momentary disappointment, grateful for the chance to spend a few hours in the kitchen with Yuyo learning to cook from this woman who certainly knows a thing or two about Mexican cuisine.

I first came to Morelia more than ten years ago to learn Spanish. During my summer here, I befriended Yuyo's youngest son Pablo, who at the time worked as a guide for the language school I attended, and was the first person I met in Mexico. On his way to Mexico City to meet me and accompany me back to Morelia, the bus he was riding veered off the road and crashed into a shallow, muddy lake. No one was seriously injured, but when Pablo entered the lobby of the Hotel Reforma, his cream-colored jacket, light-gray pants, and white sneakers were smeared with large splotches of dried mud. Despite his appearance, Pablo greeted me with a smile and a warm "Welcome to Mexico." During our bus ride to Morelia, Pablo's outward confidence and friendly demeanor melted. Shaken and unnerved by the harrowing events of the morning, he clearly needed to talk. Between his broken English and my rudimentary Spanish we somehow managed conversations about life, death, fear, mortality, the possibility of an afterworld, and fate. I spent my first night in Morelia in Pablo's living room, sipping Yuyo's hot *champurrado* with his brothers and beginning a friendship that has endured despite the burdens of time and distance. Yuyo likes to think of my friendship with her son as destiny.

Since that first summer I have returned to Morelia as often as possible. Even if I visit Mexico and my primary destination is elsewhere, I manage to make my way back to Morelia. Recently, I went to the port city Veracruz on the Gulf of Mexico to celebrate Carnaval.

After a few days of excess and revelry, I stumbled onto a bus and didn't wake from my stupor until I had arrived fourteen hours later at Pablo's house where Yuyo's spicy and bracing *menudo* nursed me back to sobriety and reality. I remember telling Yuyo then that I would return one day so that she could teach me all of her cooking secrets.

Now, Yuyo approaches, shaking her head disapprovingly. I'm at small table in the corner of her kitchen, furiously jotting down everything that transpires on a legal pad. She wipes her hands on her white apron and adjusts the pins that hold her silver-white hair in a tight bun.

"The secret to cooking you can't write down," she says, taking away my pad and pencil.

I protest mildly, insisting that I have to write things down or else I'll forget something important later. I don't want to blunder the same way my friend Suzanne did when she made her first marinara sauce. She thought a clove of garlic meant the entire head. But Yuyo is patient. "*No te preocupes*," she says. Don't worry. "I learned by watching my mother. You watch me."

Yuyo lays a few *chiles poblanos* onto a cast-iron skillet and toasts them carefully. We char the chiles, turning them until their skins are covered with black blisters, then we place them in paper bags. Before I can ask her how long we'll keep them inside, Yuyo turns my attention to the Dutch oven where chicken pieces braise in a mixture of garlic, olive oil, and red wine vinegar. Yuyo hands me marjoram, thyme, bay leaves, and a *chile serrano*. I add them to the pot. The sharp smells that jump out at me slowly mellow and meld into a potent, unusually fragrant and earthy aroma that smells nothing like any Mexican food I've had before. Sensing my curiosity about the dish, Yuyo answers the question in my head.

I suggest to anyone deciding to travel to befriend a local who will invite you into their home and cook for you. Margarita consoled me with food and also wisdom. Nights when I couldn't sleep for homesickness or altitude sickness I would stay up talking to her. She would respond with ghost stories or stories of how she learned to cook from nuns in Catholic school. I not only received a crash course in Chilean cooking, I learned a fair amount of Chilean history as well. The relationships one makes with the locals and the food make all the difference for a traveler.

—Heidi Schmaltz, "Life in a Chilean Kitchen"

"*Pollo en cuñete*," she says and nothing more. I nod. Chicken something, I translate in my head, remembering only later that "*cuñete*" means clay pot. When I ask her how she adapted the recipe without the clay pot, Yuyo ignores the question and asks me to make sure the *caldo* on the back burner is not boiling. Inside the stockpot is chicken broth steaming with garbanzo beans, carrots, garlic, onion, *epazote*, and smoky *chiles chipotles*. I have trouble adjusting the stove settings and the *caldo* comes to a roiling boil.

"It's still boiling, Señora," I say, a slight hint of panic in my voice. We've only begun cooking and already I'm afraid I've ruined the meal.

"Ay, Augusto," Yuyo says with a sigh. She presses her fingers to the lines on my forehead and chuckles slightly. "These will become permanent unless you stop worrying."

"But I want everything to turn out perfect," I say.

Yuyo smiles, pats my arm, and turns the knob on the gas range. The flame subsides and the bubbling *caldo* settles down into a slow, gentle simmer.

"You could burn everything and the boys would still eat it," she says. "What matters most to them is that you're here with us."

As we talk, I watch Yuyo go through the motions of preparing ingredients. She starts a task, then hands it to me; I simply imitate what I've seen. It's a curious cooking demonstration, not unlike watching a Saturday morning cooking show with the TV volume on mute. My mind races with questions; I don't feel like I'm really learning how to do things because Yuyo doesn't talk me through the steps or give me directions. I yearn momentarily for the wild and colorful antics of Emeril Lagasse. Even the carefully paced, measured narration of Martha Stewart would be welcome right now—at least she is thorough and describes every important step. But over the next few hours, Yuyo and I don't talk about food, or recipes, or anything remotely related to cooking. She never divulges any culinary secrets. She never describes her technique for stuffing chiles, never explains the varied uses of the herb *epazote*, and doesn't bother to say how she makes the *chicharrón* that flavors her guacamole. Instead, we take this nostalgic walk down memory lane, swapping stories about our families, our friends, and our lives.

My frustration with Yuyo mounts; for an instant, I regret not taking a "real" cooking class where I could get actual recipes or more specific training in culinary skills and techniques. Before I can scold myself for such a lack of gratitude, Yuyo has another task for me. She sets up an assembly line of sorts on the counter. I stuff a mixture of rice, onions, diced squash, and bits of *queso manchego* in the *chiles poblanos* we'd roasted earlier. Then I dip each one into a light batter and Yuyo

> Epazote *(chenopodium ambrosiodes) is an herb regularly used in both Mexican and Caribbean cooking. Easily grown in home gardens throughout North and South America,* epazote *is a carmative and acts as an anti-gas agent. Consequently, it is a frequent flavoring in beans, as well as* moles.
>
> —SB

fries them with oil in the cast-iron skillet. Under her watchful eyes, I take over the cooking completely.

"You've learned a lot today," she says. "The boys will be impressed."

Hiding my disappointment, I flash her a grin, hoping it conveys a sense of humility and gratitude, even though I'm resigned to the fact that a real cooking class in a more authentic Mexican kitchen will have to wait.

At quarter to two in the afternoon, the family begins filing into the house. Ricardo returns from the family *panadería*, his shirt dusted with flour. He sneaks into the kitchen, grabs a tortilla, dips it into the beans and snoops around for something else to snack on. Yuyo shoos him out. Felipe comes in, sets his books down, kisses Yuyo on the cheek, and takes a stack of plates from the cupboard into the dining room. As if on cue, Luis and Carlos emerge with bowls and silverware to help set the table. Pablo and Miguel enter from the courtyard and greet me with a hearty *abrazo*. Together we carry out the last serving bowls, utensils, and platters of food. This is a well-oiled machine, the product of practiced routines that have long since become habit. Yuyo's husband Martín appears shortly and everyone takes his place at the table.

There are nine of us for the *comida* today. Yuyo graciously announces to her family that they have me to thank for cooking the meal. A pause follows. Miguel glances at Carlos who looks across to Ricardo. Felipe puts down his fork. Luis stops chewing his tortilla. Pablo pushes his chair away from the table, stands with lips pursed, says in his heavily accented English, "Eh, I am not hungry anymore," and starts to walk away. Another brief moment of silence. I feel my heart stop. Then, he turns, looks at me, a wry, mischievous smile spread across his face. Simultaneous strains of "Ayyyy!" and bursts of laughter erupt from the table. I should have seen it coming, but I always fall for Pablo's jokes. A chorus of "thank you" and "*gracias*" and "¡*provecho*!" fills the room and everyone digs in.

We start together with the *caldo tlalpeño*, dividing shredded chicken, diced tomatoes, and avocado chunks into soup bowls; next we ladle in the smoky, chipotle-flavored broth, and finish with a generous squeeze of *limón*. After the soup, the "order" of the meal falls away—everyone moves on to a different dish. Luis and Felipe take crisp-fried tortillas and stack them with *frijoles*, dark meat strips of the braised *pollo en cuñete*, potatoes, salsa, Yuyo's guacamole, and top each unusual tostada with a dollop of Mexican *crema* and crumbled *queso fresco*. Ricardo layers sliced plantains on a bed of white rice, flavored simply with *chiles serranos*, garlic, and parsley. Pablo and Miguel cut into the *chiles rellenos* and the savory filling spills out onto their plates. In between bites and slurps and finger licking, the family doles out compliments. Carlos asks me where I learned to cook. Ricardo asks if I want a job in the bakery. Señor Martín jokes that if I stick around and cook, Yuyo will have nothing to do. We laugh and we eat, going back and forth between dishes, scooping up every last bit, clearing every platter.

Halfway through the meal, I look around the table and experience a moment of alchemy. Watching everyone eat, I slowly understand what Yuyo and I did together in the kitchen. In my time with her, I kept waiting for Yuyo to reveal some nugget of wisdom, some secret to Mexican cooking that I could take back with me and replicate at home. I wanted an experience rooted in an imagined sense of authenticity or romance, something worth boasting about. I could say that I learned to cook from a real Mexican grandmother in a real Mexican kitchen, and everyone would want to know the secrets I gleaned from her. Maybe there are secrets to cooking, some bit of magic that can turn the ordinary into the sublime. But it doesn't really matter. I can always read a Diana Kennedy cookbook, experiment with ingredients, master some technique by watching the Emerils, or Marthas, or Julias of the world. But in Yuyo's kitchen, I realize, *how* is not nearly as important as *why*.

Here are my friends, eating food that Yuyo and I have created together, from ingredients I helped prepare, the result of hours of care, respect, and attention. There is a current of humor and affection, a kind of joy that comes with the closeness of family sharing a meal together at the dinner table. Although I am a guest and an outsider, they envelop me in their warmth and humble me with their generosity. Another look around the table reminds me why I return to them again and again.

Yuyo catches my gaze and smiles, her expression as warm as the afternoon Morelia sun that angles into the room through the courtyard. "Look at what you've made," she says.

I smile at her and pull my chair in a little closer to the table.

Augusto Andres spends his time dreaming about adventures in far-off places, cooking, listening to jazz, and searching for the perfect burrito. In between, he teaches history to high school students and writes about education, food, and travel. He lives in San Francisco.

Caldo Tlalpeño
(Chicken Vegetable Soup)

Serves 4

1 four-pound chicken, cut into serving pieces

1 white onion, peeled and chopped

2 garlic cloves, finely minced

2 chipotles in adobo, chopped

½ cup cilantro leaves

3 quarts water or chicken stock

½ pound carrots, peeled and sliced

1 pound green beans, cut into 1-inch pieces

½ pound zucchini, sliced

2 ears corn, cut into four pieces

1 avocado, sliced

salt

Put chicken, onion, garlic, chipotles, cilantro, and salt (to taste) in a large stockpot with 3 quarts water or stock. Bring to a boil, lower the heat to medium and simmer for 1 hour or until chicken is completely cooked through and tender. Remove skin from chicken. Add carrots and cook for 10 minutes. Add beans, zucchini, and corn and cook another 10 minutes.

To serve, place a piece of chicken, a piece of corn, and some vegetables in each bowl, ladle in some broth, and top with sliced avocado.

A World Without Latkes

The author finds continuity and history in a simple dish.

On a flight to Chicago I settled into my seat located on the left side of the plane, on the aisle. I was looking forward to a good solid block of reading time. A steady stream of people bumped their way down the aisle, finding seats, looking for carry-on luggage space. A lady with a Nordstrom bag smiled at me. "Oh, thank you," she said as I stood out of her way. She slipped across my row to the window seat. "So many people have no manners these days, thank you." I slid her bag into the overhead storage.

Plumpish, not fat, her face was round with hints of wrinkles next to her mouth and eyes. She wore an exercise suit that was dark blue with large white stripes on the jacket. The material was of some crinkly, shiny fabric. Beneath the jacket she wore a dark red blouse. A thin gold chain flashed around her neck, diamond studs glittered on her ears. She wore white tennis shoes. Practical traveling wear; the effect was fancy casual.

She settled into her seat and I back into mine. "Good morning," she said.

Trying not to be too friendly and displaying my book, "Good morning," I said; but I couldn't help but smile as I saw her perched next to the window, wiggling to get comfortable before take off.

"My name is Esther." Her right hand was undeniable as she grabbed just the fingers of my right hand.

"I'm Bob." I got the feeling that the next four hours were not going to be my own.

"Would you like a Tic Tac?" she offered. As I declined she began a monologue. She'd been out visiting her daughter in San Jose, California. "Where do you live Bob?... Campbell? Is that nearby?" She was on her way home now. She'd had to take a taxi; the daughter and son-in-law were at work; she didn't mind. "You're going to Chicago on business? Oh, training for your company."

It wasn't a frantic jabber, but a kind of continuous chatter. Like air is for breathing, for Esther, words were always in her mouth. "I transfer in Chicago. My home is in Allentown, Pennsylvania..." She told me about her husband, Jerry. He owned a small furniture store; he was always working; she didn't mind.

Being curious and courteous, I had been looking at her over my left shoulder. "Oh, Esther, I have to turn away. I have a cramp in my neck," I said.

"That's O.K." she said and continued on. She'd left a week's worth of dinners frozen for Jerry. "He'll eat the meatloaf and the latkes," she said "but he won't touch the casseroles."

"Latkes?" I asked. I had heard of them, but I wasn't quite sure what they were. Like one of those words you vaguely know in context, but when asked to define you are at a loss. So was I with latkes.

"Latkes?" she looked slightly incredulous and bemused. "A simple dish, really, made from nothing. A treat. They're a traditional Chanukah dish. Pancakes, that's all they are. *Latke* means *pancake* in Yiddish. They are made with potatoes, onions, salt and pepper, or just about anything else you want to throw in. Fried golden brown, topped with sour cream and applesauce.

> For many Jewish families, Hanukkah, the Festival of Lights, is an eight-day holiday that is all about food—especially food cooked in oil. Oil symbolizes the rededication of the Temple in Jerusalem twenty-one centuries ago. Traditions include lighting candles, playing dreidel, and opening gifts for eight nights. It's a wonderful time to spend with family and friends, eating food typical of the holiday: latkes (potato pancakes), soofganiyot (deep-fried donuts), matzoh ball soup, kugel, chopped liver, beef brisket, or braised chicken.
>
> —Lisa S. Bach, "Oh, Hanukkah"

They're like a dessert. A world without latkes is a world without light." As she spoke a look of great distance and time came over her face.

Even though my neck hurt like hell there was something more I wanted to find out about Esther and latkes. What was that look about? Stretching and rubbing my neck I asked, "So tell me, Esther, about latkes and light."

"Would you like to know?" one eyebrow arched. "Oh, I should be cooking them for you. Some people, they're such purists they won't change a thing. True, there are certain stages...well, if you don't do them right the latkes won't turn out as good; but you can do lots of different things too.

"Start with potatoes. Everybody has potatoes. In the old days that's all you had to eat. My mother, God rest her soul, always insisted you grate the potatoes with the small holes on the grater, and the onions with the large holes. But I've used a food processor and it works just fine. Into a bowl first grate onions then potatoes, then onions, then potatoes, and so on. You do this so the potatoes don't turn brown. A little lemon juice doesn't hurt either. Let as much water as possible into a bowl. This is key, the less water the better. After a while a sediment will settle into the bottom of the bowl. Pour off the water, and add the sediment back into the potatoes and onions."

Esther was so animated telling me her recipe I could almost see her bustling about in her kitchen. I imagined the phone to her ear. Talking, talking, talking as she grated, poured, and squeezed. Maybe a neighbor sat at the kitchen table drinking tea and kibitzing.

"The traditional way, Mama always insisted, is to add flour or matzoh meal, a couple of slightly beaten eggs, salt and pepper, and that's all. Then you just fry them up quick as that. Aaaahh, but what is life without a little spice. Look around your kitchen. Aunt Birdie used to add bits of mushrooms and a little garlic."

I nodded my head thinking that anything else you could do to potatoes would probably be good on latkes. Nodding my head helped relieve the cramp in my neck.

"Aunt Birdie?" I asked.

"Mama's youngest sister, her name was Bertha. But my sisters and I called her Birdie. She was small and used to eat little amounts, a cracker, a piece of cheese, a slice of apple all throughout the day. She was always eating but she never gained a pound. We were never allowed to call her Birdie. It was our private name for her. Now it doesn't matter."

"No, why not?" I asked.

"They've passed on. My sisters, too. They're all gone now," she said.

"I'm sorry." My apology seemed not enough, but it was the best I could do.

"It's O.K.," she said. "It was all a long time ago."

We sat quietly for a while. I had recently lost my mother to cancer. Our respective losses, except for time, seemed the same. "How much flour should I use with how many potatoes and onions?" I asked.

"Portions smortions, who knows from portions. It's been so long since I looked at a recipe. Use three or four potatoes, one onion, one slightly beaten egg and one half cup flour until mixed up it looks like applesauce, salt and pepper to taste. Then add whatever spice you like. Parsley is good. Garlic, basil, and parmesan gives you a real pesto flavor."

"I like pesto," I said thinking pine nuts would be good in them also. "What about cooking them?"

"To cook them first heat your pan, then add one-quarter inch of oil. Use good vegetable oil. This is how latkes are connected to Chanukah. Oil is light."

"Oil?" I asked.

"Yes, Chanukah is the celebration of a great Maccabean victory that rescued Judaism from annihilation. Judah the Maccabee celebrated the victory by lighting the lamps of a great menorah. In those days their lamps were fueled by oil. So heat your oil, medium high heat, spoon out and flatten a latke, a few minutes on each side, until golden brown. That's all it takes."

She continued telling about this person or that relative that had used zucchini, sweet potatoes, or dill with cucumber/yogurt sauce. As she talked she rocked ever so slightly forward and back as if in prayer. Her words were ginger, cinnamon, nutmeg, and thyme, but her voice was something else.

The flight hadn't seemed half over and we were being told to prepare for landing. As I packed my unread book away... "Bob, would you like a Tic Tac?"

"Why yes I would, Esther."

The candy box was in her left hand. As she reached across the empty seat between us, her sleeve inched up her forearm. There, tattooed in black were a series of numbers from a time long ago, a time without latkes.

As we departed the plane, I said, "When I get home I'll make your latkes, Esther."

"*Kaddishel*, Bob," she responded, "*Kaddishel*."

I was to learn later that a Jewish son is affectionately referred to as "my *Kaddish*," the one who will say Kaddish, the Jewish prayer for the dead, for me.

Bob Golling is a U.S. Navy veteran of the Vietnam War and a retired telephone engineer. He no longer travels on business. He does practice his culinary skills every day on his sons.

Latkes

3 medium russet potatoes   1 teaspoon baking soda
1 large onion   ½ teaspoon salt
1 egg (slightly beaten)   pepper to taste
½ cup all purpose flour   ½ cup vegetable oil, as needed

Peel and grate the potatoes and onions alternately into a bowl. Press out as much liquid as possible and reserve the starchy sediment at the bottom of the bowl. Return the sediment to the mixture. Add the egg, flour, baking powder, salt, and pepper. Mix ingredients until it looks like applesauce. Spoon drop and flatten into medium high oil in fry pan. Fry until golden brown on both sides (2-3 minutes). Serve immediately with sour cream and applesauce.

Moqueca Feast

A Brazilian recipe for lovers.

The first time I saw Isabele Silveira passing the hostel in Bahia, Brazil, I thought about beauty and about the ocean, while certainly not thinking about cooking. And who could blame me? The dark, thin girl was carrying a surfboard on her head, heading for the beach. I thought that my son would have thought she was pretty, but I was alone.

That night, I had *moqueca*, the Bahian fish stew, for dinner.

It is not my habit to inquire after the cook or ask for recipes. When I travel, I enjoy the distance from my kitchen. But that *moqueca* was too perfect to be ignored. The sauce was hot, salty, and slightly sweet, the fish was just right—not too raw but not overcooked—and the vegetables enhanced the natural flavor. I couldn't resist, and I asked to see the cook.

It took me a moment to recognize the girl I had seen that morning. Her long black hair was now tucked under a white cap and her efficient movements had no trace of her swinging walk.

"I wanted to thank you. Your *moqueca* is incredible," I told her.

"Thank you, *senhora*. It's my favorite dish," she said. Her name was Isabele

"The pumpkin filled with shrimp the other table had looked great, too."

"But *moqueca* is for lovers," she laughed.

Now it seemed even better. "Is the recipe a secret?" I asked.

She looked around her with a gleam in her eyes. "You want to share it with a lover?"

I laughed. "If I can get it right, I promise you I would."

"Come tomorrow," she said and winked.

I waved at her the next morning, when she passed by. That time, I was thinking with anticipation about the culinary adventure.

In the evening, I joined her inside the kitchen. She seemed rather happy to have company. It was a modest kitchen in a small hostel, and the two waiters were serving the tables.

She mixed two spoons of Dende oil with hot spices she chopped expertly: three cloves of garlic, one green pepper, and three sprigs of cilantro, then added a spoon of vinegar to the mixture, while explaining that the hot taste should catch "him" up at his chest.

With a patient movement of her fingers, she peeled a tomato skin, squeezed the tomato to a paste and added it to the mixture.

In the meantime, she also heated a coconut, hit it with a hammer, poured its water through the hole into a bowl and grated the meat out of the shell. She poured half a glass of water into it, and let it into the bowl as well. Then, she filtered it all through a cloth, to prepare a cup of coconut milk. "The coconut milk should ease his fiery sensation," she said, smiling.

She mixed all the ingredients, and cooked them in a large pan, adding a bit of salt and a bit of pepper. After a few minutes, she arranged the haddock fish filets on it.

The rice was steaming in another pan, and the scent was making me hungry.

"Now you can eat, and then go home to your lover," she sent me out of the kitchen, pouring the sauce on the fillets.

Two days later I went home, indeed, for a nice *moqueca* feast.

Isabele knew what she was talking about.

Avital Gad-Cykman is from Israel, but has lived in Brazil for the past several years. Her work has been published in Glimmer Train, Happy, Prism International, Imago, AIM, Nemonymous, Raven Chronicles, BigNews, Wild Strawberries, *and* Snow Monkey, *as well as online in* Salon, In-Posse Review, Zoetrope All-Story Extra, Salt Hill Review, Carve Magazine, Pindeldyboz, Vestal Review, Absinthe Literary Review, *and* 3am.

Moqueca de Peixe
Bahian Fish Stew

Serves 4-6

2 pounds white fish fillets: cod, scrod, haddock, flounder

2 tablespoons dende oil or ¼ cup of olive oil

3 garlic cloves, finely chopped

1 green pepper, chile or bell pepper, seeded and chopped

1 medium onion, chopped

1 medium tomato, peeled and chopped

1 teaspoon vinegar

1 cup coconut milk

3 sprigs cilantro

1 teaspoon salt

fresh-ground pepper

Heat the oil in a large, heavy pan. Add the garlic, pepper, onion, and cilantro, stirring occasionally. Cook until onion is soft. Squeeze the tomato to a paste and add it to the mixture. Heat through. Add the vinegar and coconut milk to the mixture. Add salt and pepper and cook for 5 minutes on medium heat. Add fish fillets and allow to simmer covered for 5 minutes or until fish is done. Serve immediately, with white rice.

Tastes of Generosity

Immortalizing family recipes.

Spanish verbs run amok in my brain. My husband Jim and I are only two weeks into a three-month commitment to learn Spanish in Oaxaca, Mexico. I suggest a getaway day to explore the food of this region where at least fifteen indigenous groups contribute to its diversity. We get lucky. A call to local cooking diva Susana Trilling of *Seasons of My Heart* fame results in a journey into the secrets of Oaxacan cooking. Now our teacher sits in the front seat of the van, her long black braid brushing the top of my knees.

Her driver weaves through city traffic where blaring horns and exhaust fumes pollute the air. Soon our intimate group views the rural outskirts of the colonial city. Expectations are high as the three other Americans chat about the two days they have already spent with Susana. I listen to their enthusiasm and eagerly await a calm day in her cooking school kitchen. I intend to watch, listen, eat, and grab a fistful of recipes to take home.

Susana gives us a sketch of her past sixteen years living in the valley of Oaxaca. Her Mexican grandmother introduced her to the wonders of complex spices and recipes while growing up in the United States. Now, she shares recipes from the women who welcome her into their homes to eat and cook together. The collection of knowledge from all seven regions of the state of Oaxaca comes together at her school, where students begin to understand the value of food passed on through generations.

We anticipate our first stop at the house of Dominica in the village of Etla. The menu here includes *atole*, a chocolate-corn drink, fresh country cheese, and more. Inside the slatted wood fence, Dominica's house sits open to a courtyard of dirt where chickens, sheep, and goats roam freely with a resident dog. She leads us to the back where her husband works a shovel, leveling the dirt for a pile of cement bricks that will partition a now-open room. A white votive candle illuminates a religious icon, fake greenery, and a small vase of dusty plastic pink roses. This is the family altar, a private nook, yet not closed to us. It's as if we're old friends.

A cheerful yellow-and-red oilcloth covers the long wooden table where our attention focuses on Dominica and her punch bowl. I recognize the green glaze that coats the vessel as being from the village of Atzompa. She pours a milky corn liquid into it and begins the whipping of the drink we are about to taste. We all take turns twirling the *molinillo*. I feel the worn wooden handle spin between the palms of my hands. Froth climbs the bowl now, mixing with a smidgeon of chocolate. None of us wants to be the first to take a sip. In unison, we share the moment by raising our mugs. It's clear this hospitable moment matches the recipe's original intention. Figuratively, we've stepped on a welcome mat that embraces both of our cultures.

A young girl around eight sidles up to her grandma Dominica. She clutches a doll that holds a miniature gold saxophone. Both she and the doll look with dark eyes that

O axaca is famous for its variety of moles—each one distinct in its own way.

- Coloradito, *basic in taste, is red in color with a tomato base.*
- Rojo *is a spicier red-brown mole and includes chocolate.*
- Mancha manteles, *also a red but with the strong flavor of ancho chiles, is served with plantains.*
- Verde, *a green mole based on tomatillos, is the lightest in taste.*
- Amarillo *is a more complex green mole made with four types of chiles.*
- Chichilo *is very dark in color, and is prepared with chile seeds that have been toasted to ash.*
- Negro *is the most complex in the bunch with over thirty ingredients used in its preparation, including six types of chiles.*

—Susan Brady, "The Seven Moles of Oaxaca"

sparkle under thick black lashes. She smiles and tilts her head downward as she peeks at us, drawing us closer to her family. Dominica's sisters and a neighbor who makes cheese from her cows' milk join the patter of conversation that turns melodious in my wandering mind.

We stand around the table to husk, one by one, the cacao beans as they come out of the roasting pan. Grinding the chocolate comes next. Jim manages the pre-Hispanic style *matate*. He diligently rolls and grinds the beans in the hot sun, stooping his tall frame to the ground while sweat pours from his forehead. Soon the chocolate shines and sugar and cinnamon bark are added. Our noses preview the sweet taste to come. Chocolate is poured into individual banana leaves and wrapped for its journey to Susana's cooking school.

The neighbor lady squeezes and strains the cheese until the consistency is perfect. She covers the smooth hunk with a tea towel. I notice the care. No plastic wrap or aluminum foil, only a towel, laundered and bleached white by the sun. It balances on the top of her head as she carries it to our van. We'll use it for a special dish at Susana's. I feel the love that accompanies this food. Future families and friends will continue meeting around a table such as Dominica's and be grateful for the experience.

Before leaving, we enter a vented smoke hut constructed of cactus stalks where a *comal* (a flat unglazed ceramic griddle) perches on an open fire in the corner and is tended by a tiny older woman with gray braids. Her Zapotec-style apron protects her clothes. With short arms that barely reach the hot tortillas, she slathers them with lard and bean paste. We sample the smoky *botana* (snack). Susana points out that the tortillas here were made from the corn the family grew. She describes how they remove the outer layers of the corn kernels so they can be more easily digested. Tedious work, I think. I'm a bit surprised that the old ways are preferred to the convenience of buying a can of digestible corn from the market.

I think of the packages of tortillas on the shelves of supermarkets at home. I'm sure these Etla tortillas taste better because of the ingredients coming straight from the earth. Susana gives hugs and kisses to the women of the house as we pile in the van for the next stop of our journey. I am impatient to hear more about her connection with these generous people. She doesn't disappoint.

"This family is only one of many that I have met during the last sixteen years. I've haunted the local markets and researched family specialties. Many have been kind enough to invite me into their homes to teach me their ways," Susana says. I'm touched by her story and with renewed enthusiasm, look forward to the remainder of this special day.

The van suddenly turns west at the pueblo of San Lorenzo. We see an era stopped in time. Oxen with yolks, burro-driven carts, mangy, homeless dogs, semi-open huts with corn growing alongside. A boy of about ten is chasing a rabbit. His slingshot is in ready position for the kill. Susana covers her eyes, but still watches. "He is trying to kill the poor bunny," she says. I want to pause here and take it all in, but we must continue to Rancho Aurora where Susana and her husband Eric live. A screech of brakes interrupts my dreaming as we barely avoid slamming into a bull whose eyes stare straight into the front windshield of our van. Susana switches to Spanish and scolds our driver for not being more attentive. It seems they've had previous conversations like this, and on one occasion he made road kill of a village dog.

Through a deep arroyo, barely lined with water, the van changes gears and the engine surges, climbing the steep hill to Susana's school. We see the immense red dome loom skyward like some sort of religious shrine and marvel at the ambitious project of building such a massive structure here in nearly inaccessible terrain. I try to picture the laying of wires for electricity, tapping water from deep in the ground, and hauling building supplies. Susana's husband, Eric, was the master planner and builder for the project. They achieved an impossible dream with grit and determination. We climb the steep stone stairs to the front door. Inside, I can't believe the expanse of this space. The open room: part kitchen, part eating area, is surrounded by windows that frame the brilliance of bougainvillea and greenery growing in contrast to the dusty hills. Enormous earthen pots tempt our parched mouths to drink fresh fruit waters of hibiscus, orange, and watermelon. Gnarly wood baskets hold fresh garlic, shiny white onions, chiles, limes, and fresh pineapple, which must be ripe, because I smell its sweetness.

Oscar, a chicken farmer invites us to watch him prepare his own special rendition of a drink called a *michilada*. In halting English, I only hear, "Be sure to add *salsa bufalo* to the beer, stir in the spices and enjoy." We soon hold our own samples of this drink. The burn on the way down my throat stays most of the afternoon. Oscar proudly tells us that his chickens are yellow because he dyes their feed with marigold coloring. Today he is dressed in waiter-white shirt and black pants. His posture projects confidence and pride in his work as part of the kitchen staff. Susana joins him and explains how the recipes we'll prepare today were once shown on her PBS series in the States. Helpers from the village place bottles of cold beer on the counter. We are welcome to serve ourselves. I think I'll float after all this liquid.

I slip into a state of nirvana, wanting to drift back to our morning and the kindness we experienced, but instead, Susana talks rapidly and with such purpose, I come back to reality. She's giving us a quick overview of the six recipes we'll prepare and eat. I'm beginning to see there is no way to escape active participation. An attitude adjustment is in order.

I agree to prepare an appetizer with a Mexican/Thai influence called *Platanos Fritos con Crema de Jengibre y Jalapeño* (fried plantains with ginger jalapeño cream). It appeals because I think it's manageable and I'm lazy. I gasp when Jim volunteers to make the *Pastel de Tres Leches* (three milk cake). In order for it to achieve its full potential, he must perform numerous complicated steps. At home, Jim excels as a chopping assistant, but in our forty-two years of marriage, I don't recall him as a standout baker. But I quickly decide that it is not my problem. I'll simply concentrate on my own little project.

Each of us finds a spot in the airy kitchen where splendid tiles of navy blue faced with bright sunflowers accent counters and splash boards. Local stones create a façade for the giant island in the center of the kitchen. The use of subtle shades of pink, yellow, and blue presents a calming effect. Everywhere I look, a different view of the barren hills and valley below attacks me with a sense of mystery. Lila Downs sings *"La Sanduga"* from a boom box on the floor. I'm easily distracted. A woman from the village hands me skin-grasping gloves so I won't burn myself deseeding the jalapeños. I chop the juicy peppers and they join the fresh garlic and ginger already sitting in the blender. Next comes cream cheese, but the amount seems skimpy. Susana agrees that I should double the recipe. Others are struggling with sticky flour-and-water *masa* for tortilla appetizers. Susana directs us to start assembling the *Ensalada de Nopales Asados* (grilled nopales salad). She says that the women in the market clean the prickles from the fruit. She claims the fruit is good for lowering cholesterol and weight.

I hear Jim ask for help in separating eggs. I avoid looking his way for fear I'll be brought into his dilemma. Others scramble to help him and I see a counter covered with bowls and dairy products ready to measure. I slice the bananas and set them aside to fry. Already two hours have passed and there's more to do. The *Quesadillas de Flor de Calabaza* (fresh cheese and squash blossom turnovers) are ready to stuff. It looks easy until I try folding in the soft white cheese we brought from Dominica's. It's a coordination problem. While placing the cheese inside the tortillas, one must also place the squash flowers on top. I see the cheese oozing out of mine onto the *comal*. My hands feel too big and like a child in school. I'm happy to leave this task to hands that are more adept. I smell *pollo asada* on the grill and spot an inviting hammock that swings from the veranda. It must be *siesta* time somewhere, but not here.

Eating sounds better all the time. The resident dog slithers by and plops his long brown body in front of the door so that we must step over him. He has a good view of Susana's son and village kids romping near the farm machinery and assorted cars below.

I'm ready to fry my bananas. Oscar instructs me to pour the oil one-inch deep in the cast-iron pan. It must be hot before adding the fruit. I hear the oil pop and immerse the sliced bananas in the oil. The slices start blurring at the edges as if they were melting. I know something is wrong. Why aren't they crisping up? Here I am doing the simplest of recipes and I've already screwed up. What a disaster! I think about dumping the greasy mess out the back door, hoping the dog will slurp it up. I see one spare banana on the counter. For a moment, I entertain the thought of starting over, but one banana isn't enough.

Susana gently shoves me aside and with a long-handled spoon begins lifting bananas out of the oil on to a plate. "You must not put so many in at one time," she says. "They are crowded and cool the oil." I feel stupid. Why didn't I know this simple thing? Now I have ruined our dish. Susana smiles, "It's all right. If they don't crisp up we'll put them in the oven for a bit." I decide I'm not the first to make this mistake. The lesson is learned.

Meanwhile Jim is in the final difficult stages of cake preparation. He must top the cake with fresh kiwi, mango, berries, and whipped cream and then roll it for the refrigerator. I can imagine the cake splitting in half and all the ingredients ending up on the floor. He smiles, but his teeth clench in the effort.

Eric comes in from laying water pipe in a neighboring village. He and his helpers sit down, ready to eat. The long table is set with woven coverings, bright red fresh flowers accompany the plates of food before us. Jim's cake is a hit. A long day's effort, but well worth the struggles. Susana joins us and makes the appropriate compliments for our work, being kind enough not to mention my soggy bananas, which did crisp up in the oven. I savor a *flor de calabasa* in my mouth and stare straight out the window to a spot on a faraway hill. "Do you see the ruins?" asks Susana. "That is our ancient Monte Alban."

Our idle chatter ceases as we ponder the wonder of the moment. Twenty-five-hundred-year-old ruins are alive with a rich history while a modern cooking school successfully perpetuates old recipes for generations to come. The fistful of recipes I plan on keeping will forever trigger the places and faces that shared their heritage with us for just one day.

Judy Ware likes nothing better than to hunker down in a Mexican town long enough to recognize the fruit and vegetable vendors at a weekly farmer's market and the children walking home from school for a midday comida. *She writes about life experiences shared with her husband as they poke around the globe. Her work has appeared in* Empty Vessel Full Vessel; Standing; Poetry by Idaho Women; Frankische Unzeiger, *a regional German publication; and several regional magazines.*

Mole Verde
Green Mole

Serves 8

This mole, from Susana Trilling's Seasons of My Heart, *is one of the seven legendary moles of Oaxaca. Unlike the dark moles with their voluputuous richness, this one tastes fresh and bright, vibrant and, somehow, green, even when you close your eyes.*

1 white onion, sliced

1 garlic bulb

1 carrot, peeled and thickly sliced

3 celery ribs, with leaves

1 bay leaf

1 whole allspice

1 chile de arbol

5 black peppercorns

kosher salt

1 pound baby-back ribs, cut Chinese style

1 pound boneless pork shoulder, in 2-inch cubes

3/4 cup dried small white beans, soaked overnight and cooked in salted water until tender

1 pound fresh tomatillos, husks removed

1 pound green tomatoes, cut into chunks

1 medium white onion, cut into chunks

1 garlic bulb, cloves separated and peeled

9 large fresh jalapeños, seeded

2 tablespoons sunflower or vegetable oil

8 ounces prepared corn masa for tortillas or 1 cup masa harina for tortillas mixed with ½ cup plus 1 tablespoon warm water

½ cup fresh Italian parsley leaves

½ cup fresh epazote leaves

½ cup yerba santa leaves, ribs removed

black pepper to taste

Pour 3 quarts of cold water into a large soup pot and add the sliced onion, whole garlic bulb, carrot, celery ribs, bay leaf, allspice, chile de arbol, whole peppercorns, baby-back ribs and pork shoulder. Bring to a boil over high heat, reduce the heat to low and skim off any foam that forms on the surface of the liquid. Simmer, covered, for 1 hour.

Use tongs to transfer the ribs and shoulder to a plate. Increase the heat to high and simmer 15 minutes more. Strain the stock into a clean container and discard the vegetables. Season the stock to taste with salt.

Put the tomatillos in a 2-quart saucepan and add enough water to just cover them. Bring to a boil over high heat, reduce the heat to low and simmer until they just change color, about 10 minutes. Remove from the heat, drain and place in the container of a blender, along with the green tomatoes, chunks of onion, garlic cloves, jalapeños and 1 cup of the reserved pork stock. Puree until smooth.

Pour the oil into a large soup pot set over high heat. When it smokes, add the pureed tomatillo mixture and stir continuously until hot, about 10 minutes.

Put the masa in a blender and add 2 cups of the pork stock. Puree until smooth and stir into the tomatillo mixture. Simmer over medium heat, stirring continuously, until the mixture thickens, about 10 minutes.

Put the parsley, epazote, and yerba santa in the blender and add enough pork stock to blend well. Pour the herb mixture into the tomatillo mixture and simmer over low heat for 15 minutes more.

Add salt and pepper to taste. At this point, the mole should be thick enough to coat a spoon but no thicker; if it seems too thick, thin with a little of the reserved pork stock.

Return the ribs and shoulder meat, along with the cooked white beans, to the stock and simmer gently to heat through. Ladle the mole into soup plates, making sure each serving includes a rib and a piece of shoulder topped with lots of sauce and beans. Serve immediately, with hot corn tortillas alongside.

SARAH PASCARELLA

Nawlins

Ingenuity and substitution are the hallmarks of a good cook.

My fascination with New Orleans began, naturally, with food. During a visit to my home in Rome several years ago, my friend Christina offered to cook dinner. I eagerly agreed, as she is a fine cook.

"I'm thinking crawfish étouffée, my granddaddy's recipe," Chris said. "Where can we get crawfish?"

It was a Sunday. Most stores were closed, including the seafood shops, plus my limited Italian skills didn't cover the word *crawfish*. We walked to the nearest open market in Trastevere, my beloved Rome neighborhood, and searched for good substitutes.

"Shrimp will do," Chris said, pointing to several plump ones on display in the seafood section. The teenage girl manning the counter bagged up several, with both of us using hand signals to negotiate the correct amount. We then scanned the spice racks, with Chris choosing the right ones by sight and smell. After a quick gathering of fresh vegetables, we headed back to my kitchen.

Chris cooks by sight and taste, and, that day, worked from memory. I watched over her shoulder as she chopped vegetables, the red pepper juices staining her fingertips. I shelled shrimp as she tossed garlic and olive oil in a pan, the pungent aroma filling my little kitchen. Chris added a few onions to the stewing mix, and the salty-sea smells made me imagine weeping willow trees, hot humid days, and glasses of sweet iced tea. I pictured myself sitting on a wide front porch, fanning myself from the heat, and taking a bite of her dish, as hot as the afternoon sun.

"With the family dishes, it's just done granddaddy's way, not from a recipe book," she explained, tasting a spoonful of étouffée and adding a pinch of several spices—pepper, cayenne, and more garlic—until it was to her liking. "When we used to go to New Orleans for visits, I loved to watch him cook." She pronounced it *Nawlins*.

"And do they all eat this way, every day?" I asked.

She nodded. "Collard greens, gumbo, red beans and rice, étouffée," she put a pot of water on to boil, in preparation for rice. "When you go, you *must* order the crawfish étouffée. Shrimp is good, but the crawfish! You'll think you've died and gone to heaven."

Chris hovered over the pan, watching it carefully. "You don't want to let the sauce thicken too quickly," she noted, and began stirring it thoroughly. "It's not a dish where you can just step away and do something else. You have to keep an eye on it." We took turns stirring, having sips of wine while the other cooked. I marveled at the sauce's caramel-like color, an earthy hue flecked with bursts of flame-red from the pepper, crisp green from the celery, and silvery-pink from the shrimp.

The shrimp turned out to be a fine substitute, and I savored the dish's contrasting textures and flavors: The salty crustaceans blended well with the vegetables' sweetness; the sauce's heat was tamed by a bed of fluffy white rice.

Chris transported me, in my little Roman kitchen, to the southeastern United States, and through its superb cuisine made me nostalgic for a part of my native country I had never seen. I decided, once back in the States, to take a trip there myself, purely for gastronomical reasons.

A few short months upon returning, I made my first pilgrimage to New Orleans. While cold weather and snow raged in the Northeast that November day, it was pleasantly cool in the city. So pleasant, in fact, that my friends and I decided to have dinner outside, on the balcony of Patout's, a small restaurant on Bourbon Street.

It was my first meal in the city and I was stumped over what to order. Every item on the menu called to me, like an old friend, each wanting proper attention. I had four days ahead of me and knew that if I didn't order a particular dish here, I would have the opportunity to eat it elsewhere. I vowed not to order the same meal twice, and chose shrimp gumbo to start, plus a locally brewed beer.

Bourbon Street was pretty rowdy, even on a Thursday night. At 10:30 P.M., I was eating on the later side, and leaned over the balcony for a few minutes to take in the drunken revelers while awaiting the much-anticipated gumbo. Men, young and old, waved beads to anyone with breasts walking by, lazily tipping drinks both into their mouths and onto the ground. Some strutted, some staggered, all leered. The scene was full of colors—feathered boas in electric hues of purple, blue, and pink encircled the necks of many passersby; neon signs advertising live music, good food, and smut parlors flashed throughout the street. We were the only ones dining on the balcony that night. Most patrons chose to see the Zydeco band playing downstairs. The music's dominant Cajun accordion and drum, frenetically paced, drifted up to me, accenting the rhythm of those out walking on Bourbon Street.

The gumbo, when it arrived, was lovely. The tomato base was light both in flavor (the shrimp got first priority) and consistency. While the gumbo approached stew-like thickness, it is its own proper weight, appropriate to be served traditionally over rice. There was little competition for density between the shrimp, rice, and tomatoes, all worked in concert to highlight the dish's alternating spices and peppers. The beer was a clean finish, still crispy cool in the night air.

> New Orleans is home to two of America's indigenous cuisines: Cajun and Creole. Originally from France, Cajuns came to New Orleans via Nova Scotia and settled in the least desirable area of New Orleans, the swamps, to avoid being relocated. Their food reflects their environment, and is basic country cooking, usually one-pot meals, which includes produce of the season, as well as whatever was shot or trapped. Jambalaya, gumbo, and grillades are typical of Cajun cuisine. Creoles, on the other hand, are descendents of European aristocrats and were generally more educated, intermarrying with the Spanish and African immigrants. Their cuisine tends to be more complicated with more spices and sauces. Bouillabaisse, mirlitons, and sauce piquantes reflect this style of cooking.
>
> —Susan Brady, "The House on Bayou Road"

I sat back contentedly, tapping my foot to the swinging music below. I'd had my first Nawlins meal.

"What would you like?" the waiter at Napoleon House asksed, drawing out vowels in a slow, syrupy tone. I'd spent the morning walking the French Quarter, gazing at the Mississippi River, and ducking into churches and shops. After hours of taking in Nawlins, as Chris would say, I was famished.

The waiter lingered patiently. He was impeccably dressed, as all the waiters were, in a stiff white shirt, black bow tie, and black slacks. His hair was a light gray, traces of sandy blond still showing in places. Small wire-rimmed glasses framed his eyes. His attire, the restaurant's aged decor, the dim glow of oil lamps, and soft classical music playing gave the room a Dickensian feel. Were it not for the strains of jazz and Zydeco in the distance, I'd have expected to see Bob Cratchit round the corner any moment.

This was an old restaurant. Founded in 1797, Napoleon House is named for the former emperor, who was offered the building as asylum by its first owner, Nicholas Girod, in 1821. While Napoleon never claimed the offering, the name remains, and the restaurant has been an enclave for poets, artists, and writers seeking a space for creativity and community.

Of course, people also came for the food and spirits. "I'll have the red beans and rice," I finally decided. "And..." I hesitate, my Yankee accent already on full display. Pointing to the beer menu, I attempted the local brewery's name, Abita. "Is it Ah-bee-tah?"

"Uh-bee-ta." The waiter gathered the menu and was gone; the dim lighting hid my red, frustrated cheeks.

I was no longer frustrated when the food arrived, though. I only discovered the greatness of legume dishes in my twenties, as my parents never enjoyed their textures and thus were never part of my childhood diet. Perhaps they never had a meal of beans in New Orleans, where the red wonders, steeped in a tasty gravy, surround a bed of white rice and two spicy sausages. I sliced a sausage carefully, in small bites, and placed all three foods on my fork for the first taste. There was a burst of chile and garlic, fragrant pepper, and hints of parsley, onion, and seasonings from the pork. The sausage was tender; the beans firm. The Abita was a fine brew, clean and full-bodied.

I noticed my waiter had sat down at a neighboring table, having a meal before going home for the day. He also had red beans and rice. We smiled at each other as we lifted our forks to our mouths.

I decided to save the crawfish étouffée for my last night in New Orleans. The Gumbo Shop, a small restaurant at the edge of the French Quarter, was rumored to have some of the best traditional cuisine in town, and I headed there feeling a mixture of excitement and sadness. Like all trips, this one was too short, and as always, I felt there were several places (in this case, restaurants) I had not had time to visit.

Excitement won out, however, once I stepped into the restaurant and smelled the rich hues of garlic, pepper, meats, and seafood. Most of the patrons were dressed conservatively: golf shirts and khakis, jeans and light sweaters. My friends and I, in full celebration mode for our final night in the city, sported boas, bead necklaces, and sparkly makeup. For good measure, I wore a tiara. My hostess did not bat an eye, however, and kindly showed us to our table.

I glanced at the menu for propriety and ordered the crawfish right away.

"What is étouffée, anyway?" one friend asked.

"It's stewlike," I began, recalling Chris all those years ago. "A stock base with cream added…primarily fish or chicken stock for the seafood étouffées. There are peppers, garlic, parsley, onion, and whatever seafood you like. Apparently Chris thinks crawfish is best suited to it—or maybe the novelty of crawfish is what makes it especially good. And like so many dishes here, it's over rice."

My friend nodded. "Sounds O.K. I'll have a bite of yours."

The dish was exactly as I remembered it, and Chris's preference was right. Small, tender crescents, the crawfish silkily blended with the étouffée, an excellent marriage of spices, textures, and flavors. My friends tried a bite, and then another. One looked down at her pasta dish, then over to my plate. "I should have ordered that," she sighed.

"We'll just have to come back soon," I replied.

On my final morning in New Orleans, I rose early and headed out to Café du Monde for one last meal of chicory coffee and beignets. I had the streets to myself, my footsteps echoing in the bright stillness of early, pre-bustle morning. The sunlight kissed the pavement and homes, reflecting off the intricate iron double-decker porches and lush potted plants, washing the streets in golden glow. I was reminded of the canals of Venice, with palatial balconies opening to fine greenery, and the brightness of light off the water.

Did Chris know what she started, back in my Rome kitchen? From that gastronomical paradise, I was introduced to another, learning how much food can create the character, and flavor, of any place. Food is so much a part of New Orleans and Italy, and as I saw the café up ahead, I gave silent thanks for having made both gastronomical trips.

Sarah Pascarella, a Boston-based writer and editor, is currently planning her next trip to New Orleans. She is an associate editor at SmarterTravel.com, and her work has also appeared in The Bark *magazine,* Italian America *magazine, and* USA Today. *She also has a novel in progress.*

Chicken and Sausage Gumbo

Serves 8–10

This recipe is from the New Orleans Cooking Experience (NOCE), and their wonderful chef and instructor Chiqui Collier, a native New Orleanian. NOCE, housed in an historic 1798 French plantation house turned B&B, offers single half-day and full-day classes, series classes, as well as complete vacation packages. (www.neworleanscookingexperience.com)

- 1 cup all purpose flour
- 1 cup bacon drippings or vegetable oil
- 1 gallon chicken stock
- 1 ½ cup chopped celery

1 ½ cups chopped yellow onion

1 ½ cups chopped green bell pepper

1 bunch green onions, thinly sliced

2 tablespoons chopped garlic

1 bay leaf

1 teaspoon dried thyme

1 teaspoon dried oregano

1 teaspoon ground white pepper

1 teaspoon Worcestershire sauce

1 teaspoon hot sauce, or to taste

$^1/_8$ teaspoon cayenne

salt to taste

1 pound andouille or smoked sausage, sliced and lightly browned

1 pound sliced okra, fresh or frozen, sautéed in oil

3 pounds grilled chicken, diced or shredded

Add oil or bacon fat to heavy bottomed 2- to 3-gallon soup pot. Adjust heat to high; when oil is to the smoking point, very carefully stir in flour using a wooden spoon to make the roux; reduce heat to medium high. Use extreme care while stirring, avoiding splatters. Continue to cook the roux until it reaches a dark chocolate color. Carefully add onion, then vegetables, garlic, spices and approximately 1 ½ teaspoons of salt. Stir the roux and the vegetable mixture to insure all is well combined. Cook 4 to 5 minutes over medium heat, stirring until soft. Add the browned sausage and sautéed okra and whisk in the chicken stock. Return to high and whisk until the roux is incorporated into the stock. Bring to a boil then reduce heat to medium and cook for 1 hour, skimming any oil or foam that rises to the top during this time.

After an hour check the taste, add salt if needed. Add hot sauce and Worcestershire. Just before serving, add the chicken and heat through. Ladle gumbo over rice.

Making the Small Tortilla

A gringa learns that the tortilla says it all.

It had been hot—unbearably hot—a deep down stinky, sticky hot that makes you breathe shallow and lie still so the mosquitoes won't hear. But finally got a reprieve from the triple-digit temperatures and almost matching humidity. A "cold front" blew into the steamy village and brought the temperature down into the reasonable mid-seventies. My husband, Norm, and I could breathe and move again. The locals brought out their sweatshirts.

It was almost our third month in southern Belize. We had worked relentlessly to turn a corner of a dilapidated old building into a temporary medical clinic. Then, while I provided medical services in the makeshift space, Norm worked with the local men to build a new, permanent home for the much-needed facility.

That's when we met Martin. Side by side, under the scorching sun, the men cleared the ever-encroaching rainforest, dug a foundation with hand tools, and poured concrete by the wheelbarrowsful. As the concrete walls were built, a single block at a time, a special bond began to cement between Norm and his new friend, Martin.

Toward the end of the clinic construction project, Martin invited us to come to his home for dinner. "My wife, she will cook the tortilla for you," he said proudly.

We were delighted to receive an invitation into a Mayan home. We made arrangements for the following day.

Early in the morning little boy voices awakened us calling, "Mr. Norm, Mr. Norm." There stood Martin's sons, Elcerio and Mariano, politely waiting outside the fence that encircled our yard, straight black hair neatly combed, broad smiles on their sweet brown faces. They looked smart in their clean school uniforms. They shouted excitedly, "You are coming to dinner tonight! Me pa got a chicken for you!" I felt humbled. Eating meat was obviously not an everyday event. The chicken was to honor us.

When we arrived at the home that evening, the children were all atwitter with the excitement of having dinner guests. Martin sat outdoors by the fire warming himself against the frigid cold front of the 70-degree weather that we were enjoying.

His wife, Cecilia, was busy forming tortillas from the corn mash she had ground that morning. With the ease of a woman doing a task by body memory, she deftly shaped and fried the tortillas on a heavy round metal griddle over the open fire.

After introductions, I asked if she would teach me how to make tortillas. With a mannerism I came to know as Cecilia's trademark, she covered her face and giggled, "Of course, I be happy to teach you."

Taking a small amount of cornmeal paste from a large plastic bowl sitting on the ground beside her, Cecilia began to roll it in her hands forming a ball. It looked easy enough, but perhaps there was more to it than first inspection revealed. I could tell she was pleased to be teaching this woman from so far away. Making tortillas was something she did well. She had watched her mother prepare the revered maize and make tortillas since she could barely toddle about their dirt-floored hut. When she turned six, her mother allowed her to help, and every day of her life, for the past thirty years, she had made tortillas.

> The tortilla is the bread, the plate, and the spoon of Mexico. With cheese it becomes a quesadilla. Simple, but exquisite. Filled tacos; layered tostadas; stuffed gorditas and panuchos; sopes and garnachas; the more elaborate enchiladas—the choice is endless and each region has its own specialties.
>
> —Marilyn Tausend,
> Mexico: The Beautiful Book

Corn is venerated in the Mayan culture as the very essence of life itself. The Popol Voh, the Mayan Bible, declares that man is made from corn. When Cecilia kneels each day beside the fire and begins to grind the limewater-soaked corn into a smooth pasty meal, she partakes of a centuries-old tradition. She is grateful for the corn; she is grateful to the corn. With corn her family will not be hungry.

"Do this," Cecilia said as she began to form a ball with the meal in her hands. I reached into the bowl, pulled out my own wad of dough, and begin to mimic her action. Immediately Cecilia covered her face with her forearms, since her hands were full of dough, and began to giggle.

"What? What am I doing wrong?" I asked, laughing along with her.

Blushing, Cecilia continued to giggle as she told me, "Take only a small bit, Miss Nancy. You must make the tortilla very small." She reached across my lap, pinched a bit of dough from my ball and threw it back in the bowl. Then she nodded her head and resumed her demonstration.

She continued to roll the dough into a ball, then patted it round and round until it formed a thin, perfectly circular patty. I attempted to mimic her by patting my tortilla round and round. Although mine came out much less than perfect, it still received praise from my teacher—praise and plenty of giggles.

We continued to form the cornmeal patties until we had enough to fill the round piece of metal over the open fire she used as a stove. Each time I reached into the bowl for a wad of dough, Cecilia checked me and smiled if the amount was small enough. If I pinched off too large of a wad, she would giggle and take a pinch of it back.

As we worked she explained the importance of making the tortilla small. "If you make the tortilla too big, then your man will know that you are lazy. All men want a woman who will make the tortilla small," Cecilia said earnestly. I began to understand that making the tortilla was much more than simply preparing a meal. The tortilla is an indication of who a woman is. The tortilla says much more than simply "Dinner is ready."

After the tortillas were formed Cecilia showed me how to cook them on the ungreased grill over the open fire so they didn't burn. She showed me how to check them frequently, turning them with her bare hands. When the tortillas turned a lovely beige color, with dark brown speckles, they were done. She removed them from the grill with her bare hands and placed them in a towel-wrapped bowl to keep warm.

When the tortillas were ready she shyly invited us into their home leading the way up a ladderlike ramp into the rough-cut lumber hut raised with eight-foot stilts to keep out the rain and the animals. Thickly thatched palm fronds formed the roof overhead. She then returned outside to fetch a large, covered black pot and dished up bowls of stewed chicken and broth for everyone. Cecilia placed another bowl containing an orange-colored liquid in the center of the table. "We will share," she said as she set it down. Following Martin's lead we squatted around a small table barely large enough to hold the bowls.

"Eat," said Martin. "Take your time. We have plenty."

First, we watched to see how it was done. Soon, we were dipping our tortillas into the savory stew and scooping up the delicious chunks of chicken. The stock appeared to be seasoned with cilantro and another leaf I did not recognize. Achiote colored the stew a fiery red.

Giggling, Cecilia covered her face with both hands. "Wait! Wait! I forgot." She ran back outdoors, and returned with tiny roasted peppers perched atop a tortilla. "It is for the chicken," she said as she demonstrated how to smear the pepper over the achiote-stained meat. Just a tiny smudge lit my mouth on fire and I reached hastily for the bowl of orange drink in the middle of the table. The family laughed heartily at my reaction. Such a wonderful family they were, sharing a special meal with us and honoring us with a chicken and the small tortillas.

In our modern world of instant gratification, I am not certain the quiet pride, or the simple joy, this woman feels as she prepares the corn tortillas for her family can be understood. I am not certain that I understand. I do know that I would like to make it mine.

Nancy Leigh Harless is a retired nurse practitioner who loves to travel, volunteer along the way, and write about her experiences. When home, most of her writing is done in a towering maple tree in a tree house built specifically for that purpose by her husband, Norm. Her writing has been included in many popular anthologies and in several nursing journals. Nancy is currently in the final edits of her first book, Womankind: Connection and Wisdom Throughout the Americas. *It is the first, in a trilogy of short story collections, about the people met along her journey who have illumined the way.*

Thin flatbreads were the original breads, and are still a major source of nourishment in many countries throughout the world. The essential characteristic of flatbreads is that they cook very quickly, in as little as two minutes, on a simple hot surface, whether a pan, an oven floor or wall, or a mass of hot pebbles. The heat is often very high and this means that tiny air pockets in the dough are puffed up by rapidly vaporizing steam, essentially leavening the dough without the necessity of fermentation (though many flatbreads are made with leavened dough). This puffing, and the breads' thinness, make them tender; and since neither requires a strong gluten, flatbreads can be made from all kinds of grains. Despite short baking time, the high temperatures develop a delicious toasted flavor across the extensive surface of flatbreads.

—Harold McGee, *On Food and Cooking: The Science and Lore of the Kitchen*

A Foodie Lesson in Philo

Learning to play well with others at a B&B.

When I told a friend who works as a chef that I was taking three days of cooking classes in the Anderson Valley for a vacation, his response was quick and typically tart: "I wish you'd told me first. I need help in *my* kitchen."

Wisecracks aside, I understand that some might find the idea of a "cooking vacation" counterintuitive. Who would want to worry over a stove with a group of strangers in the heat of summer?

But generally I find the step-by-step process of putting together a meal relaxing. I'd first learned of the class during a trip to Mendocino County a few years back. We made a quick detour from quirky Boonville to the Apple Farm in nearby Philo, thirty tucked-away acres just far enough off California 128 to feel like a genuine discovery.

We meandered through the lush grounds edging up to the orchards. Then I happened upon the Apple Farm's vast, sun-flooded kitchen: its large chopping-block work islands; huge old Montague stove; well-stocked pantry; row upon row of gleaming baking pans; stacks of gorgeous, handmade crockery. Looking around this well-appointed, obviously professional kitchen in the middle of a fairy-tale-in-the-woods setting, I took it all in. "What," I wondered, "goes on *here?*"

I finally indulged my curiosity and called. It turns out that cooking classes at the farm are run by Sally Schmitt, who, with her husband, Don, owned and operated the French Laundry, the famed Yountville restaurant. After sixteen years, they sold it and "retired"—entrusting the business to chef Thomas Keller—who did them proud and brought it international acclaim.

Heading into the California hills, you get your first whiff of the woods—firs and evergreens and, finally, majestic groves of redwoods. The road narrows and serpentines dramatically the farther you climb, enough perhaps to make even the most road-hardy carsick.

I arrived with a friend well before the 5 P.M. start time. We had our choice of the three A-frame cottages close, but not too close, together, and all a quick walk from the farmhouse kitchen. (We nearly took the one with the private outdoor shower.) Each high-ceilinged cottage is simply appointed with a sort of rustic elegance: wood four-poster beds covered with cheerful quilts, wood floors covered by rag rugs, and small bouquets of lavender that scent the room.

After cleaning up in the old-fashioned sink, I headed to the farmhouse kitchen—blessedly air-conditioned—where I collected my apron and met the rest of the eight-person class. We assembled around the large island, where Sally had set out a crate of ripe, fragrant peaches.

Don trudged in wearing a workshirt, boots, and dungarees and started things rolling by uncorking several bottles. We sipped and he told us what notes to look for in the Sauvignon Blanc from Husch Vineyards not far down the road.

Our group had two men and six women. One couple had come from Seattle for

According to BedandBreakfast.com, the Napa Valley in California is among the Top Ten most popular B&B destinations in the world. Combine that with some of the best restaurants and wine in the world and you have an unbeatable combination. In addition to classes offered at Casa Lana (Calistoga), Cedar Gables Inn and Oak Knoll Inn (Napa), among others, there is the wonderful COPIA: The American Center for Wine, Food and the Arts. COPIA offers tastings, exhibitions, hands-on classes, and dining in Julia's Kitchen (named in honor of that grande dame Julia Child). And if that's not enough, head on over the Culinary Institute of America at Graystone, where cooking demonstrations, wine tastings, and rotating special events occur. (Graystone also offers an impressive catalog of culinary tours throughout the world.)

—SB

their third experience. We all made an introductory " *Love Boat*, here's to the journey" toast.

Sally spoke in comforting, buttery tones as she handed each of us a folder of recipes. That's when we realized what we'd gotten ourselves into: That night's dinner would be a three-course affair. The next day, it would be five courses, but with a three-dish lunch to prepare and consume before that. One couple began planning a morning run among the redwoods up in the nearby Hendy Woods to jog off the cream and butter damage.

Sally simply plunged forward, going over the evening's menu: poblano chile soup, bacon-wrapped scallops, peach gelato. She got one group started peeling peaches, then started another on the next segment of the recipe. This technique, though it seemed democratic and logical at first, didn't account for the overzealous in class—the first to take charge, the first to tell you how they do it at home.

The thought began to sharpen in my mind: I've chosen a vacation of hard, intimate work with a group of strangers. As I sloughed the skin from the ripe peaches, I couldn't seem to get the phrase "plays well with others" out of my head—especially as we were surrounded by precision German and Japanese knives. "Playing well together" would be the unspoken, though absolutely necessary, ingredient of the weekend ahead.

This was not *Love Boat* at all. More like *Survivor*.

After a couple of hours, though, we fell into the rhythm of the "behind you…hot plate" dance of the kitchen. As dinner emerged from its skillets and baking dishes, Sally's daughter Karen Bates gave us a lesson in presentation, how not to crowd the food, how to avoid leaving fingerprints on the plates. We delivered the first course to the table right around 9 P.M.—just as Don reappeared to open a Pinot Noir. After the gelato, served with a sprig of lemon verbena, Sally sent us off, sated but exhausted, to our comfy beds under a startling blanket of stars.

Though the rooster crows around 4 A.M., we weren't expected back in the kitchen until 10. After tea and toast and a metabolism-boosting walk to visit the goats, chickens, sheep, and pigs, we reconvened to start in on lunch and dinner.

First came a summer pudding—layers of fresh, warmed raspberries over sourdough bread that needed to chill for several hours. Then we turned our attention to lunch:

oven-roasted salmon with sorrel sauce and blanched *haricots vert*. The French potato salad included scallions and Italian parsley that we pulled from the garden—an elegant tangle of herbs, greens, berries, flowers, and vegetables that looked as though it had grown from the pages of an English children's storybook.

Sally gently showed me the way to position the knife to keep the onion and lemon slices for the salmon paper-thin. Then she demonstrated the way to roll the sorrel leaves then cut at a diagonal, *chiffonade*-style, for a garnish. We hit a collective groove balancing dinner and lunch tasks. Consequently, our midday meal was served almost precisely at noon, and we ate it outdoors under a canopy of mulberry trees.

By 5 P.M., some of us were surreptitiously finding places to perch or lean, to rest our feet or lower backs, as we confronted the most complicated meal of the weekend: twice-baked soufflés, lamb in eggplant rolls with tomato *concassé*, a green salad, and the summer pudding.

The enthusiasm of our most fervent foodies hadn't flagged—they chopped, they grilled, they sautéed. But if any one of us got too far afield, Sally in her kindest voice nudged, "Now, what does your recipe say?" or "Come close. Listen." In this kitchen there were no mistakes, only adjustments.

Joining us for dinner was Karen's husband, Tim, who fielded questions about the farm's day-to-day operations over the pillowy first-course soufflés. By the time we started in on the eggplant and lamb, Sally and Don were indulging our queries about their years at the French Laundry and the challenges of sustaining not just a farm but a way of life.

Come Sunday morning, we were all showing signs of getting a bit crisp around the edges. Even the most eager of our pack seemed ready to cede some responsibility: "Oh, you guys can do that," one woman said. "I don't want to get goat cheese under my nails."

When it came time to add the flour for the *clafouti* mixture, I put the scoop into the glass flour canister, but before I could get too far, an overeager classmate attempted to grab the cup out of my hand. "You'd fail home ec!" she cried, launching into a lecture about technique.

"And you know what you learn?" said Sally, coming to my rescue. "That really it doesn't make too much difference."

I thought about this—this subtle gift, courtesy of the Bates and the Schmitts—as we gathered a final time under the mulberry tree. The corn salsa with a bite of lime and jalapeño was a hit. The savory *clafouti* was complex. But the smiles all around—acknowledging the hard work, the collective accomplishment, a new ease and confidence—overpowered any bitterness.

Lynell George is a senior writer at The Los Angeles Times West *magazine.*

Clafouti

Serves 12

1 cup butter

2 cups fruit*

2 cups all-purpose flour

2 cups granulated sugar

½ teaspoon salt

4 teaspoons baking powder

1 ½ cups whole milk

Preheat oven to 350°F. Barely melt butter and pour into a 9 x 13-inch baking pan, coating bottom and sides of pan. Whisk together the flour, sugar, salt and baking powder in a large bowl. Whisk in milk until well blended. Pour into prepared pan. Arrange fruit on top of batter. Bake 50 to 55 minutes, or until batter rises over fruit and is well-browned.

Best served slightly warm with vanilla ice cream or lightly sweetened whipped cream.

raspberries, blueberries, blackberries; halved, pitted cherries; halved, pitted apricots or plums, sliced peaches; halved ripe figs; or combination of fruit

PART TWO

EUROPE

Drowning the Snail

Trying to impress your future in-laws should never be this hard.

I was up in the cherry tree on a Saturday morning, blissfully filling sacks and sacks with beautiful *cerises*, when Jean-Charles stopped below me. He wore a paint-splotched t-shirt and baggy shorts, his gray hair flying every which way around his head. My fiancé's stepfather was a professional restorer and remodeler of houses, a stocky man who could move things a weightlifter might flinch at. Baggy, paint-splotched clothes were his favorite attire. "I don't hear you whistling," he called up. "You know, in France, cherry pickers are supposed to whistle to prove they're not *eating* all the cherries."

I coughed a cherry pit out of my mouth discreetly and tossed it into the bushes behind my back. Of course, as my white shirt had been indelibly stained in various places with cherry juice, this wasn't very convincing. "Maybe you should whistle when you walk by, too," I counterattacked. He had already culled a half dozen of the darkest cherries automatically and was popping them into his mouth as we spoke. So when he exclaimed, "Oh, there's a nice one!" I naturally assumed he was talking about a piece of fruit. I turned, hoping I could grab it first.

A big fat brown snail was oozing its way up the Burlat cherry trunk. Jean-Charles dumped cherry pits out of his palm hastily and snatched it. "One for my collection," he grinned and disappeared into the back of the garden.

I didn't follow him because I didn't trust Jean-Charles. He kept telling me things about his culture that turned out to be true. It was unsettling.

Take snails, for example. Everyone knows the French eat snails. I once tried one in French Polynesia and decided that eating snails was similar to putting gold leaf on perfectly good chocolate. Neither tastes good, both have a lousy texture, and both are clearly priced for showing off rather than for their culinary value. But Jean-Charles never ate anything just to show off, so either he was playing with my mind about French-snail stereotypes and was going to put on a beret next, or...he genuinely collected snails?

I chose not to have my leg pulled and went back to picking cherries. I would find it more reassuring to take the French culture on as an in-law if, even once, Jean-Charles turned out to be actually pulling my leg.

The next morning I was sunning myself on a bench he had made, contemplating attacking the cherry tree again, when he passed en route from the tool shed to his remodeling project in the kitchen. He stopped, grinning at me as if I was his sister and he had a big bug in his hand. "So do you want to see my snail farm?"

Well, actually, I did. Maybe I hadn't yet fully grasped what getting married to a Frenchman would mean and still hoped seeing a snail farm would be a once-in-a-lifetime opportunity.

I followed him behind a flowerbed to an old plastic paint tray set on top of a plastic crate that was turned upside down over an old plastic bucket—not a store-bought plastic bucket, which wouldn't have suited Jean-Charles's sense of frugality, but one that had once held some kind of remodeling project goop. Behind the bucket towered two oil barrels, which saved Jean-Charles $50 a year off his water bill by collecting rain. I was still looking around for the snail farm when Jean-Charles picked up the paint tray.

Glistening pale flesh oozed up around the holes in the plastic crate as half a dozen snails tried to squeeze their bodies through the bars of their cell. Jean-Charles flipped the crate right side up and plucked these escapees off without even an instant's hesitation about touching them. He dumped them back in with the rest, and I peered down at nearly one hundred snails, crawling over each other at the bottom of the bucket, crawling up the sides, drawn into their shells, or sprawled out sloppily. Or...doing some other things, I think. I'm not an expert on snail interactions, but I'm pretty sure I glimpsed snails in more positions than I was old enough to see.

"I put them in there to fast," Jean-Charles explained.

I eyed him sidelong. My previous experience with fasting consisted of Good Fridays, Ash Wednesdays, and any week prior to wearing a bikini, and these acts seemed entirely too ritualistic for the mob of slime below me.

"For a couple of weeks," he added. "Not less than a week. Empties out their intestines."

If one thing is vital in the process of preparing snails, it is, as I would learn, emptying out their intestines. "You see that slime they leave when they move?" Jean-Charles asked, no doubt referring to the sticky puke-colored trails on the bucket and other snails' shells. "You don't want to eat that."

No, I didn't. In fact, now that I got a closer look at the raw material, I was beginning to regret that snail in French Polynesia.

"Slime," Jean-Charles said, "is not one of the better flavors. Which you'd know if you ever got a mouthful of an improperly cleaned snail." He poured the snails from the bucket into the plastic crate as he spoke.

"It's good I have you here to help me; this is usually a long job." I jumped, but he didn't notice. "First we have to wake them up and make sure they're all still alive and worth eating." He dipped the empty bucket into one of the rain barrels and dumped water over the plastic crate full of snails. "The water gets them to stick their heads out."

They didn't have to stick their heads out far for Jean-Charles to spot a live one. In fact, they barely had to start looking moist. Staring down at a slit of flesh starting to open, I had a brief, flashing image of the female sexual organs but decided I really didn't want to go there.

Jean-Charles gave the snails about ten minutes, then dug his hands in. I was impressed. I mean, I, personally, would have used gloves.

He paused, his hands full of snails, one of which curled immediately around his index finger. "You are going to help, aren't you?"

A pair of gloves didn't seem to go with that question. "Er...um...yes. I was just trying to get a good idea of how it was done first, that's all. Wouldn't want to accidentally mix up a live snail with a dead one."

I had a strong suspicion Jean-Charles was giving me a gift. But it was a challenging gift. Could I take his culture straight, undiluted for foreigners? And if I could, here was a shot of it in all its fascinating richness.

I inspected the snails carefully and then selected the biggest, brownest one, with the cleanest shell, and delicately closed my fingertips around it. I flinched. My choice had gotten slimed on the far side by a fellow *escargot*. I placed it as quickly as possible into a second crate, where the live ones went; but having lost my snail-slime virginity, I felt I might as well keep trying to impress my future in-laws and so continued picking out snails.

Sébastien, whose fault this was because he had been worth changing my life, wandered into the backyard at that moment and spotted what was happening. He grinned and sat down on the bench to watch, a safe distance from the proceedings. I glared at him. He stretched out his legs and blew me a kiss.

"Now," his stepfather Jean-Charles announced, once all the live snails had been triaged into the new crate, "we've got to make them drool."

"I beg your pardon?"

"Drool," he said. "*Baver.* You know, vomit their insides out."

"Oh, *do* we?"

Jean-Charles *tsked* and shook his head. "Don't want to eat that slime."

To accomplish the vomiting part, he propped the crate at an angle against the cherry tree and sprinkled a healthy handful or two of *gros sel* or rock salt over the snails, then splashed them again with a little water. Pretty soon, foam emerged from the shells, followed by the snails themselves, and last their drool. When Jean-Charles lifted the crate fifteen minutes later, snail drool dangled through its holes like multitudinous strings of pizza cheese, although oddly enough, less appetizing—at least to me. Sébastien would later have some things to say about American pizza commercials that would make me realize all was relative.

I was actually getting into this endeavor by now, but here I ran into a problem in my exploration of the snail-cooking art. Fifteen minutes before my encounter with Jean-Charles, I had promised to go shopping with the others. No one seemed very understanding of the fact that I didn't want to go anymore because I wanted to stay in the garden and watch snails vomit.

"It'll take a while," Jean-Charles said. "I have to keep splashing them with salt and water every half hour or so, for a couple of hours. You go on."

Naturally we got stuck in Paris traffic, and by the time we returned, the snails had finished vomiting and sat cold and dead, a sickly gray-brown, in the refrigerator. Jean-Charles had washed them off without me and boiled them for half an hour. He gave me well-relished descriptions of the white and yellowish mess that had covered them and that he had washed off under repeated doses of running water. Living in Paris must have developed a sado-masochistic streak, because I felt aggrieved to have missed it.

Fortunately, even an American in Paris could be satisfied with the exquisite unpleasantness of the next step. The snails might be washed and cooked, but they were still in their shells. We had to get them out, in the process separating the part we wanted to eat (I use the "we" loosely here) from the part we didn't.

Jean-Charles brought out the equipment to do this, making me feel culturally underprivileged. Never, in not a single American kitchen, had I ever seen little two-pronged forks designed exclusively for popping snails out of their shells. "Don't watch too closely," Jean-Charles said as he demonstrated this instrument. "It's never nice to get a face full of dead snail juice." He stabbed his fork into the dead snail flesh, forced it halfway out, and just when things were looking too easy, pressed his thumb down on the second half of the snail and ripped the two halves apart. "Hepatho-pancreas," he said. "Don't want to eat it."

I stared at this, then at the bucket of nearly one hundred snails, feeling queasy. Jean-Charles paused and raised an eyebrow at me: "You asked how snails were prepared." I had? "So you're going to help, right? There's a lot to do."

I took a deep breath and plunged my tiny fork into a snail corpse. Popping it out was easy enough, but it took me a long moment before I could squish my thumb down on the hepatho-pancreas and rip away. I quickly rid myself of the hope of a clean break. The two parts separated easily enough, but bits of innards and stringy things dangled and curled.

"You've got the cutest expression on your face, *crevette,*" Sébastien said from well out of snail juice range.

I gave him a dirty look. "Why aren't you helping?"

"Do you see anybody else in the family crazy enough to do this? I was raised by Jean-

Charles; I've had all the experience with snails I need for a lifetime, thank you."

"Not easy, snails," Jean-Charles admitted. "That's why they're so expensive in restaurants. Plus, anybody who's willing to prepare them has to be well-paid."

"No," I said. "You're kidding me."

He grinned. "*Normally*," he admitted, "the person who prepares the snails never eats them."

"Really? I wonder why."

"But I'm not going to do all this work and not enjoy them. They're delicious."

> *The French approach to food is characteristic; they bring their consideration of the table and the same appreciation, respect, intelligence and lively interest that they have for the other arts, for painting, for literature, and the theatre. We foreigners living in France respect and appreciate this point of view but deplore their too strict observance of a tradition which will not admit the lightest deviation in a seasoning or the suppression of a single ingredient. Restrictions aroused our American ingenuity, we found combinations and replacements which pointed in new directions and created a fresh and absorbing interest in everything pertaining to the kitchen.*
>
> —Alice B. Toklas (1877–1967)

As I settled into a rhythm with the snail-innards-ripping part, I could focus on the question that had been needling me ever since I had watched snails vomit the day before: what could possibly have inspired the first Frenchman to think, "Look at all those snails ruining my garden. You know, I bet if I starved them for two weeks, made them vomit for a few hours, washed them repeated times, boiled them, ripped them out of their shells, and cooked them again in the right ingredients, they'd be delicious."

"Probably the siege of Paris in '70-'71," Jean-Charles responded promptly. "They ate anything that winter, even rats, even the two elephants they had in the Jardin des Plantes!"

Although I later did some research and found references to snail recipes at least one hundred years older than 1870, I still think he had the right idea: famine. Perhaps the main reason the great Paris siege famines of 1870 and 1590 get so much attention from casual historians is that they reduced the bourgeois and aristocrats to eating rats, too. The average French peasant underwent extreme famines regularly. Someone had to try snails at some point; what awed me was that they had figured out how to make them taste good. I had to hand it to my prospective culture-in-law. Other regions have gone through famines, and possibly other people have eaten snails out of desperation over the course of history; but only French peasants could turn them into an internationally known delicacy.

The rest of the snail preparation was comparatively easy: we had to wash them again several times and then simmer them for an hour and a half in water, garlic, herbs, cloves, and white wine. Next we had to squeeze them back into their shells, which Jean-Charles had boiled clean as a surprise for me. Normally he just stuffed the snails into little white *pots à escargots*, yet another thing you don't often find in American kitchens. We smothered them with enough garlic-parsley butter to make anyone but a Frenchman gain weight, popped them into the oven long enough to heat them through and let the butter melt, and then...*à table*.

"This is the life," Sébastien said happily, gazing at his gastropods. "I don't know how Laura survived until now. Do you know, when I was in the U.S., I saw this documentary on American sandwiches? You would not believe what those people eat. They even showed a sandwich that combined bacon, peanut butter, and bananas."

The Elvis! *That's* what my mother could make Sébastien the next time he visited. Sébastien really did need to experience a bit more of the U.S. soon, if you asked me. I didn't want to keep hoarding all these culturally enlightening experiences. Sometimes, especially when those culturally enlightening experiences included snails or hours waiting for my number to pop up in an immigration office, I couldn't help feeling selfish.

I took a deep breath and poured the snail and its butter into my mouth. Interestingly, now that I had spent hours torturing snails and mutilating their bodies, my tongue, even through rivers of butter, could identify every part of this one as I hurried it through my mouth. Fascinating anatomy lesson, really.

"It's the sauce that's delicious," said my skinny mother-in-law-to-be, dashing a shot of melted butter down her throat.

"Yes, but couldn't you have put it on *chicken*?"

Sébastien's family looked at me with polite tolerance and shook their French heads. "It just wouldn't be the same."

"That's my point."

They all exchanged glances. "Maybe she didn't get a good one," Jean-Charles said doubtfully. "Here, try another."

"*Another one?*"

"Where's my camera?" Sébastien asked gleefully.

"Wait for me!" Justine ran to get her own.

"You know, when I agreed to marry you, I never intended to become a zoo exhibit," I told my fiancé. I took a deep breath and picked up the second snail, recalling vividly the impression of an eyespot on my tongue from the last one. I dumped the snail into my mouth and tried to concentrate on its butter and garlic while Sébastien and his sister captured a whole series of grimaces on film.

Sometimes you have to impress your future in-laws any way you can.

Laura Florand has lived in Tahiti, Spain, and France and traveled many other places. For further adventures with her French in-laws, see her book, Blame It on Paris. *Her work has appeared in previous Travelers' Tales anthologies under the name Laura Higgins.*

Classic Escargots

Serves 2-4

3 garlic cloves

½ teaspoon salt

½ cup unsalted butter, softened

1 shallot, finely minced

1 tablespoon fresh flat-leaf parsley, finely chopped

¼ teaspoon black pepper

1 tablespoon dry white wine

12 to 16 snails (from a 7- to 8-oz can)

12-16 sterlized snail shells

2 cups kosher salt

Put oven rack in middle position and preheat oven to 450°F.

Using a heavy knife, mince and mash garlic to a paste with ¼ teaspoon salt. Beat together butter, shallot, garlic paste, parsley, remaining ¼ teaspoon salt, and pepper in a small bowl with a hand mixer until combined. Beat in wine until well combined. Divide half of the garlic butter mixture among snail shells. Stuff 1 snail into each shell and top snails with remaining butter. Spread kosher salt in a shallow baking dish and nestle shells, butter sides up, in salt.

Bake snails until butter is melted and sizzling, 4 to 6 minutes. Serve immediately in escargot serving dish (or on a bed of kosher salt).

Tomatoes

A time-honored ritual in Sicily is shared.

Making the year's supply of tomato sauce is *the* most important domestic ritual in the Sicilian summer, and each housewife believes in the efficacy of her favorite method with fervor equal to that with which she believes in the efficacy of her favorite saint. There are basically two rival schools of thought: the one favors passing the scalded tomatoes through the tomato mill, then sterilizing the filled and capped bottles in boiling water; the other prefers to heat up the empty bottles, fill them with boiling hot tomato sauce, and then lay them in a nest of woolen blankets, so well wrapped that they will take several days to cool off. Then of course there are many minor variations: some prefer to add a few onions to the cooking tomatoes, some don't cook the tomatoes at all but pass them, raw, still others disdain the widespread habit of putting a sprig of sweet basil in each bottle.

Preparations begin early, in the spring actually, when cracked pots and old five-kilo sardine tins are seeded with the tiny-leafed basil that is preferred for sauce making; these are assiduously watered into big and brilliant balls of green. Then crate after crate of empty beer and soda bottles are lifted down from the lofts, rinsed out, and left upside down to drain in the July sun for at least two weeks, so as to eliminate the least bead of moisture. At the same time the Wednesday morning street market at Alcamo is crowded with outside gas burners, huge aluminum and copper cauldrons, gigantic ladles, and mammoth colanders.

Sauce making is no small undertaking for the average peasant family, which in one day will put up anywhere from 50 to 150 bottles, or even more if there are married daughters to be supplied, or the padrone to be served. In fact, when I was first in Sicily, the little sauce that sufficed for my in-laws' needs came from bottles prepared by [our friends] the Pirrellos or by Peppino. (One year the bottles Peppino left in homage in the stairway behind the front door at Alcamo exploded, painting the entire staircase red, and I have often wondered whether it was chance or, like the green fruit, one more act of guerrilla warfare.)

It was therefore not my mother-in-law who initiated me into the rites of sauce making, but [our neighbor] Teresa Vivona, Turiddu's wife. When we were first at Bosco, Turiddu had not yet inherited the piece of irrigated land where he now grows their family vegetables, and each summer he would plant tomatoes and other vegetables at Bosco, for their use and ours. As soon as Turiddu announced that a sufficient number of tomatoes had properly ripened, the whole family would arrive at dawn to do the picking and then, when ten or fifteen crates were filled, we would set up our assembly line in the shade of the almond trees. Teresa, Franca, and I hosed down the tomatoes in large plastic buckets and plucked out the star-shaped green stems, which have a bitter taste, while Turiddu ignited the fire under our big copper cauldron, its bottom black from years of smoke, and spread out an old iron bed trestle the enormous sieve he had made by wiring thin young canes together. Gino, Felice, and Francesco carried out tables and strung an extension cord from the kitchen for the electric tomato mill that a thoughtful friend had once given me.

And there we worked, across the morning and on into the early afternoon, stirring and ladling and passing and capping. Teresa was in charge of the cauldron, filling it with tomatoes while she stirred until it was time to ladle them out onto the canes, so as to drain off the incredible amounts of watery juice that these plants had managed to suck up from the dry soil. Felice, still young enough then to be fascinated by *any* form of machine, operated the mill and sent the thick red sauce cascading into a plastic bucket, while I spooned it into the bottles into which Franca had first poked a sprig of basil. Turiddu and Gino capped the bottles and lowered them gently into the big oil drum, each layer covered with straw to keep them from cracking against each other in the boiling water. Francesco and Natalia ran errands for as long as their interest held out, then disappeared, not to show themselves again until all the bottles, filled with sauce and covered with heating water, lay in the oil drum and the last remaining sauce was being ladled out onto big plates of pasta. Our meal was interrupted by frequent trips out to shove the flame-consumed logs farther under the drum and to see if the boiling point had been reached and we could begin to keep an eye on our watches.

After forty-five minutes of boiling the fire was scraped away and the Vivonas went home, leaving the drum and its contents to cool off in the night air. The next day Turiddu came back to lift out the bottles and wipe away the bits of wet straw that clung to them, separating the green glass of mine, formerly filled with my mother-in-law's mineral water, from the sturdier brown of the beer and *gassosa* bottles that Teresa preferred, and I would carry mine into the house and set them in rows on the shelves of the *palmento*, where I could give them a proud glance each time I passed.

I must confess that sauce making lost much of its appeal when the Vivonas no longer came to share it with me, and after two years of solitary efforts that left me flattened for three days afterward, I proceeded to put aside my cornucopia complex and make a hardhearted estimate of our real consumption. It is thus without too much grief that Natalia and I pick, cook, and pack three crates of tomatoes this morning, and when Tonino and Francesco return from commitments elsewhere to do their part, they find some twenty-five bottles of sauce, an adequate yet unostentatious supply, waiting to be loaded into the drum and boiled.

Mary Taylor Simeti is an expert on the culinary history of Sicily. She is the author of numerous books including, Travels with a Medieval Queen, Sicilian Food: Recipes from an Abundant Isle, *and* On Persephone's Island, *from which this is excerpted.*

Italians are fiercely proud of the regionality of their cuisines. They'll also tell you that a meal prepared at home is infinitely better than any you'll find in a restaurant. So how is a culinary traveler to find an authentic Italian meal these days? Thankfully, today you can enjoy a traditionally prepared Italian meal in an Italian household, becoming one of the family for an evening. Egaria Di Nallo, a professor at the University of Bologna, created Home Food, an organization of over two hundred members that offers genuine regional Italian home-cooked meals for a small monthly membership fee (that fee allows you to sign up for as many meals as you want across the country for that month). The Cesarina, as the mostly female hosts are warmly called, must demonstrate deep knowledge of and pride in their region's cuisine in addition to being great cooks. Participating families are peppered across the country, making this a fun new option for the world-weary food traveler.

—Emilia Thiuri, "Meeting Alex"

DEBORAH GARFINKLE

Mushrooming Before the Fall

A Bohemian's culinary guide to fungi.

I know they are out there somewhere beyond our town limits—caps tipped in deference to the Emperor of the forest like Chinamen—their silky robes: fawn, alabaster, ochre, dappled, pallid as a swooning maiden and opalescent as the moon. When they first come out, they shyly hide their faces to protect the anonymity of their tender flesh. But once they age, they abandon all pretense of modesty, exposing themselves like frowsy hot mommas under great gaudy parasols. They can show off if they like because they're past their prime. But the delicate ones who've just nudged their heads out of the mulch are in constant danger of being snatched and so camouflage themselves from the keen eyes of peeping Toms and their prying fingers. They can't help their obsession; once you've partaken of the sublime delicacy of their flesh, you forget about the Beluga pearls and Nova nibblets dressed in their gaudy packaging and hawked in swank emporiums like Harrods, Bloomies, and Fauchon.

From the first time I went to hunt mushrooms beyond Světlá nad Sázavou, the town in the Czech Moravian Highlands where I lived for three years, mushrooms in their myriad forms have haunted my dreams: *houbová polévka* enriched with succulent cubes of potato, spiced with marjoram or added to a meat broth seasoned with caraway and bay leaf and pungent garlic. The Campbell's cream of mushroom soup of my youth, reconstituted with dark bits of god-knows-what floating on its surface and a heaping dose of salt added to conceal its blandness, is a sad imitation that pales in comparison; diced mushrooms cloaked in a web of freshly scrambled eggs accompanied by a thick slice of Czech rye and a slab of sweet butter; *řízek*, mushroom cutlets, breaded and pan-fried as if they were schnitzel; *houbový guláš s kysanou smetanou*, mushrooms drowned in pools of sour cream and ladled over fluffy *houskové knedlíky* (bread dumplings), that you use to mop up every dollop of that divine sauce; *Jihočeský hubovec*, bread pudding stuffed with mushrooms and cooked to perfection by my friend Jarka, served fresh from the oven golden brown and piping hot; jars of *nakladené houby*, slippery chunks of pickled mushrooms we'd eat to keep away the hair of the dog during the long winter nights when we drowned our sorrows in *pivo*, the fresh frothy lager, a staple of the Czech diet. In the dead of winter, these were our only sources of warmth and consolation.

But now it is late summer. Dusk overtakes the bright emerald landscape and softens it to heather. The dun-colored wheat that is now almost as tall as I am rustles briefly as a breeze passes over the sheaths. In August, the sunflowers bow their heads, doing penitence until they are absolved of their guilt and turn their faces toward the sky where the light is quickly dying.

After living there for a time, I realized that every aspect of existence in Světlá is governed by light, even the town's name means literally, the *light* village. According to legend, Světlá was founded by Charles IV, the Emperor of the Holy Roman Empire who is famous world over for his eponymous bridge, the quintessential Prague landmark. Once while tracking a stag he had wounded, he got hopelessly lost in the dense forest. Since night was fast approaching, he knelt down and prayed that if God would show him the way out of the labyrinth of spruce and pine, he would dedicate the place. As if by a miracle, a ray split the darkness and lit his way to safety and Charles returned to complete the construction of his great capital. To commemorate his salvation from perdition and as a token of his faith, he named the place *Světlá*, light. My twist on the legend has God turning his divine spotlight on a *lycoperdum perlatum*, the snowy puffball, which Charles nimbly dislodged and used as an improvised light source. I insist on the puffball because all Czechs know its taste is hopelessly bland. Had the light fallen on a more delectable specimen such as the *pýchavka obecná*, perhaps Charles would not have elected to be saved at all. He would have set up camp, lost forever to dreams of sautéed fungi and the fairies singing him to sleep. And in his absence who knows what bridge would span the Vltava, shepherding the hordes of tourists on their package deals to and from Prague's Greater and Lesser Sides.

My journey to Světlá was far more prosaic. I arrived there from Manhattan one cold November in 1990, to teach English at the elementary school. According to my friend Vladimír, I was the first American to breach the town limits since the war. Whenever he says this, I always think of myself in combat fatigues passing out Bazooka and Hershey's to a gaggle of half-starved children. But I know the facts; Patton was forced by Eisenhower to stop at Plzeň and the troops who liberated Světlá were not Yanks, but Soviets, the hard reality my friends live for whom February 1948 and August 1968 mark bitter anniversaries. However, we, who truly embrace country life know that each returning August does not symbolize Russian tanks or armies. The invasion of their territory is by a far stealthier adversary: neighbors armed with wicker baskets and their genetically imprinted knowledge of the mycology of the region. It is mushroom season, and according to Jiřina, my native informant, when it comes to sharing where the best places to hunt are, *one doesn't even know one's own brother.*

Today Jiřina and I have a date to go mushrooming in a patch of forest just on the outskirts of town. The weather is perfect. Fair and sunny, not even the least hint of the fall that is soon to come. I have always loved what I thought were mushrooms, the ivory button-capped fungi I bought home from my local supermarket. But those *mushrooms* are what people here call *šampiony*. It is a word I can easily remember because it has been taken from the French *champignon*. I like them because they are not linguistically illusive. I can ask for them by name no matter where I order or recognize them on the menu because they do not use the generic term, *houba*. But as Jiřina explains, any idiot knows that *šampiony* are not *real* mushrooms; real mushrooms are hidden beneath thick blankets of fallen conifer needles where their heads gently nudge out of banks of moss that flank the spruce and pine. The ones that are most prevalent in the thick forests that ring our town are, Jiřina tells me, *hřiby* (singular, *hřib*, *hříbek* in the diminutive)— almost impossible for non-natives to pronounce because of the hard first consonant and the palatal "r" that only exists in Czech language.

We approach the patch of forest which she believes, based on her vast experience, will yield results. She is much faster than I am despite her age. I follow her up the hill, almost out of breath. As we come closer to the juncture of grass and field, we cross paths with a young boy. He is walking back to the road and has nothing in his hands. He is wearing a t-shirt and sweatpants that hang off his slim frame like a pair of old gym socks. To me he looks like all the other Pavels, Honzas, and Petrs in my English classes at the local elementary school, but he's not one of mine. Jiřina, who knows many of the kids in town from teaching in the other school, eyes him suspiciously.

"Have you been in the forest?" she asks him.

"No, Ma'am," he replies without looking her square in the face.

She pauses for a moment and then she blurts out rather anxiously, "Do you know if there are any mushrooms in the forest?"

He meets her with a pause of his own, weighing just how to respond and still remain within the limits of propriety. There have been some workers in the forest, he says without any emotion, then adds, "I think they've picked the lot of them. Good-bye," he says as he calmly stalks away with his hands shoved in his sweatpants' pockets, cool as a cucumber.

Jiřina turns to me, explains their exchange and then says bitterly, "He's only pretending so we don't go looking." I shrug my shoulders, but I can feel the mixture of her disappointment and angst. I, too, want to find hidden treasures. I want my share of the real mushrooms. My heart begins to thump and I have butterflies as we plunge into the deep shade of the spruce forest.

I come across my first discovery. It is a lovely flashy mushroom with a reddish cap and white spots that is standing right in the middle of my path. It looks as if it's right out of the Enchanted Forest. "Jiřinko," I joyfully yell out into the dense growth, but she is lost rummaging in her own patch of forest and has left me to fend for myself. I can hear her huffing and chuffing off in the distance. By the quick pace of her footfalls on the leaves and needles, I can tell that she is not having much luck. "Jiřinko," I call out again, filled with glee that I, the neophyte, might be the first one to discover the first true mushroom of the season.

When Jiřina finally comes stomping over to where I am standing, she waves her infamous dismissive hand. "Deboro, that's a poisonous one," exasperated that I have ripped her away from her quest for such an ridiculous reason. Why would the damn thing be standing there in pristine condition in broad daylight, brazenly displaying its colors if it weren't a completely inedible specimen?

"Sorry," I say, chastened by her better judgment and disappointed by the fact I have lost this round of the treasure hunt.

I decide to follow Jiřina to observe just how she carries out the search. She is purposeful and very quick in her movements. Suddenly, she bends down and sticks her hand into a mossy bank beneath some deciduous trees; it's almost as if she has sensed the flora with her mind instead of her hand. She pokes her fingers into the earth, gently prodding something out of a seemingly invisible notch in the earth. It is a small brown-capped mushroom *a true (pravý) hřib*, she announces to me using the Czech term for the species because we have yet to decide on its proper English translation. She leans over to show me its delicate form. It has a thick cap and instead of the field mushroom's milky button that turns an unappealing mud color when manhandled and chocolate brown gills that turn gooey after a day in the fridge, the underside of the cap like the honey-comb of treacle candy or a sea sponge and the skin is silky smooth. It's an amazing, wondrous thing. Jiřina pares away some of the stem to see if the mushroom is a taker. After a moment's scrutiny, she places the tender little body into her wicker basket. "I knew there were mushrooms!" she says triumphantly, like Stanley who felt Livingston's presence in the heart of Africa from deep within his bones. We are ecstatic.

No one else is in the forest. As we wander deeper into the trees, the aromatic smell from the decaying foliage and needles becomes intoxicating. I rarely look up. I am far too preoccupied with trying to read the forest floor as if it were a rare old map and I were Long John Silver: go six paces east from the oak leaf that fell at 10:52 A.M. on August 4th and then twelve paces north from the roe deer scat from the first yearling, and so on, until you come upon a soft patch of earth. There X marks the spot. Because human minds are so bent on making order when confronted with confusion, we wrack our brains until we can create the meaning out of chaos; we see mushrooms through the trees, even when they are not even there. So I bend down to take a closer look, focusing my gaze as if the whole patch of floor in front of me can be viewed like a stereogram map to mushrooms waiting to pop out before my very eyes.

After staring for what seems an eternity, I see it appear as if by magic from out of nowhere! A small fawn-colored *hříbek* sitting surrounded by the umber litter of pine needles and starry moss. I'm in love with my find. I know this time I have not bungled the identification because I am sure it resembles several of the other edible mushrooms Jiřina has placed in her basket. I gently ease the stem from the ground and call to her to confirm what I already know.

She stomps over to me miffed that I have once again interrupted her search. "Show me," she orders so I stick out my hand. Her voice softens immediately softens once she realizes that she has not been called away from her searching in vain. "Yes, yes, Deboro, it's a *hřib*," she says happily, patting me on the back. She is proud of her student who has finally managed to come up with fruitful find after such a long quest. Her mood is almost jubilant, but that would be too much enthusiasm for the competition. She takes the mushroom from my hand, pares down its base and checks for worms. I wait on pins and needles for her approval, wondering if the worms have got there ahead of me. But no. This one is going to be the first to grace my empty basket. Here you go, she tells me, handing me back the mushroom which I place on the bottom of the basket as if it were a sleeping infant. I have not been this happy since I was twelve gorging myself on handfuls of wild blueberries I picked from the crest of a 3,000-foot mountain in Maine.

We keep searching, but neither of us has a great deal of luck. I have less than a quarter of a basket. No more than six or seven. Jiřina has about twice as much. Not a good showing for someone who's been at it seriously for more than a half a century. Today has not been propitious for seekers. After what seems like hours, we eventually stumble out of the forest. We have combed the whole floor, but pickings have been fairly slim. Jiřina keeps going over in her mind what factors might have contributed to the poor yield: the interns from the agricultural school have been out and about before us; the foresters did, indeed, spirit them all away in the wee hours of the morning; the barometric pressure has dropped; the humidity is too low; the evenings have been too warm; the Gods are against us. It is August, which everyone here knows has the potential for being the cruelest month to those who wish to roam the countryside, living life free as a bird. As we leave behind the forest, both of us must face the end of summer and civilization's contradictions, heartbreaks, and divisions. And the local children are sullen because vacation is almost over and school will begin again in just a few short weeks.

"*Tak, pojd'*," Jiřina says to me as we slowly make our way back into town to her house. Such a disappointing day. But despite our failure, I still I feel elated because of the warm summer sun than beats down upon us as if it will never grow cold again.

I take a look at my watch. It's only one o'clock and I am famished. When we arrive home, Jiřina begins the preparations. I watch as she cleans our catch, paring away their imperfections and worm-eaten patches with a surgeon's skill. With so few found on this excursion, we can't waste a bit of edible flesh. She sets asides a small pile, then begins slicing up the majority of them to dry, the first of her provisions that will have to last through winter. I want them now, but Czech preservation takes precedence over my American city slicker's yearning for instant gratification; I am the prodigal grasshopper to Jiřina's prudent ant.

Once the mushrooms lay drying on baking sheets near the window, she dices the ones that remain and throws them into a pot of boiling stock. My mouth is watering and soon the kitchen is filled with humidity that fogs up the window. I undo the latch, open out the large pane of glass to let the steam escape and I smell the freshly mown lawn, the heat of summer mingling with the smell of rich mushroom soup. I go back to the table to slice the rye as Jiřina ladles out the mushroom soup into our shallow bowls, almost too shallow for my yawning appetite. As I take my first spoon, the woody essence of wild mushroom reconstitutes the whole expanse of forest on my palate and I find consolation even in defeat. I know that tomorrow they will still be out there hiding, daring me as they had Charles IV to breach their domain before dark, before it's too late.

Postscript: A note on the word *hřib*. I have long since learned that the Latin for *hřib* is boletus (pl. boleti). There is, to my knowledge, no vernacular equivalent in English. In my local upscale grocery they are sold under their Italian name *porcini* (little piggies) for $35 a pound.

Deborah Garfinkle is a poet, writer, and translator living in San Francisco. Her creative work has appeared in several publications including The New Orleans Review, The Prague Post, Two Lines: A Journal of Translation, The Dirty Goat, *and others. She is currently*

working on a collection of short stories based on her experiences living in Central Europe called Accounting For Germans and Other Tales of Mittel Europa. *In 1990, she left Manhattan and her position as the Associate Manager of New Accounts for Bloomingdale's to live in Světlá, a small town in the Czech Moravian Highlands, armed with two words of Czech and an adventurous spirit. Fifteen years, a Master's Degree (English - Poetry) and Ph.D. (Czech Literature) later, she teaches composition and creative writing at De Anza College.*

Whether *you call it* bolet *or* cepe, *or* boletus, cep de Bordeaux, *or* tete-de-negre *(politically incorrect, it may be, but not a single French neighbor knows the* boletus aureus *by any other name!), this fungus is the ultimate, the 24-carat, the creator of superlatives. In the Ariege it is called* cep. Cep *appear only when the weather is perfect—such precision of circumstances is required to produce them that a whole folklore exists around their uncertain emergence. It's true that they only grow where pigs travel, so unless the* sanglier *cross your land, you will not be rewarded with bowling-ball sized fungi that taste of smoked bacon but have a texture all their own; incomparable. That taste, the villagers claim, is produced— alchemically—from the dung left by the pigs.*

Because we have sanglier *in our woods, we also have* cep. *And that is where the cultural chasm emerges. My father believes that a man's land is sacrosanct, and good fences make good neighbors. Every Ariegious also believes both those things to be true, unless one's neighbor has something like* cep, *or cherries, or wild strawberries, or chestnuts or walnuts…at which point, the rules change. If you have a wild crop and you don't appear to be harvesting it, or it is obvious that you can't use all of it yourself, or if your land was once owned by a distant cousin of theirs, then the average Ariegious feels they have a sacred duty to uphold the proverb "waste not, want not" and to help you out with the harvesting, storage, and consumption of that produce.*

The rest of my family still see these incursions onto our land as larcenous. Back home, when we wanted to visit neighbors, we would use the main drive, but villagers here arrive from all directions. Back home, we'd call this theft. Here it's called nothing—it's just the law of the land. If your neighbor is too busy, lazy, or stupid to harvest nature's products, you just help yourself. Then, when the time is right, you repay whatever benefit you've gained.

—Kay Sexton, "Mushroom Hunters"

JOAN HALADAY

Look Until Done

Persistence pays off in Portugal.

With the taste of twelve Portuguese lessons on my tongue and four weeks of a vacation in Portugal still digesting inside me, I knew that I wanted to take cooking lessons in Lisbon. However, how to do it proved to be more like the old-fashioned recipe instruction "cook until done," than a precisely worded modern recipe. At first, I did try to be methodical about my search for a cooking school. Before leaving Ninho das Águias, the Lisbon pension below the Castelo where I began and ended my first trip, I tore out a page of the Yellow Pages from the phone book in my room. The page contained two listings under the heading *"Escolas Culinárias"* (Cooking Schools), and as soon as I returned home I worked up my place-enhanced twelve language lessons and wrote to both schools in Portuguese.

A letter sent to one listing, a woman's name, never received a response, while the second listing, which I also treated like a woman's name, produced a letter of regret that no cooking lessons were being offered, as well as a little commercial pamphlet of suggested recipes for a week's worth of meals. In Lisbon, that letter must surely have provoked laughter because with my limited language skills, my salutation in Portuguese had read something along the lines of "Dear Margarine Dairy" as I mistook and treated the name of the local margarine factory and research facilities like a personal name.

While my first leads failed to produce a cooking school for the following year, I contented myself through the winter and spring with preparations based on faith by acquiring a large food-related Portuguese vocabulary from reading recipes during private language lessons from the cookbooks purchased during my trip. This turned out to be a boon—albeit a slightly one-sided one—to language learning and made me realize that following a passion, interest, or hobby made language learning easy and natural. Fortified with so many linguistic culinary ingredients, I felt energized to look for a cooking school again.

My next strategy involved using travel books in libraries and bookstores to look for a cooking school. When those efforts also produced no harvest, I contacted the Portuguese National Tourist in New York City, but that approach revealed only another empty larder. The agent I spoke to offered to send me a list of language schools instead. I declined that offer. However, convinced as I was that there was a cooking school-in-hiding waiting for me to find, every six months or so I would call the tourist office again, and once more be told that there was no information available on culinary schools. In between calls, I went to Portugal for the second time and attended the annual national gastronomy festival in Santarém which, rather than satiating my Portuguese food

> The evolution of the internet makes it simple and quick to search for anything you need. Bring up a search engine such as Yahoo or Google and type in what you are looking for and voila!, within 10 seconds you can have 100,000 web site hits. However, it can be daunting. We have provided you with a Resource section which is a great place to start. In addition to the web sites for cooking schools and culinary tours, there is a section with clearinghouses full of leads and a bibliography with books devoted to descriptions and contact information on schools and providers around the world.
>
> —MAJ & SB

cravings, just made my interest more like an addiction. Once I was home again, the period between my telephone calls to the tourist office became shorter, until one time an annoyed agent, tired of saying no to someone who didn't seem to understand the word in English or Portuguese, put me on hold.

It turned out to be the most fortuitous hold of my life thus far. When I heard a voice again, a man identified himself as the director of the office. When I explained the reason for my call, it both amused and charmed him. He didn't think American women liked to cook or that anyone who wasn't Portuguese would want to cook Portuguese food. He asked for my telephone number saying he would get back to me, and he did. A colleague's mother just happened to teach cooking in her home. That three-year-long scent I followed put me on the trail to Vera Sousa's home-based cooking school in the Amoreiras neighborhood of Lisbon.

The first time I attended class I was late. Instead of walking, I took the tram, which ended up stuck in Lisbon's rush-hour traffic. I finally found her apartment building at dusk. The other students were already assembled in the kitchen, among them an affluent woman wearing pearls and oozing perfume who was learning to cook in order to better instruct her servants, two retired gentlemen who had eaten well in restaurants during their working years and had taken up cooking as a hobby, a girl still in high school who became the pet of the group, and a woman about to be married. During my five-week stay I joined them one evening a week for the basic cooking class that proceeded through soups, *açordas* (a category of Portuguese bread soups that can be appetizers or one-dish meals), sauces, omelets, and more.

On Wednesday and Friday mornings I had two private lessons that Senhora Sousa tailored to my special interests: *salgadinhos*, literally "little salty things," which included such bar snacks as *pastéis de bacalhau* (codfish-potato fritters), *rissóis* (meat, fish, or shrimp-stuffed fried pastries prepared from a cooked dough), and *empadas de frango* (diminutive tartlets filled with chicken in white sauce), and seafood dishes such as *lulas gratinadas* (gratin of squid in tomato-cream sauce), *lulas recheadas* (squid stuffed with sautéed onion, carrot, chorizo, and rice), and *bacalhau bem bom* (gratin of shredded cooked dried codfish and fried straw potatoes in white sauce).

On those days, the senhora regaled me with tales of her own cooking past. She, too, once took lessons in her youth, and from a much stricter teacher. She talked about her many children, the recent marriage of a daughter, and her own pleasure in enjoying nightlife in spite of many years of marriage and childrearing. She shared her fears about the health of her aging mother who lived on the premises, told me of her visit to New York to see her son and of her experiences trying out New York street food sold from carts during that trip, and gossiped about how when an American journalist once visited her as a source of recipes, they had to do a photo shoot in the bathroom because it was the only room in her lovely but modern apartment that had the requisite "atmosphere" created by the *azulejos,* or tiles, that a foreigner would expect to accompany photographs of Portuguese food.

After my first late arrival, I realized how close Amoreiras was to my pension if I walked, so I walked to the rest of my cooking classes. Depending how much I dawdled, the walk was a pleasant twenty- to thirty-minute appetite teaser from my pension in Bairro Alto. I loved the walk, its repetition which became like the perfecting of a walk as a recipe, too: each day a form of perfecting a skill as well as an exercise in subtle variations. It gave me time to become intimate with Bairro Alto and Rato, the neighborhoods that I passed through en route to Amoreiras, and I felt a sense of belonging while in Lisbon that I hadn't had since my college summer abroad when I studied French.

For Joan Haladay, home is a place within walking distance of the Hudson River. Away from home, she is a food-centered traveler, who especially loves to wander in and write about Portuguese-speaking places. She is working on essays about Lisbon and the Azores. Her story, "Theater of the Air," about traveling to Brazil, appeared in the anthology In the Air, Your Stories. *"Food for Diversity, Food for Thought," an essay about culture, food, and identity was published in* Under the Sun. *She has written book reviews for* Small Press *and* Independent Publisher, *culinary pieces for* The Brasilians, *and anecdotes for the "Metropolitan Diary" column of* The New York Times.

Pastes de Bacalhau
Salt-cod Fritters

Makes 20-25

1 pound dried salt cod

2 cups milk

4 medium Idaho potatoes

1 large Spanish onion, finely chopped

2 garlic cloves, minced

1 handful fresh flat-leaf parsley, finely chopped

1 handful fresh cilantro, finely chopped

2 large eggs

freshly ground black pepper

vegetable oil, for frying

lemon wedges, for serving

Twenty-four hours ahead, soak the dried cod in cold water, changing the water several times to remove the majority of the salt. To prepare, drain the cod, rinse, and put it in a large pot. Add the milk and enough water to cover by one inch. Simmer gently over medium-low heat for 20 to 25 minutes, until the cod is tender and pliable. Drain and rinse well, then flake the cod into a bowl with your hands, removing any bits of skin and bone.

While the cod is cooking, pour 1-inch of water in a large pot fitted with a steamer insert. Add the potatoes and simmer on medium heat for 20 to 25 minutes until very tender. Drain the potatoes, peel, and mash well. Add the cod to the potatoes, along with the onion, garlic, parsley, cilantro, and eggs. Beat the mixture firmly with a wooden spoon so that it well combined. Season with a pinch of pepper. With lightly moistened hands, shape the cod mixture into egg-shaped balls.

Heat 3 inches of oil in a deep heavy skillet or pot to 370°F. Add a few of the balls at a time to the hot oil, turning them 3 or 4 times to evenly brown them. Lift the cod fritters out of the pan with a slotted spoon and place on a platter lined with paper towels to drain.

Repeat. Serve hot or at room temperature with lemon wedges.

Mincing Garlic

A lesson in food, a lesson in self.

You might wonder, as do I, just how I ended up somewhere in the mountains of Catalonia trying not to cry. This Spanish town and the circuitous route by which I arrived in it are, at the moment, a proverbial blur.

Let me be more specific. I am visiting a small cooking school and home-stay inn called Catacurian. It has three rooms for students, a beautiful dining room and garden, and a kitchen that made it into an article in a Spanish magazine praising it as one of the ten best kitchens in the world. I like it because it is small, modest and efficient, every inch designed for both beauty and function.

I have just finished mincing garlic, an activity I should have declined given my state of sleep deprivation. But I can mince garlic in my sleep, I think to myself, and so I accept the assignment from the diminutive and feisty proprietor, Alicia Juanpere. I finish my task quickly.

As I walk to the sink to wash my hands, I hear her thick Catalan accent.

"You have not done a very good job," she announces crossly from across the room.

Under normal circumstances I would have accepted the tease and simply laughed. Instead, I want to cry.

I want to slap her and walk out. Tiredness is like that; proportion is a fast victim.

I have just completed a round of cooking classes at home. I am in my teacher's frame of mind, yet suddenly I am a student, feeling small and mildly ashamed. I would never humiliate a student, ever, or anyone in a jet-lagged stupor like mine. I cannot focus on the humor. I can only pretend to take it calmly.

"Would you like it smaller?" I ask.

"Yes, please, make it smaller," she says.

I wash the knife that has grown sticky with the juice of the garlic and return to mincing, reducing the already small bits of garlic to something very close to a puree.

Juanpere makes no further assessment of my kitchen handiwork. She gives me other tasks—making a bouquet garni, slicing and peeling tiny green garlics, making the *picado*, a mixture of crushed garlic, hazelnuts, and almonds that is essential to many Catalan dishes—and soon brings me a stool, instructing me to sit as I work. It is apparent how exhausted—and likely, how close to tears—I am.

We continue to cook the *ficandó*, a traditional Catalan stew, and soon we are drinking *cava*—the low-alcohol sparkling wine of the region, a delicious bubbly balm I could drink around the clock—and eating small grilled chiles drizzled with local olive oil and coarse, solar-dried sea salt from France.

I watch as a fellow student completes her task, peeling, seeding, and dicing tomatoes. If she were my student, I think to myself, I would show her how to do it properly. She is cutting the tomatoes incorrectly—through the poles instead of the equators, so that only a portion of the seeds and gel come out—and chopping them into chunks that are too large.

The student, a precisely manicured woman who appears to be in her early seventies, looks immensely pleased with herself. I can tell by a subtle sideways glance in my direction that she is competitive.

Juanpere says nothing. I take another long sip of *cava*.

A sweet man from New York fries the veal he has floured. A tall, gray-haired man from Sacramento cleans wild mushrooms with a brush. The student of the tomatoes moves on to parsley.

At a moment when everyone's attention is elsewhere, Juanpere discreetly picks up the bowl of chopped tomatoes and hands them to a woman from Washington, D.C., who has been staying at Catacurian for a week.

"Chop them into smaller pieces," she all but whispers.

I am the only other person who hears.

I know there is both wisdom and humor in all that she has done, but I am too tired to quite put my finger on it. Later, when we are all sitting around the dinner table sipping more *cava* and savoring our stew, she and I chat and I am simply happy to sense that she doesn't think I'm a fool in the kitchen.

Juanpere was a dancer for many years, I learn, first as a student of classical ballet and modern dance and later as a teacher, with her own school in Barcelona. She gave it up when she turned forty and two years ago bought an old house in the village of El Masroig, where she spent summers as a child. She and her husband, Jonathan Perret, remodeled the building with its ancient pine beams, creating one of the most charming and diminutive cooking schools I have seen, with a gorgeous cellar and tasting room in the basement. People come here from all over the world to enjoy Juanpere's classic Catalan cuisine, based on the recipes she learned at her grandmother's and mother's sides.

She is charming, intelligent, complex, and kind. I forgive her the garlic comment yet still, as I drag my tired self out into the dark night, now heavy with rain, I can't help but wonder what it was about me that made the admonition about my mincing technique acceptable yet silenced her when it came to the clumsy tomatoes.

I still have a lot to learn, I think to myself, even if how to mince garlic is not one of those things.

Michele Anna Jordan is the author of numerous cookbooks, including San Francisco Seafood, The New Cook's Tour of Sonoma, Williams-Sonoma Complete Pasta Book, *and many more.*

Ficandó

Serves 6 to 8

1/3 cup picado (see recipe below)

2 1/2 to 3 pounds boneless veal, cut into randomly- sized slices

kosher salt or sel gris

1 cup flour

4 tablespoons olive oil plus 3 tablespoon lard

3 shallots, thinly sliced lengthwise

1 onion, thinly sliced lengthwise

3/4 cup dry vermouth or white wine

2 or 3 tomatoes, peeled, seeded and minced (about 1 cup)

3 cups veal or beef stock

bouquet garni of 1 bay leaf, 3 thyme sprigs, 1 3-inch celery stalk 1-
inch leek, white part only, wrapped and tied with kitchen twine

4 garlic cloves, minced

3/4 pound golden chanterelles

First, made the picado as directed below and set it aside.

Season the meat all over with salt and dredge it in flour, shaking off excess but being certain the meat is thoroughly coated. In a large pot or a traditional Spanish *casuela* set over a ring on top of a burner turned to medium high heat, heat 3 tablespoons of the olive oil with the lard. When the mixture is hot, saute the shallots and onion until limp. Season with salt, add the meat and pour in the vermouth or white wine. Cook until the vermouth or wine is nearly completely evaporated. Stir in the tomatoes and beef stock and add the bouquet garni. Simmer, uncovered, until the meat is very tender, about 1 hour. Add the picado and cook until the juices have thickened, about 15 to 20 minutes.

When the *ficandó* is nearly done, pour the remaining olive oil in a saute pan set over medium heat, add the garlic and saute 15 seconds. Add the mushrooms, season with salt and saute, stirring frequently, until the mushrooms are limp. If they remain firm, add a splash of vermouth or white wine, cover the pan and cook for 3 minutes. Season with salt and stir into the stew.

Picado

Makes about ⅓ cup

2 garlic cloves, peeled and crushed
pinch of salt
¼ cup hazelnuts, toasted and peeled
¼ cup almonds, toasted and peeled

Put the crushed garlic in a mortar or other hand grinder, add a generous pinch of salt and crush the garlic to a paste. Add the nuts and use the pestle to crush each one. After the nuts are crushed, continue to grind the mixture until it forms a nearly smooth uniform paste. Set aside until ready to use.

Open House

Who knew all recipes' key ingredient is confidence?

Chatting, charming, and teasing the clerks as she shopped, she plucked a bundle of leeks from her favorite grocer, a perfect chicken from the good butcher, a crunchy loaf of bread from the best baker.

Oh, yes, and we'd better get some of those bright green apples. And parsley…. She stuffed everything into her rolling market cart and trundled home, talking fast, French-accented English to us all the way.

The "us" in this Parisian adventure was Deborah Morgan, a marketing consultant from New Jersey who is a good amateur cook, and I, who am not, and never will be.

Ms. Morgan and I chanced to sign up for the same one-day class in French cuisine, and Paule Caillat ("pole" and "kay-yah" are as close as I came to pronouncing her name) deftly tailored her teaching to suit us both.

Back at her apartment in the Marais district, we unpacked bouquets of produce and a mass of paper-wrapped bundles, spreading edible treasures all over her antique, scrubbed wooden kitchen table.

We peeled, diced, mixed, and cooked. Then we ate. The result was delicious, but so was the day.

It turned out to be far more than a cooking class, more even than a way to demystify

French cooking. It was an excellent way to get inside Paris and into the mind of a French cook.

Ms. Caillat rendezvoused with us at a small café near the Oberkampf Metro station on an October morning.

I was interested in basic things; Ms. Morgan wanted more advanced material. She wanted, for example, to know how to make the classic apple dessert *tarte tatin*.

It's complicated, mused Ms. Caillat, noting that she prefers a much easier version of apple tart. I was instantly certain I would, too. So Ms. Caillat agreed to teach us to make both. We shared coffee and hot chocolate, made a game plan, and walked to her favorite street market on Boulevard Richard Lenoir.

Paris has a long tradition of small, floating street markets. They're put up for a morning in one neighborhood, taken down by afternoon and moved to another neighborhood for the next morning, moved again the next day, and so on.

On any given morning somewhere in the city, even in winter, vendors display their wares outdoors, under striped awnings, around some compact square. Shoppers browse pears, peppers, and tomatoes as bright as jewels, as many kinds of mushrooms as there are in a forest, succulent red meats, fresh, silvery fish, and a fair sampling of the world's best cheeses.

The French like quality ingredients and they like them fresh, so good cooks shop daily. "Nothing goes into the fridge," was how Ms. Caillat put it. That's why so many French apartments have refrigerators not much bigger than ones made for a college dorm room.

In addition to the street markets, everybody has a short list of favorites among the myriad food shops—grocers, butchers, and cheese mongers—that line the streets in every neighborhood.

And bakers, of course, because baguettes are mandatory with meals, and they stay fresh just one day.

Now, for an admission: I don't have any recipes to share. Although we used recipes— Ms. Caillat's own adaptations—that wasn't what the class was about. It was more about attitude.

As she charged down the market aisles, popped into shops on side streets and bustled around her kitchen, Ms. Caillat dropped pearls of cooking wisdom. It was like listening to a philosophy of life:

"If I could, I would cook and eat something new every day!"

"Cooking is combination more than invention."

"I am against unnecessary steps."

"If you want low-fat, you make low-fat. If you're going to eat, you eat."

"The secret to the flavor of meat is in the bones."

"Putting Camembert into the fridge is absolutely going to kill it."

"Just cook until it's cooked."

"Life is a permanent class, anyway."

"The guests wait for the soufflé. It's not the other way around."

Ms. Caillat came to teaching by an unusual but perfectly French path: fashion. She spent eighteen years as a buyer for Bergdorf Goodman in its Paris office and ten years as a sales manager for Paris fashion stores. But about five years ago, she was ready for something different.

She started with classes in her apartment, then branched into giving food-oriented tours, mostly in Paris but also in Provence. Almost all of her students are Americans.

"A lot of couples come," she said. "Very often, it's the men who cook or want to cook."

But Ms. Caillat has been noticing how squeamish Americans are. They even object, she said, to the uncooked eggs that go into a classic chocolate mousse.

Ms. Caillat calls her kitchen her "salon"—her living room—and it did have some dream elements: limestone floors, yards of pink-and-black granite counters, two sinks, enough room for a sofa, and more cupboard space than I have in my entire house.

But the space inside those cupboards looked comfortably familiar: well-used pots and pans, stacked inside one another, so she had to juggle them every time she took one out.

Not that this mattered. It was clear that when you really know how to cook, you can do it in a soup can, in the dark, over a campfire. The skill matters more than how the shelves are arranged.

The menu we cooked for lunch was poached chicken and leeks drenched in a subtle cream sauce, cheese soufflé, and the two apple tarts—all washed down with white wine.

The first tart, a classic *tarte tatin,* is like a one-crust upside-down pie. Big chunks of apples are packed tightly into a round pan, slathered with butter and sugar and cooked on the stovetop until they soften, subside, and are just this side of caramelized. Then you put a lid of fresh pastry on top and pop it in the oven.

For what I thought of as "tarte easy," you make a piece of pastry, put apples on it and bake it till the edges brown. *Voilà.*

Served warm and drenched with crème fraîche, the thick, slightly tangy delicacy that puts our whipping cream to shame, both tarts were so good that I had trouble deciding which was better.

As a finale, Ms. Caillat escorted us to Dehillerin, a cooking-equipment emporium that continues to be one of the most quaintly frustrating stores in Paris. Even Ms. Caillat called it "intimidating."

We went there because I wanted a pair of killer oven mitts like hers: thick sueded leather with padding so effective I thought it must be asbestos.

They were firemen's gauntlets, Ms.

Monsieur Courtois, director of the Ecole Supérieure de Cuisine Française-Ferrandi, giving a tour of the facilities to a group of illustrious French government "big toques," guided them to my work station. "Et voici, messieurs/dames," he explained, using his laser pointer to indicate that I was Exhibit #1, "is our main attraction. Mais non, he isn't the best of the new chefs, but he is a lawyer! And he is, évidement, not a poulet de printemps anymore." Even "not a spring chicken" is easier to take when expressed in French. Ah, French subtlety, who could not love it? The guests caught on fast. Remember those spectacular Busby Berkeley musical extravaganzas with hundreds of coordinated dancers and swimmers performing perfectly in-sync like an école de poissons? Now think about a group of those French dignitaries equally in-sync giving the Gallic shrug, chanting, "Bizarre! Bizarre!"

M. Courtois then administered the coup de grace, "And…he is…américain!" The heads turned to each other, bobbed knowingly. "Ça explique tout!" There is, after all, only so much one can expect from foreigners. I was given no blindfold for this, like in the movies.

—Atticus Madison, "Will You Be Having Pinstripes with Your Canard?"

Caillat explained, and Dehillerin had them for a steep price for oven mitts, but cheap for a unique and useful souvenir.

The storefront is a wooden classic, like those that dotted Paris in the eighteenth and nineteenth centuries, and inside on towering racks is a jumble of cast-iron pots, copper pans, oddly shaped strainers, escargot pans, brioche molds, and nearly every other conceivable weapon in the *batterie de cuisine.*

Thanks to heavy publicity in American gourmet magazines, Dehillerin is almost always crowded with Yanks. Men in blue smock coats bustle around helping you find things, and everyone converges at the front for a slow but time-honored process of payment.

First, your helper takes your purchases to a small wrapper's counter; you get a slip with the total on it; you take that to the equally small cash register counter, stand in line, pay, wriggle back to the first counter and trade the receipt for a nicely wrapped purchase.

That's a lot of work for a pair of oven mitts.

But I thank Paule Caillat every time I put them on. Never mind that what I'm taking out of the oven is a frozen pizza, not a *tarte tatin.*

Catherine Watson took her first trip at the age of five, by train, from Minneapolis, Minnesota, to Grand Forks, North Dakota, in a blue suit her mother had sewn and a new white straw hat. She has been fascinated ever since by the relationship between "home" and "away." She is the award-winning travel editor of the Minneapolis Star Tribune *and the author of* Travel Basics.

Classic Tarte Tatin

Serves 6 to 8

Tarte Tatin, one the France's greatest contributions to world culture, should be dark golden brown. This version, offering a shortcut, calls for commercial puff pastry, available in the freezer section of most supermarkets, and gives excellent results.

½ cup unsalted butter

1 cup granulated sugar

6 apples, such as Golden Delicious or Gravenstein, peeled, cored and quartered

1 pound puff pastry

crème fraîche or vanilla ice cream, optional

Preheat the oven to 400°F. Melt half the butter in a 9-inch frying pan, preferably cast-iron, set over high heat. When the butter is melted, use a wooden spoon to stir in the sugar; continue stirring until the mixture takes on a golden color, like light caramel. Remove from the heat and let cool for 1 to 2 minutes.

Arrange the apple slices in concentric circles, working from the inside of the pan outward. If any apple slices are left over, scatter them over the first layer. Cut the remaining butter into small cubes and scatter the cubes over the apples. Bake for 35 minutes, remove from the oven, and let cool.

Cut a circle of puff pastry that is one-inch wider than the frying pan and about ¼-inch thick. Fit it over the cooled apples, tucking the edges inside the rim of the pan. Bake for 35 minutes more, or until the pastry is flaky and golden brown.

To serve, put a large flat serving plate on top of the pan and carefully invert everything, so that the tart drops from the pan onto the plate. If any apples stick to the pan, carefully remove them and tuck them into their proper places. Cut into wedges and serve neat, or with crème fraîche or vanilla ice cream alongside.

CATHERINE ANN LOMBARD

Giuseppa's Secret Ingredient

The author learns more than a time-honored recipe.

Wherever I go in Italy, recipes seem to follow me. One spring morning I stand with the village women at the meat truck to buy my husband's *prosciutto*, raw ham sliced thin. One of the women asks for rabbit and wants to know if it is fresh. "*Carissima*, they're from last night," the butcher announces proudly as she pulls two skinned, earless rabbits from the refrigerator. The limp beasts lie on the counter like newborns, their pink flesh gleaming.

The women exclaim how beautiful and fresh they are and immediately ask if I eat rabbit. I don't have the heart to tell them I'm a vegetarian. "Well, no," I say, "but my husband likes it." Then the recipe follows: Fry the rabbit's liver with wild fennel and garlic. Then stuff the rabbit with the savory liver. Sew up the rabbit's belly and cook it slowly over a low fire with a little bit of white wine. Turn it once or twice. It's ready when the meat falls off the bone.

These are the kind of colorful, yet imprecise recipes that keep following me. One day I was invited for a coffee at Signora Giuseppa's house, when she offered me a piece of *crostata*, which means "crust" in Italian. It is a delicious and popular tart which consists of a flour-based bottom crust covered with a thin layer of homemade jam and baked until golden. This particular *crostata* was decorated with pieces of hazelnut and walnut which Giuseppa had gathered in the autumn from her eleven trees. On top of the nuts were pieces of golden dough shaped as stars and half moons. It was delicious.

Giuseppa is seventy-eight years old, a round and sturdy widow with small, yet broad strong hands. She is one of the few people I have met in my life who is really present when you are with her. She talks and talks to me in Italian, maintaining her normal speed, even after someone else in the village suggested she slow down so I might understand her better. She knows I don't always understand, but perhaps what she finds more important is our time together.

While I munched on the delicious cake, she asked if I wanted the recipe which had come from a friend of hers. Giuseppa had added her personal touch of nuts and celestial decorations. I naturally said yes, and she handed me the recipe on a small scrap of paper along with a pen and piece of paper so I might write it down.

The recipe, of course, was in Italian. After writing it down, I studied it a moment, and then paused, realizing something was missing. "Excuse me, Giuseppa," I said. "isn't there flour in here?"

"Yes, of course."

"But, then," I stumbled. "How much flour do you use?"

"Oh, I don't know. Not too much and not too little. Just when it feels right. When it doesn't stick too much to your fingers. *Quanto basta*." ("When it's enough.")

"And doesn't it have to go in the oven? How long do you bake it? And what's the temperature?"

"Why, I never look at the time. After all, every oven is different. The oven has to be hot. But not too hot. You cook it not too much and not too little. You just look and see if it's done. *Quanto basta*."

I started to laugh. This was the craziest recipe I had ever seen.

"And the lemon," she said smiling, knowing what an amateur she now had on her hands. "Of course, you don't put in a lemon. You grate a lemon peel. And the nuts, well like I said, they were my idea. And the stars and half-moons, well, I just did that because it was entertaining and looked nice."

What could I say between my laughter? "Giuseppa, next time you make the *crostata*, please tell me because I want to come and see how you do it."

"Oh, Caterina," she said, quite wisely. "Next time you want to make the *crostata*, you tell me, and I will come and show you how. After all every oven is different and you should know how to cook it in your own oven."

She then gave me her phone number and I jotted it down below the recipe. This seemed only right. Giuseppa, after all, had become the essential ingredient to making a perfect *crostata*.

A few days later I decided to ask Giuseppa to come and give me the *crostata* lesson. I knew that in the afternoon I could find her at her farm where she goes every day after lunch. I wandered down and sure enough she and a companion were sitting in the shade taking a short rest from the hot April sun. She had been planting tomato plants, since the nights had now grown warmer and the plants were safe from frost.

She greeted me and we chatted for a while about the weather and tomato plants. Giuseppa finished her planting and then went to water her lettuce seedlings. Soon she was generously filling a plastic bag with lettuce, new garlic and onion, spinach, and *rucola* for me. Naturally, recipes followed. "Chop the *rucola* up fine and mix it with mayonnaise. You can add a little olive oil if you like. Toast bread and spread the mixture. The taste is so delicate! Chop this garlic up fine, mix it with wild mint and a little hot pepper and olive oil. Put it inside the artichoke and cook it slowly. It's more delicious than meat!"

I then felt the time was right to ask for help the next morning in making the *crostata*. Giuseppa was free and happy to come. "Have you already made your jam?" she then asked.

Made my jam? Before even starting, I had failed my cooking lesson! Months ago I had purchased a jar of 55-percent-less-sugar strawberry jam at the local supermarket and it had been sitting in my refrigerator ever since. I thought the *crostata* was a perfect solution to finally rid myself of this jam.

"Oh, Giuseppa, I bought the jam at the shop."

She looked at me as if I were a small child who tried too quickly to finish her chores. "And do you have nuts?"

This question seemed a bit fairer to me, after all I couldn't possibly make nuts myself.

"No, but I asked Giovanni to buy me some." Since my husband's name Kees is impossible in any language but his native Dutch, he has adopted Giovanni as his Italian alias.

"Oh. Don't worry about the nuts. I will bring you some. And the pan? What kind of pan do you have?"

"I have pans for making pizza. Will they do?"

"I'll bring my pan. What time should I come? Is nine o'clock fine?"

I kept thinking how I would have to have the kitchen and the rest of the house spotless before Giuseppa arrived. "Nine o'clock is a bit early. How about ten?"

"*Bene. Bene.*" We were set for the next morning at ten.

Right on time, Signora Giuseppa swept into the house the next morning with the energy of a twenty-year-old woman. Inside the bag slung under her arm was her pan and a large bag of nuts. In addition she had brought her own apron, spotlessly pressed (mine hung soiled and wrinkled around me), and her own nut cracker. On the kitchen table, I had laid out all the ingredients and a bowl.

She didn't waste a moment, whipped on her apron and started cracking the nuts. *Crack, crack* went the nutshells under her strong tutelage and soon I had six, seven, eight nuts lined up waiting for me to dislodge them from their shells. Giovanni showed up to say hello and steal a nut from the bowl. I protested, but Giuseppa carefully shelled a walnut herself and handed it to him.

Once half of the nuts were shelled and chopped (the other half was a present for me), it was time to start the dough. I gave Giuseppa a clean bowl, but she put it back on the table. She first wanted the flour. I handed her a sack and she poured a large amount through a sieve and onto the table. Then with her hands, she created a hole in the center

I find that little of what I cook is based on my heritage. The lone exception to this is my great-grandmother's shortbread, which she brought with her from Scotland to America. This recipe is the one thing that ties me to our collective past and may link us to our future, as I've passed down the recipe to my children. My hands work the buttery dough as she would have done and the rich smell permeates the kitchen. The taste of it with a cup of tea binds me, however slightly, to her and my cultural and familial history.

—Susan Brady, "The Ties that Bind"

of the hill of flour and asked for the eggs. Cracking the two eggshells together, she let the eggs drop onto the table inside the middle of the flour. With a fork she started to whip the eggs. I watched astonished to see the flour actually become the bowl.

She continued adding all the ingredients except the jam and then slowly, with her fingers, added more flour to what now looked like a yellow crater in a mountain of snow. The flour began to swirl and thicken the yellow egg paste and gradually, almost magically, she had a round piece of dough sitting on the table before my eyes. She slid the remaining unused flour to one side. I reached out to handle the dough, trying to imprint its consistency into my palm and fingertips.

Of course, all this time, Signora Giuseppa was talking. "When I was a young girl during and after the war, we had to make everything. If you wanted to eat pasta, you had to make it. My mother taught me how to make everything. The bread, the pasta, the pizza. I started when I was very young. You just need some experience. You just need to become used to it. It's really very simple."

Well, it looked simple enough, but I had my doubts when left on my own. I could imagine my mountain of flour becoming a blob of sticky glue, with the egg running all over the table and onto the floor.

It was time to light the gas oven. Giuseppa came to inspect the oven settings when I explained that the oven was old and had only two temperatures: high and half-high. She selected high and continued working.

Next she spread olive oil on her large round pan and started to stretch the dough to form the bottom crust. The pizza pan would not have worked after all; its sides needed to be higher. The dough spread perfectly and was just the right amount to cover the pan's bottom. Next was the jam. At first she thought it might be a bit too thick so she asked me for wine to thin it.

Next came the decorations. Together we pinched and pulled dough into stars and half-moons and decorated the jam filling. Finally, we covered the entire *crostata* with nuts, leaving the dough decorations free to show. We placed the tart into the pre-heated oven and she suggested we check it after twenty minutes.

I thought we might pause here for a cup of coffee or tea, as we had been standing the entire time, but no. The remaining flour sat on the table and Giuseppa turned to me and said, "Why don't we make Giovanni some homemade pasta for lunch!"

I actually thought Giovanni should came down to the kitchen and make his own homemade pasta for lunch. Wasn't the *crostata* enough for one day? After all, he was bound to enjoy most of the large tart. But what could I say? "Oh, what a great idea!"

Signora Giuseppa moved the small pile of flour back into the middle of the table and added a bit more before once again making a deep hole. She then asked for wine. "We'll make pasta without egg. White or red wine will do. Red will just color the pasta. But then you have all different color pasta. Spinach will make it green and red wine will make it red. Does Giovanni like pasta without egg?"

Giovanni surely would not refuse homemade pasta, with or without egg. "Of course," I said, reaching for the opened bottle of red wine. She poured the wine into the "flour bowl" and started to mix the ingredients, once again, with her fingers and hands. Under her care, a round ball of dough once more appeared on the table. I reached out to feel it as she started to knead the dough with her strong broad hands.

"You see, Cateri, my husband was in a car accident when he was only forty-three. For three days he lay in a coma. We didn't know if he would live or die. He had broken a vertebra in his dorsal spine. My son was only two years old."

Thud, thud, thud. The rose-colored pasta dough thumped the table. "My son needed his father and I needed my husband to help raise him. Afterward, of course, I was left to do everything. In the house. On the farm. In those days we raised our own pigs. Everything. It was years before my husband could move again, and, in the end, he had to use a wheelchair."

I listened and watched closely, the rhythm of the kneaded dough marking her staccato words. "I'd come home tired, and he would be waiting for me. 'Are you tired?' he'd ask. And I'd say yes. 'Are you too tired to make me some pasta?' he'd always ask. And of course I always made it for him."

Giuseppa smiled now with the memory of her husband, someone, I had been told, who was kind and generous. "He'd always ask. And I'd always make it. Now, where is your rolling pin?"

Oh, dear. Store-bought jam, dirty and wrinkled apron, and now, no rolling pin. Giuseppa's head shook as she looked once more at me with a mixture of humor and disapproval. We needed a rolling pin to roll out the dough into a flat sheet. Once it had dried a bit, we could then cut strips of pasta. Instead, we were faced with rolling small pieces of dough into long strings of spaghetti by hand.

"This is the work of patience," said Giuseppa as she cut off the pinkie-size pieces for us to roll. The *crostata* had now filled the kitchen with the smell of sweet cake. I checked the oven, but it wasn't yet brown enough, and I was told to leave it for a few more minutes.

We began to roll dough into long worm-like strings, which we then placed on a tablecloth in the sun to slightly dry. Giuseppa started to teach me all the different names for such pasta. "In Bomarzo, they call this *scivolati*, because '*scivolare*' means to slip or glide. Here in Mugnano, we call it *rescivole*. In Umbria, it's called *strangozzi*. '*Strangolare*' means to strangle, and I suppose these are long enough to strangle someone if you had to," she laughed.

I kept repeating the names as she said them. *Scivolati. Rescivole. Strangozzi.*

"In Roma, they call this pasta *tornarelli*, because you turn and turn the dough to make it. And in Viterbo, they are called *umbrighelli*. Of course, some people like to call it, *strangola il prete*." She stood laughing alone until I took my pocket dictionary and looked up "*prete*," which means priest. Some people like calling the pasta "strangle the priest."

All of these towns are within twenty-five miles of one another, and yet each had their own descriptive name for the spaghetti. By now the *crostata* was done baking and sat on the counter as we continued for the next hour rolling the *scivolati, rescivole, strangozzi, tornarelli, umbrighelli*. I wondered how women fifty years ago found time to do this between making their bread and *crostatas*, minding their children, watering their hogs, and working in the fields.

"There are pasta machines that you can buy," I timidly suggested.

"Oh, they are not the same as homemade. They take too much water out of the pasta and leave it dry. There is nothing like homemade pasta," she said.

I thought about all our sharing that went into the pasta dough. Perhaps while telling her story, some of the love Giuseppa felt for her husband had worked its way into the dough. No machine could have substituted for that.

"Cook this pasta in boiling water until it rises to the top. It doesn't take long. The best sauce is one with tomato and chile peppers, a little parsley, salt and pepper. It's too early for basil, but it is also good with tomato-and-basil sauce."

Could another recipe enter my head? Long strings of pasta covered the kitchen table. Our work was finally finished. Giuseppa flipped the *crostata* onto a large plate and protested while I insisted on washing and drying her pan. Before placing it back into her bag along with her apron and nut cracker, Giuseppa removed a small item. "I brought you this, Cateri, so you could remember me." She handed me a crocheted doily that, naturally, she had make herself. The handiwork was fine and delicate, the piece spotlessly white and tidily pressed. "You put it inside a bowl when you want to serve cookies or bread. Do you like it? At night, when I am sitting alone by the fire I make things like this. My hands are always busy."

What could I say? That I would never forget her cracking the eggs into the pile of flour on my kitchen table. That every time I ate *rucola* and mayonnaise I would think of her. That her energy and good-will astounded me. That I had nothing to give her in return but her clean pan.

"Thank you so much. It's beautiful. I love it," I said kissing both her cheeks. "Thank you for coming today and being my cooking teacher. Giovanni will love the pasta."

It was noon and she bustled toward the door. "We are planting more tomatoes today. I must go home now." Giovanni came down to admire his promising lunch and to sniff longingly at the tart. We all said goodbye and walked Giuseppa to the gate.

Since that day, I have made the *crostata* so often that I no longer need a bowl and have grown comfortable with the idea of *quanto basta*. But, no *crostata* has ever compared to the one I made that warm April morning with the secret ingredient called Signora Giuseppa.

Catherine Ann Lombard writes, gardens, cooks, and teaches yoga in Italy where she lives with her husband. Besides Italy, she has lived in Ireland, Egypt, and Japan. Her essays have been published in Italy Magazine, London's The Guardian Weekly, *and numerous other publications.*

Crostata

Serves 8

Pasta Frolla

2 cups flour

½ cup sugar

²/₃ cup unsalted butter, room temperature

1 egg + 1 egg yolk

grated zest of 1 lemon

Filling

2 cups jam (raspberry, strawberry and plum work best)

½ cup chopped nuts (walnuts, pecans, hazelnuts)

Mix the crust ingredients until they form a ball. Refrigerate for 1 hour, if possible. Roll out dough on floured surface to ¼-inch to ½-inch thickness. Cut a round and fit into 8-inch round pan. Spread with jam. Take leftover crust and re-roll. Cut into strips to form a lattice on top, or cut into shapes and place atop jam. Sprinkle with nuts. Bake at 350°F for 20 to 25 minutes until dough begins to brown. Cool and serve.

ANN MCCOLL LINDSAY

Kitchen on Wheels

Two bibliophiles trade in John Keats for Elizabeth David.

One thing should be understood right from the beginning. We had no interest in cooking when we started on the journey. Absolutely none. Poetry—that was our whole impetus. To burn intensely in the moment, to pay homage at the shrines of the writers, that was our aim. For seven years we had been teaching English Literature. Now we were going to live it.

David had arranged to pick up a camper van overseas. September and October we'd tour Britain, experience a Dickensian Christmas in London before crossing to the continent to follow the sun in the footsteps of the romantics around the Mediterranean. Not a single piece of cooking equipment was packed in our blue trunk. Small velvet pouches of jewelry went in instead of a can opener, fur-trimmed coats rather than anoraks. Nothing practical was included. *The Oxford Book of English Verse* took precedence over *The Joy of Cooking*.

Living in the confines of the van that first week brought us close to divorce. Behind the passenger seat was a doll-sized sink and food storage cupboard. When the side door slid open, a tray could be popped up on the side of the van to hold the two-burner stove that ran on camping gas. Behind the driver's seat hung a table which could be flipped up onto a leg when needed. We used this table for writing and playing chess, but most meals were taken perched on the suitcases outside the van to view the ever-changing scenery. Because of our lack of implements, we did more snacking than dining on the upended Samsonites.

We ate our breakfast rolls on the banks of the Firth of Forth, crunching along the beach on a bed of mussels before the tide came in. We lunched on fruit and cheese in a gazebo in Pittencrief Park, a lush garden of globe thistle and coreopsis. A fish-and-chip supper, wrapped in newspaper, was a dinner treat on the crags of Stirling Castle. The prospect of an entire year in which every meal offered a different view made Hemingway's *A Moveable Feast* a reality.

That golden autumn as we drove through Britain, I could feel a personality change coming on. At the country houses listed in literary guidebooks, our intention was to stare at manuscripts in glass cases. But once on site, something drew me below stairs where social history was on a more intimate level. In an Adam's mansion, while the group upstairs crowded around the El Grecos and Murillos, we snuck down to a cool cream-tiled kitchen, as chaste as a temple, lined with open shelves of blue-and-white china. I experienced an unaccountable urge to put on an apron and fill that swirled white porcelain mold with a vanilla cream or poach a skate in the huge triangular copper fish poacher. From then on, in every historic house we visited, I headed for the narrow stairway that led to the realm of scullery maids and cooks. Cinderella in reverse, I began to realize that the room of one's own that Virginia Woolf had been going on about was, in my case, the kitchen.

On our run down to the south coast of England, the van became a stockroom of pedigree utensils that hardly qualified as essential camping gear. A china ham stand from a butcher's shop in Nevis, a carved bread board and knife from Sheffield, a pair of ridged butter hands from a farm store, a silver cake stand from a jumble sale in the crypt of a church. They all told a story about a lost way of preparing and serving food. They filled a gap in our sketchy culinary pasts. If we had to go on a buying spree, better to choose domestic objects that could be used rather than useless fripperies. When we reached the south coast, we perched outside the van on the cliffs of Dover and picnicked on ham, bread, butter, and cakes from the correct serving pieces. But I still couldn't cook in them.

A few days before Christmas, we visited the British Museum to view the Sutton Hoo Burial Treasures, but ended up in the tea room tucking into scones with Dr. LeMire, my professor of Victorian literature. He invited us to spend Christmas Eve with his family in their apartment on Mecklenburgh Square. When we arrived, their apartment house was full of overseas professors and their families. None of us expected the unconventional cooking class about to take place.

Dr. L. proposed that he prepare Crèpes Suzettes as was his custom on this special night. The group of us from different continents gathered around the chafing dish to watch our prof roll the thin pancakes that he had just made in a small cast iron pan, soak them in cognac, then briefly flame in the chafing dish. In that precise moment, like a flash in the pan, I realized that simple ingredients with proper equipment could create a festive atmosphere. As soon as I saw Dr. LeMire transforming flour and milk into a celebration, I knew that my future would involve food preparation.

When Dr. LeMire noticed my interest in his cookware he made a fateful suggestion. "You are staying in South Kensington? That is quite near Elizabeth David's Kitchen Shop on Bourne Street where we bought this Crueset crèpe pan." She had presented Britons with one of the world's first specialty kitchenwares store just a few years earlier, and I could barely wait for it to reopen after the holidays.

This innocent morning's shopping expedition turned into a lifetime obsession. We had spent that fall admiring the lives of writers. Now we were about to meet a woman who had converted the lyricism of her writings on food into a concrete business ethic. She has been called "Keats in the Kitchen." With a sense of venturing into the unknown, I bought *French Country Cooking* and a French marmite, that tallish casserole whose silhouette is featured as the logo on E.D.'s paper bags. *French Country Cooking* represented a brave leap into the world of real ingredients. The introductory chapter on *batterie de cuisine* justified my previously incomprehensible urges to buy old bits of kitchenware.

Once we made it onto the continent, we found out what to do with our collection of utensils. Our kitchen skills were on the fast track now since most Spanish restaurants and bars obligingly keep the *cucina* open to view. In one small bar, a talented waiter prepared several *tapas* of mushrooms, fish, shrimp, and sausage using only the top of a burner plate and some saucepan lids. He flipped the cap off a beer bottle onto the ceiling, and caught it while sliding the bottle to us down the bar. His sense of fun was infectious and he had a healthy irreverence toward food preparation that dissolved any lingering hesitation we may have felt regarding our new passion.

Some of our unorthodox classes happened out-of-doors strictly by chance. At a later date, we had the good fortune to be on the beach at the same time as an ex-marathon runner named Ayo was preparing a gigantic paella over a wood fire on the sands at the edge of the Mediterranean. His athletic prowess was put to use as he scampered along the beach collecting wood and ingredients for his production. The theater involved in the preparation was heightened by the suspense of the serving logistics. Although this flat iron pan spanned more than five feet, a loyal clientele of fifty strong were waiting to dig in. It was tantalizing to watch this tall, athletic Spaniard in swim trunks kindle the firewood, toss the rice in oil, add the freshly caught shellfish, pour on the broth, quicken the flames, deftly dance around the perimeter, without having any assurance that a serving would be available for you at the end of it all. Anxious diners sat at tables bordering the sea, swilling Sangre de Torres, devouring baskets of crusty bread, while

Passing by a typical Sevillan bar, I was engulfed by the smell of frying garlic and coriander leaves. I peered through the open doorway. Huge legs of jamon serrano (cured ham) hung from the rafters, and barrels of wine were stacked off to one side. The tables were empty. A woman with intense black eyes and a crisp white apron informed me that the restaurant would be open in an hour.

Returning later that night, my friends and I encountered crowds spilling out onto the street. We squeezed our way to the bar, which was covered with plates of tapas. The noise of laughter and chatter was deafening, confirming, in my mind, Spain's reputation as the second loudest country in the world. We ordered glasses of wine and began feasting on the grilled portabella mushrooms, marinated olives, delicate slices of Spanish omelet, and squid soaked in saffron and wine. When our glasses were empty we moved down the street to the next bodega, and then onto the third.

Tapas, traditionally served in bodegas, or wine bars, range from octopus boiled with paprika to almond and garlic soup with grapes. The popular small plates originated in Seville (today the tapas capital of the world) when little dishes were placed on top of wine glasses to keep fruit flies out. Over time, cooks began putting appetizers on the plates to please the customers—and a new tradition was born!

—Suzanne Dunning, "Seville, Spain: Going *Tapas*," Tangodiva.com trying to catch Ayo's eye. The regulars, who came every Sunday after Mass, were served first; the Virgin and her heavenly host made sure that the plates of the faithful got filled. Saintless, we could only rely on chance. The level in the pan was dangerously low. But magically he scraped up enough clams and saffron rice to make two Canadian Presbyterians happy.

After we pitched camp near the sea at Alicante, we followed a path through the grounds to a trio of campers sitting out in front of an English caravan, engaged in making marmalade. The gentlemen rose to greet me as I approached.

"This is the month for Seville oranges," the tall frail one explained. "We go through jars of it over the rest of the season. Been here since before Christmas and don't intend to return to England until Easter." He resumed his seat in the canvas chair next to an elderly lady who was passing curls of peel from the mountain of huge oranges in front of her to the two gents, so that they could cut it into proper size slivers for the jam. A large copper preserving pan bubbled on the camping gas stove, sending out waves of a sweet syrupy citrus fragrance. I perched on a stool in front of the assembly line and was instructed patiently in the fine art of preserving.

By the time we sailed into Copenhagen (Merchants' Harbour in Danish), we felt as qualified as MBA graduates to toss aside our teaching fellowships and enter the food business. We sailed home with $500 left in our pockets in May of 1969, opened one of Canada's first kitchenware stores in August of that year, with a real kitchen in which I honed my newfound craft and eventually even gave cooking lessons. The smorgasbord of culinary information that we had absorbed that year on the road, supported us until our retirement in 2002.

The lessons Ann McColl Lindsay learned on the road in "Kitchen on Wheels," informed her writing career. After several years in business, she wrote a guide to the use and care of over two hundred pieces of kitchen equipment, including recipes for each, and illustrations by David Lindsay. Exposure to street markets equipped her to write an introduction to the Covent Garden Farmers' Market cookbook, Cooking with the Seasons, *and a historical chapter on the role of this market in downtown London. Ann's articles urging architectural preservation have appeared in newspapers and periodicals.*

Crèpes Suzette

Makes 6-8 crepes

Crepes

1 cup flour

pinch salt

1 tablespoon sugar

1 ¼ cups milk

2 eggs

2 tablespoons melted butter

1 tablespoon grated orange zest

butter for cooking

Sauce

4 tablespoons butter

¼ cup sugar

1 tablespoon grated orange zest

2 tablespoons Grand Marnier

Place all crepe ingredients in blender and mix thoroughly. Let rest refrigerated for 30-60 minutes (up to overnight).

Heat 6- or 8-inch skillet over medium heat and add a small pat of butter. Pour several tablespoons of batter onto skillet, swirling it around so that it covers the bottom of the pan. Once it starts to dry out, turn and cook the other side for 15 to 30 seconds. (Do not let crepe get too brown on either side.) Remove to a plate, and repeat, separating each completed crepe with wax paper.

To make sauce, melt butter with sugar, and add zest and liqueur over low heat until sugar is melted and all are combined. Fold crepes in half, and in half again, forming a triangle. Add to the melted mixture stirring to cover. Serve two crepes to a plate, pouring excess sauce over all.

MELISSA KRONENTHAL

Basque Tortilla

A homesick exchange student finds solace and passion in the kitchen.

The first time you step off the plane into the cool, humid air, you could be forgiven for thinking you've arrived in the wrong country by mistake. The landscape is the first clue, particularly if you've traveled here from other parts of Spain: parched, arid plains have given way to close-knit, brooding mountains, green and hemmed in by rain clouds. The cities are tucked in between them, huge apartment blocks challenged in height only by the aging black spires of the industrial infrastructure. There is no endless sun, no evening bullfights here; the people you encounter are quieter, more reserved. Signs on streets and doorways mock your grasp of Spanish with their incomprehensible strings of letters containing multiple *k*'s and *x*'s, and words like *kaixo* and *eskerrik asko* filter their way into the conversation of those around you. And if that's not enough, when you start talking to people they all ask you how you enjoyed your time in Spain. But, you stammer, I haven't left Spain! Yes, they assure you, you have. You haven't just crossed into another province of Spain, you've entered a place that is emotionally, intellectually, and linguistically its own country—the Basque Country, or Euzkadi, as the locals call it.

I was sixteen when I arrived here, exhausted from the transatlantic flight but tingling with both excitement and terror. Ahead of me stretched a year in this strange new place where I would have to learn to function in a new language and adapt to a new family's routines. I was well prepared for the culture and language shock, and had even steeled myself against the inevitable bouts of homesickness. What I wasn't so prepared for was learning that my placement in Spain was going to be in a region that didn't consider itself the least bit Spanish.

"The Basque Country?" I remember repeating in confusion when the exchange organization told me the location of my host family. I had read about the Basque Country once in an issue of *National Geographic*. It occupied about a paragraph in an article on Spain that mentioned that this 'dark and industrial corner of northern Spain' was best known for its 'mountains, fervent separatism, and magnificent cuisine.' It also briefly hinted at how the Basques did everything they could to distance themselves from the symbols of the rest of Spain. To be honest, I didn't really know what to think about the prospect of industrialism or separatism or the absence of anything remotely Spanish, but at least the cuisine part had me intrigued.

As luck would have it, I found myself in very capable hands in this department, thanks to my new host mother. Clari was without a doubt one of the most enigmatic women I'd ever met. Small, dark, and rotund, with piercing coal-black eyes and an encroaching colony of facial hair, she was both a fearsome cook and a stern disciplinarian. To her own family she could be fiercely intimidating, the gruffness in her voice accentuated by decades of smoking Lucky Strikes, her orders taking on a military severity as she barked them to her rebellious children. Mealtime was certainly no exception, and I often found myself mired in the middle of family food dramas. In theory the arrangement was simple: she cooked, people ate. There was no discussion about what was for dinner, no special requests taken or pickiness tolerated. Whether she produced a pot of beans or a perfectly baked fish, her family was expected to eat and be grateful; the problem was that they never were. "Why can't we ever have pizza?" the two younger siblings would complain daily. "Why do you need to use so much garlic?" the oldest sister would chime in, pedantically redirecting the most obvious pieces to the edge of her plate. "I think you used too much salt this time," my host father would grumble, pouring himself more wine. Clari would just sigh deeply as she cleared away their leftovers, shrug her shoulders, and turn to me. "Would you like more Melissa?"

It was a rhetorical question—I always did. Despite her family's complaints, I knew I had never had food this good. Clari, like most Basque housewives, cooked a fixed range of rustic, earthy dishes, things like *porrusalda* (leek and carrot soup), *alubias de tolosa* (red beans with garlic) and scrambled eggs with *perretxiko* mushrooms. She also excelled at seafood, and had even achieved some fame in town for her versions of famous Basque creations like *marmitako* (tuna and potato stew) and *txipirones en su tinta* (baby squid cooked in its own ink). For me, though, the dish that cemented her true genius was something remarkable for its simplicity, a staggeringly delicious mixture of potatoes, eggs and onions that she'd served to me my very first night with her family. "This is a typical Spanish dish, isn't it?" I had asked when she brought it out, proud to be able to identify the famous *tortilla española*. All eyes had turned to Clari, who just looked bemused. "This is a Basque tortilla. I don't think you'll find one this good in Spain." While I knew enough to be skeptical of such a casual generalization, what I tasted was certainly good enough to leave me wondering.

I began joining Clari in the kitchen as a respite from the stresses of my new life. Before school started I had several weeks to get acclimatized and improve my language skills, and my older host sister thought this would be best accomplished by giving me a month-long crash course in partying. Naturally her seemingly endless circle of friends was very curious to meet the exotic *Americana*, but my poor grasp of the language made every conversation —particularly with young people as they used so much slang and liked to have their inter-action happen in places with pounding music—simply exhausting. I began bowing out of social dates, much to my sister's disbelief, to spend some quiet time at home with Clari.

At first I just sat with her as she prepared the family's meals, soaking in the rhyth-mic efficiency of her movements as she peeled, chopped, and sautéed. We talked very little, which seemed to suit both of us fine—occasionally I would ask her for names of unfamiliar foods or dishes, but mostly I just sat enraptured. One day, though, feeling increasingly more confident about my linguistic skills, I noticed her assembling what looked like ingredients for a tortilla, so I asked if she would teach me how to make it. She nodded, and gave me a bowl and a knife. "Do you use a recipe?" I asked, remember-ing how my own mother rarely set foot in the kitchen without some kind of instructions by her side. Clari let out an explosive laugh and shook her head. "I've been making this since I was a little girl. I could do it blind."

I followed Clari's lead and set to work peeling and cutting up a pile of potatoes. "The first important thing is the size and shape of the pieces," she explained, showing me how she cut off rugged chunks. "They should be as irregular as possible with lots of corners to get crispy and browned in the oil, and they should be just the right size to cook through in the time it takes for that to happen." This was obviously a science at which she was an expert, and in the time it took me to dismember a single potato (quite inconsistently, I

might add), she had done the rest. She tossed them in a bowl with an onion that she had finely diced and reached up into the cupboard for a large bottle of olive oil. "You must use extra-virgin for this," she said, "it's necessary for the right taste." Shaking her head reproachfully, she added: "In Spain they often use *regular* olive oil." I nodded sagely, and then watched in amazement as she emptied the better part of the bottle into a large skillet. Clari shrugged. "I never said tortilla was diet food."

As the scent of slowly frying potatoes and onions drifted up from the pan, Clari relaxed her posture against the counter and turned to face me. "What does your mother cook?" she asked. Hesitantly trying to pull together the right words, I tried to explain how different things were in my house, how my mother worked and nobody really cooked, that meals were quickly thrown together out of partially-prepared ingredients and how in a typical week our dinners were from all over the globe: a little bit of Italian, a little bit of Mexican, a little bit of Chinese. Clari looked confused, and then thoughtful. Slowly, so that I would understand everything, she began telling me how she had learned to cook from her mother when she was young, and how everyone told her she had a talent for it. She'd always wanted to learn to cook other cuisines, but never had the opportunity, and so she'd spent her time perfecting what she did know. In those days it didn't matter if a girl wanted to learn to cook, Clari told me, she just did; she was expected to be able to cook all the typical dishes of her region by the time she got married, in her case at seventeen. "Now I couldn't get my own two daughters into the kitchen even if I paid them," she remarked wistfully. She then turned her gaze to me and a softness washed across her face. "You'll probably end up making better tortillas than them."

When at last the potatoes were perfectly fried, she showed me how to drain the oil and mix them with the eggs, breaking the saffron-colored yolks directly into the hot potatoes and stirring quickly until a creamy, viscous sludge was formed. She added few generous pinches of salt from the crock next to the stove, and ladled some of the mixture back into the skillet. A few minutes later as the edges were just starting to set, and after a series of deft swirls of the pan to dislodge the eggy mass, Clari clamped a plate over the top of the skillet and with acrobatic precision flipped the whole thing over. The half-cooked tortilla slid effortlessly face down into the skillet, sizzled fiercely for another minute, and then was turned out cleanly onto a new plate. She smiled and handed the pan to me. "That's how you make a Basque tortilla. Want to try the next one?"

That tortilla lesson, and the ones that followed, are some of the most cherished memories I have from that challenging, often difficult year. While it was one of the most stimulating, exciting, and horizon-broadening periods of my life, it was also very overwhelming to be so far away from everything familiar, and homesickness was often harder to ignore than I'd thought. My time with Clari in her kitchen was a blessing, however, as not only did I learn volumes about cooking seasonally, simply and instinctively, but I had a valuable insight into what makes Basques tick. Although I occasionally grew exasperated at their insistence at distancing themselves from anything and everything Spanish, I grew to understand and even admire their fierce patriotism and spirit of independence. Like that seemingly simple tortilla—which took me several years to master, by the way—I realized it is in the small details where they must find the things that set them apart, that give their identity meaning. Though perhaps transparent to outsiders, the borders they erect are really the only weapon they have to fight the ever-increasing erosion by the powerful Spanish mainstream on their utterly unique culture. By the end I didn't regret one bit that I'd been placed there instead of anywhere else in Spain—my only regret was that I'd gone there to learn Spanish instead of Basque.

I left Spain at the end of a year to return to "normal" life, and it was five years before I had the opportunity to return for a visit. I was glad to see that Clari was looking better than ever, and naturally the instant we were reunited, the first thing we talked about was food. She was fascinated to hear how my interest in cooking had developed, and what kinds of dishes I had sampled on my travels. She proudly showed me two new cookbooks she had recently bought on French and Italian cuisine, and told me they were planning a trip soon to Scandinavia. "Do you still remember how to make tortilla?" she asked me. When I replied that not only did I still make it regularly, but that several Spanish people who had tasted my version proclaimed it the best tortilla they had ever eaten, she shrugged in her typical noncommittal way. "Of course," she said, "they've obviously never tasted a Basque tortilla." I couldn't help but smile at the reminder of her stubborn patriotism. "And anyway it makes sense," she continued, "since I make it better than my mother, that one of my daughters should make it better than me. Even if she is American."

Melissa Kronenthal has either been cooking, eating or thinking about food for as long as she can recall. In fact, if you ask her about some of her earliest memories it seems that food is the only thing she can recall. A West Coast native, she somewhere along the line discovered a passion for travel, too, and since leaving home at sixteen to be an exchange student has counted Spain, Ireland, Germany, and New Orleans among her places of residence. She currently lives in Edinburgh, Scotland, with her husband Manuel, where she cooks, writes, photographs, and is nursing a Ph.D. in linguistics to completion. You can read more of her work online at The Traveler's Lunchbox (htt;://www.travelerslunchbox.com).

Basque Tortilla

Although Clari never used a recipe for this dish, instead instinctively adjusting proportions based on the size of her eggs, the starchiness of her potatoes, and the number of mouths to feed, Melissa has developed a recipe that approximates her version very closely. Note that the tortilla is meant to come out of the pan slightly liquid in the center—although this may cause red flags to go up for you, you really should try it this way—it's one of the "secrets" to a really great tortilla. Just make sure to buy really high quality organic, free-range eggs, and you won't have anything to worry about. (Not to mention they'll taste much better!)

½ cup extra-virgin olive oil

1 pound potatoes (preferably Yukon gold), peeled and cut into
 irregular teaspoon-sized chunks

1 small yellow onion, peeled and coarsely chopped

salt, to taste

4 large organic eggs, at room temperature

In a large, heavy 9-inch skillet (nonstick is best), heat the olive oil over medium-high heat. Add the potatoes and onion, and sprinkle with a hefty pinch of salt. Reduce the heat to medium, and cook until the potatoes are tender, about 15 minutes, stirring frequently to prevent sticking. Raise the heat again and cook the potatoes for a few minutes longer, until they are lightly browned and crisp around the edges. They should be completely soft on the inside. With a slotted spoon, transfer the potatoes and onions to a colander and let drain for about five minutes.

Pour off all but a tablespoon of oil from the skillet and set it aside. In a large bowl, beat the eggs with another good pinch or two of salt, then stir in the potato mixture. When everything is well combined, taste a drop of the mixture for seasoning, adding more salt if necessary (this step is obviously optional, but will help you get the right level of seasoning).

Heat the skillet over high heat, swirling the oil to coat the bottom and sides of the pan. When it is very hot, pour the egg mixture into the pan, smoothing the top with a spatula. After it has cooked for about a minute, lower the heat to medium and continue cooking until the edges are firm, about 5 minutes more (the center will still look quite runny). As soon as the edges begin to set, start shaking and swirling the pan frequently to dislodge the tortilla—it should not stick to the bottom or sides. Run a thin spatula around the sides if it does.

Remove the pan from the heat and clamp a rimless plate slightly larger than the skillet over the top. Using one hand to hold the plate in place, quickly invert the tortilla onto it. If you're feeling nervous about this, you can slide the tortilla out onto a plate first, cover it with a second plate, flip, and proceed from there. Add another tablespoon of the cooking oil to the skillet (save the remainder for another use) and place it over the heat again. When it is very hot, slide the tortilla back into the skillet, uncooked-side down. Shake the pan gently as before and cook for about 3 to 4 more minutes, or until the edges feel firm but the center still feels a little soft. Slide the cooked tortilla onto a clean plate and let cool.

Serve cut into wedges, warm or at room temperature.

PART THREE

AFRICA/
MIDDLE EAST

WAYNE MILSTEAD

Serendipity in Cyprus

A chance encounter yields delicious rewards.

Sometimes the best lessons are unplanned. Serendipity is an intuitive teacher. It has a way of stepping in where course catalogs leave off, providing what you need to know when you need to know it. In our case, serendipity came in the form of George and Lara.

Sipping Cypriot brandy next to the fire at our hotel in Polis, Cyprus, on a brisk January evening, my traveling companion, Aaron, and I glimpsed two shivering figures emerging from the beach. As they stepped out of the darkness into the muted light of the bar, we could see it was a man and woman. The man ordered Commandaria, a popular sweet wine with a history spanning ten centuries. The woman ordered a warm drink of unknown origins. They spoke Greek, so I figured they were locals. They huddled near the fire to steal some warmth and immediately introduced themselves as George and Lara.

He was a handsome man with long salt-and-pepper hair pulled into a ponytail and a thick mustache of the same color. He had the sort of look that causes you to instinctively look for the guitar case and the rest of the band. The woman had a natural beauty and air of sophistication, like the women you see in films leaping white fences on thorough-breds, doffing their equestrian helmet and flashing a devilish smile.

To say the least, this was a marked difference from the two dour German couples in hiking boots and '70s-style monochromatic t-shirts who sat quietly in the bar each night and in the dining room each morning carefully avoiding eye contact or any other excuse to acknowledge our presence. It was off-season and the hotel didn't appear to have more than six guests the entire week we were there. This apparent desire for anonymity was considerably awkward with no crowd to blend into. While solitude on the hiking trails was a major incentive in planning our trip, it was nice to finally have someone to compare notes with.

George, who grew up near Polis, agreed it was a good time to visit. He and Lara were on vacation themselves. While it got chilly at night, during the day it was t-shirt weather. With few tourists, it was the perfect time of year to explore the natural beauty of this swath of southwestern Cyprus.

Dotted with citrus groves, overlooking turquoise seas, Polis is the least developed beach resort in the south of Cyprus. What is most striking is the variety of the landscape in such a small area. It ranges from rocky promontories to lush meadows and rugged forests to sleepy monasteries and quiet beaches.

The famous Akamas Peninsula is just down the road. Set aside as a preservation area, it is a wild finger of land jutting into the Mediterranean, with a network of nature trails and the Bath of Aphrodite, a waterfall and pool where legend says the goddess escaped to bathe when not entertaining lovers.

Lara asked what we had seen of the island.

We told her how we took advantage of several days of sun, during what is normally Cyprus' rainy season, by hiking through vineyards, orchards, and trails rife with wild herbs. The byproduct of the rain was a lush countryside. At the end of each hike we usually gorged on a meal of Cypriot specialties.

I'm a firm believer that you learn more about a place by eating its food and walking its streets than by staring in a thousand glass museum cases. It was the cuisine and the hiking that attracted us to Cyprus in the first place. So while we let our feet be the guide during the day, at night, our stomachs led the way.

The journey was tasty, but we wanted to learn more. Why was some *haloumi* cheese squeaky as the sole of your sneaker and others squishy like jelly? What's in season? Is *taramosalata* a native Cypriot dish? Why does it vary in color? How does Cypriot cooking differ from that in Greece and Turkey? We wanted to taste authentic dishes we had read about but not encountered in restaurants. The original pre-departure plan was to take a cooking class in Cyprus, but none were offered in January. As we soon learned, most Cypriots involved in the restaurant or tourist trade take the month off.

Enter serendipity.

"We own a restaurant in Yeroskipou near Paphos," George said. They only serve what he described as real Cypriot cuisine: uncultivated plants gathered from the verdant countryside and seasonal produce along with natural handmade cheeses, breads, and quality fish and meats. The types of dishes you would find in a Cypriot village home. "No chips or *taramosalata* at our *taverna*," George mused.

They were taking a break; staying in a villa at the hotel.

It was not long before George, sipping his Commandaria in the glow of the fire, began lecturing on "Cypriot Cooking 101." He explained the basics, the differences between styles of cooking, and how to find edible plants in the wild. He answered Aaron's *taramosalata* question. It originated in Thessalonica, Greece but is common in Cyprus. George explained that the color varies from white to vast degrees of pink depending on the type of fish roe used and whether or not coloring is added. There was a time when *taramosalata* in the region was made from local roe. Now, with fishing stocks depleted, most roe is imported, meaning the type and quality varies widely.

Food in the south is eastern Mediterranean in spirit. Classics such as hummus, Greek-style salad called "village salad," eggplant salad, roasted meats, and fish (on the coast) abound. While feta is common, the ubiquitous local cheese is *haloumi*, usually served grilled or pan-fried. George said its texture varies based on the amount of sheep's versus cow's milk used. The traditional style of eating in Cyprus is called "*meze*." It is best described as a revolving

Haloumi *is a salty, white cheese indigenous to Cyprus and traditionally made from sheep's milk. It is boiled and folded during production, yielding a stringy texture. Typically sold in brine, it is firm in texture and is usually grilled and eaten hot.*

—SB

buffet, consisting of small portions of as many as twenty different cold and hot dishes served as they are prepared. Traditional Cypriot cuisine is quintessential village food. Simple, tasty recipes based on fresh seasonal produce and whatever meat is available.

When we finally said goodnight, George gave us a list of places to hike, including his favorite vineyard, along with the names and locations of open restaurants where we could sample the various dishes he had described.

We couldn't believe our luck. This was exactly the type of insider knowledge that brings a cuisine alive. We couldn't wait to head out into the countryside the next day equipped with a deeper understanding of Cypriot food, culture, and the natural environment. We had no idea that the fireside lecture included a practicum.

The next evening George was waiting for us in the parking lot when we returned from the hike in the mountainous Vouni Panayia Vineyards he had recommended.

"Did you get our note?" he asked.

"No," I said. "What was it about?"

"We want to cook for you," he said. He wanted to show us what he had told us the night before. No argument there. The best food talking and writing can't hold a candle to cooking and eating. We agreed without hesitation.

The scent of fresh herbs and garlic tickled our noses as we entered George and Lara's villa. Earlier, when he invited us to dinner, George mentioned they had gathered some "weeds" to eat. I thought he was joking. He wasn't. The kitchen resembled a greenhouse overflowing with a lush garden of fresh wild greens, herbs, vegetables, and fungi.

It was probably coals to Newcastle, but we presented our hosts with a couple bottles of wine we had bought at the vineyard.

"Thank you. I bought some, too. We have lots to drink," George said with a devilish grin, handing me the corkscrew.

Small dishes sprouted like mushrooms on the table: olives marinated in oil and coriander, fresh tomato and celery, and slices of bread topped with sesame seeds.

"These are called baby sparrows," George said, holding a dark green plant. "That's what the Greek means. In English you call it bladder campion. Sometimes customers get a frightened look on their face because of the name. They think they are eating baby birds." I understood the name when he stripped the leaves off. They resembled tiny feathers. He then fried them in a skillet with eggs, creating an omelet of sorts.

We helped chop, dice, and open wine, while asking questions, taking notes, and tasting the results.

"See these," Lara said, pointing to a clump of weeds in a colander. "These are wild mustard greens." She sautéed them in olive oil with fresh lemon juice. An exotic grassy aroma filled the room. *That's what fresh smells like*, I thought. I savored the refreshing chlorophyll flavor as I washed them down with Alina, the smooth water-like white wine.

As we plowed through wild leeks sautéed with fresh thyme and olive oil, George filled our empty glasses with a rich, chocolatey limited-edition Cypriot red called Carmen. He bought most of the allotment for his restaurant. "It's not available anymore," George informed me. I was heartbroken. I drank slowly and surveyed the table.

There was *haloumi* made by hand in the village where George's mother lives. "It was still warm when it was delivered this morning," Lara said. There was also fresh *loukanica* sausages made by George's mother. We sampled a plate of fresh *anari* cheese. George served it deliciously plain, explaining that it is often eaten at breakfast with the locally made carob syrup, *teratsemelo*. With this new knowledge I tried this combination the next morning. It added a whole new dimension to the cheese.

Lara placed sliced avocado drizzled with olive oil, lemon, and herbs on the table. While an introduced species, avocado thrives in the region.

Next came a sauté of fennel mushrooms with olive oil, fresh rosemary, and garlic. George explained that they got their name because they grow at the roots of wild fennel plants. I had seen hordes of fennel while hiking. George said the mushrooms only grow in certain areas and that you had to know what to look for. He picked these particular ones earlier that morning with his mother. "She has the eye," he said, referring to his mother's mushroom-hunting prowess. Lara agreed. "She just walks out and points and there they are," she said.

Lara followed the mushrooms with salmon broiled with lemon and fennel.

Our pace slowed. I glanced over at the counter with a strange mix of anticipation and dread. How could I eat another bite? How could I not?

Large mushrooms that grow at the roots of pine trees roasted in the oven. They looked like golden upside down hats from a Dr. Seuss story. George served them drizzled with garlic, olive oil, and lemon juice. The infamous velvety textured Cypriot potatoes roasted with cumin and pepper followed.

George poured more wine and glowed with pride as we picked at the remaining morsels. He rubbed his back. It was sore from picking mushrooms.

As the conversation turned from food preparation to the relaxed banter of friendship, I couldn't help thinking about the power of food to unite. And to teach.

We didn't sign up for a class with George and Lara, our common love of food convened us. And the rest just happened.

Two days later George and Lara loaded their truck and headed back to Paphos. "Follow us out of town," George said. "I will show you where you should walk today."

We drove along the main road out of town, out past the beach and then turned onto the highway to Paphos. Our stomachs rolled as we barreled down the mountainous road trying to keep up with George. Finally we turned onto a gravel road and he slowed down. At the top of a hill, we pulled over and got out. We stood silent for a few minutes taking in the vista. A dam formed a small reservoir to our left and the road disappeared into the foothills to our right. An abandoned Turkish village crowned the hill before us. We turned around. The white stone ruins of a mill and medieval Skarfos Bridge contrasted against an organic green backdrop. George pointed out herbs and plants, many of which we had eaten that night in their villa. Rows of citrus and olive groves stretched along a small stream into the distance.

"Over there," George said pointing to a tree beyond Skarfos Bridge. "Before we married and had kids, we used to camp over there." His finger moved to the left. "Follow the stream along the road. Walk some, drive some. Whatever suits you. There's no traffic out here. Eventually you'll reach the edge of the forest where we picked the mushrooms."

We said our goodbyes and watched as George and Lara's truck disappeared over the hill.

We began walking. Past the oranges. Past the olives. Beyond the leeks and wild fennel. Finally, we turned back at the mushrooms.

Wayne Milstead writes from the colder climes of Europe, but thankfully it is only a few hours flight to the eastern Mediterranean.

Cypriot cuisine is similar to that of the Greeks. What distinguishes traditional Greek cuisine is a combination of the following factors: unique ingredients, the Greek philosophy regarding eating and sharing meals, as well as the country itself and the atmosphere in general.

The Greek philosophy: The time of day when the Greeks gather around a table to enjoy a meal, or some appetizers (mezedes) with ouzo, is a time held in reverence by all the inhabitants of this country. For the Greeks, sharing a meal with friends, either at home, at a restaurant or a taverna, is a deeply rooted social affair. The Greek word symposium, a word as ancient as the country itself, if translated literally, means "drinking with company." The atmosphere in typically Greek restaurants and tavernas is very relaxed, informal, and unpretentious. Food preparation, on the other hand, has its own sacred rules. Good amateur cooks are held in great esteem in their social circles. A good housewife, in Greece, means a good cook. And a good cook can spend days preparing a meal for his or her friends.

The atmosphere: Try having a glass of ouzo or wine, accompanied by barbecued octopus or any other Greek dish, while sitting beneath the shadow of a tree, at a small tavern by the sea, on one of the Aegean islands. Then, when you go back home, try repeating that experience by preparing the same dish and serving the same drink. No matter where you decide to have it, you will soon discover that it does not taste the same. Do not try again. There is nothing wrong with the delicacy of your palate or your cooking skills. The Greek meal experience, namely the combination of what you eat and where you eat it, cannot be repeated, exported, or duplicated. It is something you can only find, taste and enjoy in Greece, like the blue of the Aegean Sea.

—Greek National Tourism Organization

Honor Thy Mother

Unconditional love reaps culinary treasures.

I wanted Jamila to teach me how to cook Moroccan food, but it was not going to be easy. For one thing, my Moroccan mother-in-law worked full time, getting up before dawn to pray, preparing the day's meal to be reheated at lunch, then heading off by seven A.M. to her job as a scribe at the Fés courthouse. When her three sons and I gathered at two o'clock for a late lunch, everything was already finished. I would help with what I could, chopping tomatoes and peppers for a salad, or taking plates of spiced olives to the table, but the real work had already been completed long before I had awakened. The substance of these meals—namely Jamila's rich stews, called *tagines*, layered with delicate, unidentifiable spices, a sauce you couldn't get enough of, and meat cooked so slowly it fell apart in your mouth—remained elusive.

During the year and a half that I lived with my husband's family, I marveled at Jamila's tirelessness, at how she always managed to get breakfast, lunch, and dinner on the table, despite working. If there are daughters around, they usually shoulder the burden, but Jamila's two daughters were far away, one living in Germany, the other in northern Morocco. Sons, traditionally, are less helpful in domestic work, though my husband and his brothers did what they could, sensitized from an early age that a widow raising five children on her own needed all the help she could get. But while men will help under certain circumstances, they lack the initiative and the vast store of traditional knowledge instilled in Moroccan women from an early age. This includes anything from cleaning, butchering, and preparing an entire lamb during Ramadan to making enough *b'stilla* (a flaky, layered pie stuffed with a salty-sweet mixture of poultry, almonds, sugar, and eggs) to feed twenty people. Hospitality is still a prized virtue, and there should always be something on hand to feed guests—a sister's homemade sesame seed cookies, for example, and some tea prepared with generous handfuls of fresh mint just purchased at the local market.

Although I tried to pick up cues, I was probably a failure compared to a Moroccan daughter-in-law. Once a week I prepared lunch for the family, but quickly learned that I needed to make adaptations. Since lunch was the main meal of the day, something entire

---

I had been in Lebanon for two weeks meeting my husband's relatives. At home the cooking had been a sore point, here it was beginning to suffocate me. It was true, his mother baked bread from scratch, kneading it with her own hands and everything. I baked bread, too—with a machine I purchased for $99. I'd always thought it's better not to touch something you're about to eat. My husband and his mother didn't agree.

I walked into the cooking class with my head held high, determined to prove I didn't need lessons. The instructor stood out the front at her own little bench and began to instruct. Falafel was our first dish.

I slowly moved my hands into the wheat, then I did as she said, squeezing it in my hands and letting the water drain out of it. As I did it, I started to feel it. There was something about my own hands doing the work that felt different, special. It was a feeling I'd never gotten by using an electrical appliance. I felt like a real cook. I felt like I'd discovered Lebanon in some way. This was what Lebanon was about. Making food with your own hands, washing clothes with your own hands, working with your own hands.

That night I told my mother-in-law how I felt.

"You finally got it," she said proudly. "See, we Lebanese know what we're doing."

"Yeah," I said. "I guess you do."

—Shelley Ann Wake, "Cooking the Lebanese Way"

families came home for, it had to be substantial. And there were rules. Ideally the meal should consist of meat and vegetables, although for some, meat was a luxury. Chickens had to be eaten the day after they were killed, too soon and they would be tough. Fresh bread, purchased just before lunch from the local bakery around the corner, was indispensable. For dessert, we ate whatever fruit was in season—in winter, tiny, perfect tangerines from the north that burst in your mouth like a star; obscenely sweet melons in summer; and small succulent cherries in late spring, unlike any I have ever tasted in the States. I tried to center my own cooking around these rules, and occasionally there were successes—a roast chicken dish that my family requested over and over again, or lasagne, which, with its many substantial layers of pasta, cheese, and beef, was a guaranteed hit. But ultimately, my in-laws preferred to eat something familiar, to sit around the table and dip their bread in the communal *tagine*, to take a break from the stress of modern life in the Ville Nouvelle of Fés, where we lived.

As my Arabic improved, I began to understand what people were saying around me, and lunch suddenly became even more interesting. Jamila would talk about the criminals who had been arraigned that day in court, astounding us with stories of knife-wielding bandits attacking drunks in a poor neighborhood on the outskirts of town, or immoral pharmacists replacing antibiotics with aspirin. Fortunately these stories usually ended triumphantly, with evildoers locked away for years, the city safe again. But lunch was not just a time for city crime reports. It was also the only chance for the whole family to sit down together, to exchange news about the neighborhood, or to report on a phone call from a loved one living abroad. Due to the economic situation in Morocco, every family has someone who has left, seeking a fortune or merely just a living, outside the country. For us whenever the phone rang, we hoped it was Jamila's vivacious daughter who had married a Moroccan living in Germany. I asked Jamila once how she felt, having a daughter so far away. "Husband or wife, if you have to go, you must," she said. "Away from your family to build a life together, wherever the work is."

Once my husband and I decided to move to the States, the need to learn how to cook Moroccan food suddenly became more urgent. I felt responsible for my husband, for selfishly taking him away from his family and his job, to move to the States, where people ate solitary lunches in cubicles at work and didn't talk to their neighbors. I couldn't be a substitute for a mother, a brother, or a sister, but at least I could recreate the food.

And so I finally begged Jamila to teach me. She returned home from work early just to show me how to make all the different *tagines* that her family loved. When my husband's sister came to visit from the north of Morocco, she also gave me cooking lessons. Both women were fine cooks, especially Kenza, who could even watch cooking shows and later recreate from memory everything the television chef had done. Jamila and Kenza laughed at my little notebook in which I meticulously translated their handfuls and pinches into quantities I would be able to replicate later. I had to watch them closely, because when I wasn't looking they might toss in an extra onion or a spice that I had not written down. I learned how to make *harira*, the rich bean soup eaten during Ramadan, how to marinate fish in *chermoula*, a cilantro-heavy spice mixture spread liberally over fish before being roasted with potatoes and peppers, and how to prepare at least ten different varieties of *tagine*. Other cooking lessons were too difficult to write down, such as a recipe for the sesame-seed cookies known as *shabakiya*, whose intricate latticework of dough is folded in on itself, deep fried, and dipped in honey.

Moroccan cooking was nothing like the trendy Moroccan recipes that often appear in magazines or cookbooks, which often

Thank God for Bacha! Bacha is my sister-in-law's cook, and communication between cooks is without language, borders, or complication. An inadvertent licking of the lips and the barriers crumble. I was never confounded by Moroccan cuisine; I simply fell head over heals in love with it. Bacha would take me by the hand to the tiny, earthen-floored shop to choose tumeric and paprika from the large sacks on the floor; saffron, coriander, and cardamom from the heaped, colorful woven baskets on the shelves. She shops always with the same, trusted merchants so they can't "just pass off anything." Her eyes sparkle like her two gold teeth as she bargains for the chicken, thrown on the scales flapping and squawking. We'd strike the deal, then head to the vegetable merchant while the poulterer puts the chicken's head under its wing. Bacha would pluck it herself. Plunging it into a basin of boiled water, then moving fast from its neck to its tail, singeing the smallest feathers over the gas ring, then tackling its intestines and insides, neatly saving the liver, heart, and gizzard, peeling back the latter from its inner bag of seed for use in soup or salad.

—Diana Holuigue,
Postcards From Kitchens Abroad

call for an excess of spices and use techniques common to American cooking—such as sautéeing meat and onions in oil—but which I never once observed in a Moroccan kitchen. A typical *tagine* usually involves placing meat, onions, water, oil, and spices into a pressure cooker, known as a *cocotte*, and cooking the heck out of it for an hour. The variety lies in the spices used, in the vegetables added toward the end, or in the final technique—a chicken might be finished off in the oven, for example, while the sauce is reduced until it becomes thick and savory.

A cooking lesson with Jamila or my sister-in-law usually began with a trip to the central market, where scores of butchers, olive and spice sellers, and vegetable and fruit salesmen spread out their wares. We always bought our vegetables from the same person, a gentle old man named Mimoun who had worked in the same vegetable stall for forty years and had a sister in Seattle. Mimoun usually gave me a present, whether it was an apple polished with his shirtsleeve or a taste from the shipment of apricots he had just received from Agadir. From his stand, we walked to the butcher's and bought a kilo of beef or lamb, usually with bones and fat to give extra flavor.

Traditional Moroccan kitchens have very little counter space, and when we returned home, laden with bags of vegetables, we would set to work slicing, peeling, dicing, and chopping without a cutting board, dropping the scraps onto the tile floor and depositing the vegetables into a deep cooking pot. All the while, we talked. Several of Jamila's siblings lived in the same building, and often a cousin or an aunt would stop by to lend a hand, each one adding the flavor of her personality to whatever topic we were discussing. I began to understand that a meal was not solely about the final product, a clay *tagine* dish brought steaming to the table. The process of cooking itself provided women with a chance to gather and talk about life in a less restrained manner than they did when men were nearby. By the time the *tagine* was simmering happily away on the two-boiler stove, and cold salads of cucumbers, tomatoes, and onions had been mixed with their vinaigrette, I felt a little more like family. Jamila threw all the scraps into the garbage, and mopped the floors until they were spotless. We washed the fruit, set out plates of olives, and sent someone to bring bread from the local bakery.

Now that I am back in the States I have added her *tagines* to my repertoire. I cook for my husband, for friends, and for myself, but more than anything I imagine myself cooking for Jamila. As I look over her recipes in my food-stained notebook, I remember not one specific cooking lesson, but all of them—all blending into one long lesson about food, about life, about cooking being as much of a shared activity as eating. When I speak to Jamila on the telephone, I tell her how I prepared her *tagine m'hammer*, or her *l'ham b'il jilbana,* but really that's not what I mean to say. As with the language, and my new family, cooking Moroccan was something I apprehended gradually, until one day I realized my plane flight was a week away, just when I had finally begun to grasp the nuances of it all. Jamila accepted me unconditionally; she never expected me to be something I wasn't, i.e. a Moroccan daughter-in-law. I never learned the proper way to mop floors, to wash clothes by hand, or to handle the sacrifice at Ramadan, but that was fine with her. She loved me anyway. And cooking is the best way I know to honor her.

Rachel Newcomb received a B.A. in 1995 from Davidson College, where she twice won the Vereen Bell Award for poetry and fiction, Davidson's highest student literary prize. In 1997 she received an M.A. from the Writing Seminars at Johns Hopkins University, and from 1997-98 she held a Reginald S. Tickner Writing Fellowship at the Gilman School of Baltimore. From 1998-2004 she completed a Ph.D. in cultural anthropology at Princeton University, and in 2001 she was awarded a J. William Fulbright Fellowship to conduct her dissertation research on women and social change in Morocco. Her poetry, fiction, and book reviews have appeared in journals such as Interim, New Delta Review, *and the* Charlotte Observer. *Currently she is Assistant Professor of Anthropology at Rollins College in Winter Park, Florida.*

Tagine with Meat and Prunes

Serves 4

1 pound lamb or beef, for stewing, preferably with bones to add flavor

2 large onions, finely chopped

20 prunes

¼ cup canola oil, plus a heaping tablespoon of olive oil

1 heaping teaspoon ginger

1 beef boullion cube

dash of turmeric for color

a few strands saffron, dissolved in ¼ cup boiling water (optional)

1 heaping teaspoon cinnamon

2 tablespoons honey, or more to taste

¹/₈ cup peeled and slivered almonds, lightly toasted

Put the meat in a stew pot, chop the onions finely and place on top, and add the regular & olive oils. Start the heat on medium-high and get everything bubbling as you work. Add a heaping teaspoon of ground ginger, a beef boullion cube, dash turmeric, saffron dissolved in water, and a small amount of salt. Add just enough water to cover, bring to a boil. Cover with a tight-fitting lid and turn heat low enough so that everything is still simmering.

Meanwhile, boil the prunes in water for about five minutes. Drain.

After an hour, check the tenderness of the meat. It may take another hour if the meat is tough. When meat is tender, uncover, add prunes, a heaping teaspoon of cinnamon, and 2 tablespoons of honey, or to taste.

Cook for another fifteen minutes, uncovered, boiling off the excess. The sauce should cook down considerably until very thick and not at all runny. The meat should be fall-ing-off-the-bones soft. Add more honey or salt to taste, if necessary. Garnish with toasted almonds. Serve in a big plate in the center of the table with bread for dipping.

Cooking with Jas

The author learns the secret to a delicious curry.

J as cuts hair. She lives in an opulent house two doors outside the gate of our school compound, and she runs a salon in her front parlor. Most of our teachers get their hair chopped there, enjoying the aromatic *masala* tea and listening to Jas talk about visiting her children at the University of Maryland. Her radio is always tuned to Nairobi's Christian radio station, despite the fact that she and her husband, Mangit, are Sikh. She says Mangit, a successful international real estate developer, promised to build her a new salon beside the carport. But instead, he built a pavilion—perfect for entertaining guests during a blistering Nairobi afternoon or a torrential equatorial downpour. But the pavilion is not so good for cutting hair.

So Jas still cuts hair in her front parlor. But now she runs cooking classes in her pavilion. With its array of wicker couches and deck chairs, the pavilion can easily accommodate thirty guests under its thatched roof. It also has a full-service bar, equipped with a sink, gas stove, oven, and refrigerator. The pillars and lintels which support the roof are decorated with paintings of the East African countryside. Mount Kilimanjaro anchors the pillar behind the bar, while acacia trees, wildlife collages, and the Great Rift Valley adorn the others. The images are ably depicted, but for the most part they are not spectacular art. However, the portraits of a Maasai warrior and his mother are drawn with intricate, expressive detail. Jas explained that the artist drank three or four pints of Tusker lager while working on the landscapes. By the time he got to the portraits, he could barely stand on the ladder. But somehow, in his inebriated state, he created his best work.

A few months ago, Jas began asking her clients if they would want to learn Indian cooking. With a substantial South Asian population, Nairobi has scores of Indian restaurants. And since Asians form the merchant class, some of the most expensive restaurants in the city are Indian, including Haandi and Anghiti.

When we go to Anghiti with our friends, we always battle over whether to order *palak paneer*, spicy creamed spinach with cubes of homemade cheese. One of our best friends won't touch the stuff—I suspect because the puréed spinach and cheese chunks vaguely resemble the contents of a sacred cow's four-chambered stomach. However, my wife and I love it. Despite its unpalatable appearance, *palak paneer* has a subtle creaminess and delicate spiciness that ably counter the robust flavors of chicken *vindaloo* and mutton *rogan josh*. So when we heard that we could learn to cook *palak paneer* on our own, we signed up for the class without delay.

The class was originally scheduled to begin at four P.M. on a Saturday afternoon. Around eleven that morning, we received a message that it had been rescheduled for an hour earlier. This worked for us, but it was highly unusual. In Kenya, nothing is early. In fact, nothing is ever even on time. For instance, we attended a Kenyan wedding that started nearly two hours late—because the bride and groom didn't show up on time. We sent text messages to the other members of our cooking class, alerting them of the amended schedule. Safaricom, our cell phone network, was experiencing one of its chronic outages, so one of our friends didn't get the news until six hours later. But the rest of us were there on time, with open minds and eager stomachs.

Once the class began, we quickly discovered the fundamental ingredient in Indian cooking. I had assumed it was cumin, curry powder, or possibly garlic. But the single most abundant ingredient in our recipes was butter. No wonder those sauces are so rich.

Jas put a fat chunk of butter in each pan before she began sautéing the vegetables and spices. Then she would add another slab before cooking the meat. My mouth was watering—and my arteries were cringing—with every greasy spoonful. Throughout the cooking class, Jas told us that her husband was really the cook. She could make the *naans* and rice, but Mangit had a gift for chicken.

K enyan food is comprised of the traditional foods of its many tribes and influences adopted from the British, who were colonizers until 1963. Indian food, another common part of the Kenyan diet, arrived courtesy of laborers imported by the British to work on the railroad.

Kenya's largest tribe, the Kikuyu, are ethnically Bantus and share similar foods with other Bantu tribes. Traditionally, maize and beans were the basis of most Kikuyu meals. Special occasions call for meat, usually goat; mukimu, a mash that is a special variation on maize and beans that uses njahe, a bean indigenous to Kenya; and njohi ya muratina, a traditional beer. The diet of the Luo, Kenya's second-largest tribe who reside near Lake Victoria, consists mainly of fish and kuon, also known as ugali. Ugali has been adopted around the country due to its benefit of being a cheap carbohydrate and is simple to prepare—maize meal and water. Many of the poor in Nairobi eat ugali and sukuma wiki (kale) almost daily.

The most pervasive British adoptions are tea, fish and chips, and bangers. Every afternoon, Kenyans all over the country stop to have a cup of tea. Children come home from school for tea and bread smeared with butter and jam, or maandazi, a square donut-like treat. Fish and chip shops are all over Nairobi, and bangers on a Sunday morning are perfection. While there are many Indian restaurants in major metropolitan areas, chapatis are by far the most popular Indian food to make in Kenyan homes. Chapatis are a special treat, and to be recognized as an accomplished chapati-maker is a grand feat for a Kenyan cook.

—Emilia Thiuri, "Kikuyu Hospitality"

Just then, Mangit arrived home from a morning at the office. He was still dressed in his business clothes, slacks and a dress shirt, but that didn't matter. Mangit loves cooking chicken.

By the time he arrived, Jas had already begun sautéing the *masala* spices, including chiles, garlic, onion, turmeric, coriander, and roasted cumin. The aroma of the sizzling spices wafted around the pavilion. The first thing Mangit did after he rolled up his sleeves was add another half stick of butter to the pot.

"My secret to good curry," he said, with a wink.

After the vegetables and spices were properly sautéed, he added still more butter and stirred the chicken pieces into the simmering stew.

While Mangit was stirring, Jas showed us how to roll out the *naan* dough into plate-sized *chapatis*. I chuckled as I remembered the Indian mother in *Bend it Like Beckham* trying to teach her soccer-crazed daughter how to make proper *chapatis*. Like most bread dough, the *naan* batter was sticky and stringy. I had to scrape the batter off my fingers before I could start rolling. My first attempt bore an uncanny resemblance to my home state of California—including the Sierra Nevada mountains and Death Valley. My second attempt was vaguely oval-shaped, and almost flat. But eventually I developed a rhythm and mastered the right degree of uneven pressure on the rolling pin to spin the *chapati* with each roll.

Once we had correctly shaped *naan*, we threw it onto a glowing charcoal *jiko*. We could use a frying pan or oven, but Jas admonished us that to achieve the perfect balance of crispy edges and tender interiors, real *naan* is always made on a grill.

By the time our *naan* production line was finished, we were ready to eat. We sat down to the table with full plates of rice, *palak paneer, jeera* fish, chicken *masala*, and *naan*. On the lawn a few meters away, Jas's son and nephew were playing cricket. Each time I heard the crack of the bat, I flinched. The hard leather ball seemed eager to disrupt our victorious meal. It careened toward the pavilion a few times, but never succeeded in overturning our plates. Eventually the game ended, and I let myself succumb to the satisfying flavors of a home-cooked gourmet meal.

Since then, we have cooked Jas's dishes several times. Since Indian food is always better shared with a large family, we usually join together with friends and try to pass on our new knowledge. Our home-cooked *palak paneer* and chicken *masala* are always tasty, but somehow they never turn out quite the same. Maybe we need to add more butter.

In addition to writing about his travel experiences, Josh Flosi is an award-winning amateur ice cream maker, Jeopardy! champion, and former bus driver. In his spare time he is a high school history and English teacher now living in Sherwood, Oregon. He and his wife, Laura, spent three years teaching at an international school in Nairobi, Kenya. They miss spontaneous barefoot soccer games, ibises grazing on their doorstep, warm cups of chai on cool highland mornings, and the gracious smiles of their Kenyan friends.

Palak Paneer
adapted for Western kitchens

Serves 4

2 cups oil

1 cup paneer cheese, cubed

1 onion, chopped

1 tablespoon garlic, finely minced

1 teaspoon garam masala

1 teaspoon ginger, grated

¼ teaspoon chile powder

1 pound frozen spinach, thawed

1 tomato, chopped finely

Heat oil for deep-frying. Fry cheese cubes until light golden brown. Drain on paper towels. In large saucepan or wok, sauté onions with 3 tablespoons of oil. When softened, add in the garlic, garam masala, ginger, and chile powder. Stir to combine. Add spinach and tomatoes. Lower the heat to simmer and cook 20 to 30 minutes. Once spinach is at a pastalike consistency, raise heat and bubble lightly until oil floats to the top. Add the paneer cubes and heat through.

Flavor by the Spoonful

The author learns to appreciate slow cooking.

My hands are cramped from peeling figs, but I can't stop. The look on the chef's face tells me we are running behind and dinner can't wait. Peel those figs faster, then chop the walnuts, and run the chickpeas through the hand-cranked grinder for hummus. (Note to self: Remember to send them a food processor when I get back from vacation.) Yes, this is my vacation.

If "music be the food of love," as Shakespeare wrote in *Twelfth Night*, then surely food is the soul of good travel. As a frequent traveler, I've found the pleasures of feeling at home in a foreign country, immersed in people, culture, and food, and nowhere is it easier than in Turkey.

I arrived in Istanbul to find this city of 7 million people teeming with creative and resourceful food vendors, restaurants, cafés. Food was everywhere. In the old quarter, the Sultanahmet, street stalls offering *doner* kebabs of pressed lamb and beef, roasted nuts, and succulent melons, while rug merchants beg you to visit them for apple tea, as they throw a whirling array of carpets at your feet to admire. Locals and tourists alike press to get close to the food stalls during market days. Each merchant's pride in the artful display of their produce made me lament the lack of a cooking facility in my hotel room. Unable to purchase and cook the marvelous foods, I strolled the market, mentally wrapping myself in the texture and flavors of peaches, almonds, spices, and figs.

Street markets are just a warm-up exercise for the sensory pleasures that appear at Marco Polo's last stop on the Silk Route to Asia, the famed Egyptian Spice Market, or the more touristy Covered Bazaar, an amazing collection of over four thosand shops in a fifteenth-century covered market. As locals shopped the market for such necessities as bed linens, produce, clothes, pots, and pans, I hungrily followed them, learning how to choose olives and taste *beyaz penir*, a delicious white cheese, curiously displayed under furry goat skins.

The richness of my experiences in Istanbul were unmatched by any other travel experiences, yet my trip was just beginning. On a tour called "Behind the Veil," I was invited to see how women's roles in home and society compare to our own. Observing traditions, crafts, and the survival of people in a primitive land was humbling. By comparison, we live with such excess, yet these Turkish women are happy, and seem to want nothing more. Is it because they don't look across the fence and see a better life?

After an evening's entertainment, seeing a dervish whirl, I felt there was nothing left to discover. Then I observed women selling Fanta, jewelry, and handmade village dolls with cotton stitching for the eyes and mouth. The dolls resembled their makers, with their baggy *salvar* pants and scarves covering their heads. The women sat by the road wearing blank or sad expressions, as if their faces were sewn on, too. Yet they waved the dolls hoping to catch the attention of the few tourists in this remote region of Turkey. As I made a purchase, one woman spoke in halting English:

"You like country?"

"Very much," I said. Wearing rags, selling handmade dolls along a dirt road, this woman smiled back and said, "We have so much good."

I grew more curious about the simplicity of the lifestyle, complexity of the food, and the contentment of isolated people who grow everything they need, and use everything they grow. When the tour guide took us to a cooking session in a private home, I learned one of many customs emphasizing the importance of tradition among Turkish families. Before she can marry, a Turkish woman must be able to make *manti* (ravioli) so tiny that forty will fit on a spoon. This proves her culinary skill and makes her fit to be a wife. Surely I would never marry, since only nine or ten *manti* fit on the spoon when made by my inexperienced hands, before toppling into the fragrant tomato sauce with cinnamon.

Another part of my cultural adventure, was an invitation to accompany Erdal Gulcan, the chef from our hotel in Goreme on a shopping trip. With the help of our guide, I was soon shopping the local markets of Cappadocia, choosing grape leaves and produce for the hotel dinner menu. What a treat to watch the chef's discrimination as he selected fresh vegetables, and had a spice vendor mix a batch of his preferred seasoning blend. Back at the hotel I was invited into the kitchen and was able to share in the preparation of an exquisite menu including Turkish Wedding Soup, beef stew, hummus, and lentil *kofte*. *Kofte* translates to "a woman's thigh," and is made either from lamb, or a simple recipe containing red lentils, bulgar, spices, and onion.

I worried when the chef instructed a young boy to go out for fresh figs at 3 P.M. Would I have time to make the dessert for the hotel guests' evening meal if he had to travel far, and was that donkey by the window his only form of transport? Just minutes later, the boy returned with a basket of figs, picked from a tree in the open land.

The figs couldn't have been fresher, and the dessert took only minutes to prepare, pouring a simple sugar and water mix over the peeled figs, topping with chopped walnuts, and baking for ten minutes. Much of the cooking I observed was based on ordinary ingredients matched with fresh and inventive spices, plus a pride in the wealth of their agriculture I had never known growing up in America.

As the common language of food stripped away any cultural differences, I felt completely at home, in a foreign country, among the familiar surroundings. I worked hard to show the chef I appreciated the effort he made to include me in the kitchen chores. He didn't need to speak English to instruct me on which vegetables to wash, or how much meat to chop. While hand gestures were adequate for cooking chores, I did move beyond that to exchange a few words with a delightful dishwasher, a young boy, who enjoyed my small Turkish vocabulary as he practiced English.

While I had brought little gifts for the people I met along the way, in the hotel kitchen I really wished I had brought a food processor. While grinding chickpeas by hand to make hummus, my mind flashed to the typical American kitchen, with an appliance or machine for every task. The gifts I did bring, vegetable peelers and miniature graters, were good for a laugh, but didn't seem too practical in kitchens unaccustomed to such conveniences. As our guide Hamide translated, "To save time? Why?" seemed to be the common reaction upon presentation of the beribboned kitchen gadgets.

At home in Chicago, I would often entertain the idea of making bread on a quiet Saturday morning, only to say "Nah, I don't have the time today." Time is really put in perspective when you are invited to bake bread with Turkish women. The sequence went something like this: Wait two

> *Her diminutive body, under five feet tall, belies the strength in her hands. For more than fifty years, my husband's Lebanese grandmother had a weekly bread-baking ritual. She rose early, measuring the ingredients, kneading the dough for ten to twenty loaves of both white and Lebanese flat bread. Even as she got older and her hands became more gnarled with arthritis, she eschewed the use of electric breadmakers, continuing the tradition of doing it manually. She maintained that the breads would not taste the same, and she could not get the amount of dough into one that she needed. Not that she needed twenty loaves of bread, at least not for herself. She baked these loaves, packaged them up, and grandpa would drive her around to deliver them to extended family and friends, as gifts, food in time of illness, and to make an equitable exchange with others for bounty from their gardens.*
>
> —Susan Brady, "The Old Way"

hours for the dough to rise in a plastic tub in the living room. Work to keep the small children from bouncing on the tarp-covered tub. Dress the baby and walk to the neighborhood oven, letting the children cart the tub of dough on a wagon. Spend a full forty-five minutes finding and breaking twigs to light the fire in the shared outdoor oven. I swear I will never again groan at the thought of pre-heating the oven for three minutes to heat a pizza.

We made traditional breads, filled with potato and onion, or tomato and cheese, as the neighborhood caught the scent of bread baking. "This is the experience we came here for," I said to my friend. For once, I was glad it took all day to make bread. So, there we were, rolling dough on a floured board just six inches off the ground, chasing flies away, while the neighborhood children and adults sat around on rocks wondering when the bread would be done. Soon, women were finding paper and wrapping the warm, crusty loaves for each family to enjoy. It seemed the social etiquette to sharing an oven also required sharing the bread.

It touched my soul to share laughter while teaching a farmer to make a radish rose, to play soccer out behind the hotel, and admire the goods made by women at the market.

A journey encompassing this vast amount of local color, personal contact with local people, new friends, and culinary skill satisfied the hunger for an experience that went beyond conventional travel. Best of all, I'd brought back culinary skills garnered from first-hand experiences. Cooking and eating with locals will remain with me long after other travel memories have faded.

These days, all I need is a quick dessert of baked figs with walnuts to transport me back to the colors, culture, and cuisine of Turkey.

Helen Gallagher is a passionate traveler, writer, and computer consultant and author of Computer Ease. *Based in Glenview, Illinois, she's just fifteen minutes from the airport, and always ready to travel. Helen can slice a tomato on her knee, and can frighten chefs worldwide with her knife-wielding skills in the kitchen.*

Turkish Wedding Soup

Serves 4

6 tablespoons butter

1 pound lamb, diced fine

1 carrot, chopped finely

1 onion, chopped finely

2 tablespoons flour

5 cups beef stock

2 egg yolks

juice of ½ lemon

1 tablespoon butter

½ tablespoon paprika

pinch cayenne pepper

cinnamon

Melt butter in a stockpot, add the lamb and vegetables and sauté for 10 minutes. Stir in flour and cook until blended, approximately 2 minutes. Slowly add beef stock, stirring well. Bring to a boil, then lower heat and simmer for 60 minutes. Remove from heat. Beat the egg yolks, adding lemon juice to them. Add some hot broth to the egg yolks to temper, then gradually stir the yolk mixture into the soup. Ladle the soup into bowls. In a small sauté pan, melt butter and quickly sauté paprika and cayenne. Place small amount in each soup bowl and swirl. Lightly dust each bowl with cinnamon.

TOM SWENSON

A Scandal in Senegal

In search of mafe, *the author almost gains a wife.*

The sleepy riverside town of Ngangane, Senegal likely doesn't see many scandals, so it stood to reason I caused an uproar. For there I was, walking to market with lovely young Miriam Faye, the cook at the psychedelic Le Petit Paradis, a restaurant owned by the charismatic Amadou Faye. The women food vendors observed us with increasing amusement as we approached and picked over the stock, selecting a potpourri of ingredients. Miriam, who was sixteen, displayed an adolescent misery as she sheepishly explained herself amidst a volley of questions. The town was quickly abuzz. I didn't understand most of what was being said, as it was carefully spoken in Wolof rather than French, but from poor Miriam's posture, and the raised eyebrows, I got the general feeling. The scandal reached its pitch later that day when Babacao, my river guide through the mangrove tributaries of the Sine-Saloum Delta, knowingly informed me that it was obvious that I loved Miriam, and as her father he approved of my marrying her.

In fact, I had not come in search of a bride, but was seeking a cooking lesson. I had come to Senegal partly for the food, reputed to be diverse, savory, and spicy. I yearned for the rich tomato and groundnut stew called *mafe* poured generously over rice as I'd eaten at a Senegalese restaurant in New York. My goal was to make friends and have them impart their secrets so I could recreate the tastes of Senegal in my kitchen back home.

After several days in the Dakar area, I made my way to Ngangane, a tourist stop on the north branch of the Saloum River, approximately ninety miles from Dakar. My first stop in town was Le Petit Paradis, a restaurant I had read was run by an erudite English-speaking couple who promised engaging conversation over delicious food. It was here I would seek my culinary indoctrination. The restaurant, adorned with lavish paintings, was empty aside from the owner Amadou, his niece, and her friend who sat in plush chairs under the lofty palm-thatched roof, he quaffing wine and smoking joints and holding court while the girls listened with bored looks. Over a bottle of wine, I broached the subject of a cooking lesson with Amadou, an idea which was well received by the garrulous restaurateur. I was to return at ten the next morning to begin my lesson, which would include a visit to the market and a full meal once we were finished—my first *mafe* of the trip.

It wasn't until I had arrived at Le Petit Paradis the next morning that Amadou informed Miriam of her fate, which caused her obvious distress, though she remained poised, and took the affront with good humor. She would need it for all the good-natured heckling she would endure. With me in tow she gamely stepped out onto the sandy road to head to market. Our first stop was at the butcher, who hacked off several large chunks of mutton from the fly-covered carcass that was strung up in the back of his wooden stand. Next stop was the vegetable stands, which were no more than long wooden tables piled high with a rainbow of fresh produce. We selected manioc, onion, potatoes, carrots, chiles, garlic, and a *diakhatou*—a vegetable that resembled a small heirloom tomato. We also stopped for tomato and groundnut paste, both of which came in small plastic bags. We were met at each stand with shrieks of laughter from nearby children, knowing looks and broad smiles amidst a barrage of comments from the women. The chatter continued after we left, and the story spread like wildfire through the tiny village until it reached Miriam's father, who thought I made a worthy suitor.

Miriam was clearly relieved when we finally reached the safety of the restaurant's kitchen, and began to loosen up. Unfortunately she spoke limited French and no English so conversations didn't range far. The kitchen was spartan, with a couple well-worn metal pots, sticky bottles of palm and vegetable oils, some bowls and utensils on a narrow shelf near the rusty metal sink. Two large propane stoves stood on a bench beneath the window. A rickety dish cabinet, a work table, and an unused storage refrigerator were the only other furnishings.

Miriam set right to work, falling easily into teaching mode. She would demonstrate a step in the process, and then turn it over to me to continue. First we chopped the root vegetables, onions, chiles, and *diakhatou* coarsely and soaked them in water. She then heated some palm oil over extreme heat, threw in the chopped mutton, and cooked it thoroughly, stirring to keep it from sticking. Next she added the groundnut paste and a couple cups of water, stirred and simmered it to reduce. While it cooked we added some dried chile and black pepper to a tall hand-carved mortar and pestle and pounded it. Then she threw in garlic, onion, and two cubes of bouillon and pounded it into a paste, turning the task over to me after a few pounds. The mortar was about two feet long and the pestle a foot deep so it rested on the ground and made for good leverage. Next the vegetables were added to the lamb and covered. After about twenty minutes she added the garlic paste to the pot and covered again. The aromas began to overwhelm the small room and I couldn't resist going over to lift the lid and give our concoction a stir, which caused Miriam to laugh every time. While it cooked, Miriam rinsed off some *netetou*, which is a small, fermented lentil-like grain that is a common condiment in Senegal, and pounded them in the pestle. Finally she added the tomato paste and *netetou* to the pot, stirred vigorously, covered the pot partially and proclaimed us finished. The concoction would simmer for the rest of the day.

My lesson was over but for the eating, which came later. I had written everything down and double-checked the ingredients with Amadou, and looked forward to trying it at home. Along the way I had created something of a scandal in Ngangane, and put poor Miriam through a fair bit of teasing. I had also been offered her hand in marriage, though I'm sure she wouldn't have appreciated that. Amadou offered up her services for the next day as well, when the meal of the day would be *thieboudienne*. However I was moving on up the river to Mar Lodj in search of a new teacher, new friends, and more adventure, and had to pass.

As I sat under the high ceilings of the restaurant later that day, drinking a Gazelle beer and eating the delicious plate of *mafe*, I was sated. Even if a man shopping for and cooking the day's meal caused a scene in Ngangane, I knew that in New York it would bring back the memory of my trip in the most delicious way possible.

Tom Swenson is a New York-based software project manager and travel writer who seeks cooking lessons on every journey—having been successful in Kenya, Morocco, China, Puerto Rico, and Senegal. For all his culinary explorations, he admits to having been taught most of what he knows in his mother's kitchen.

Mafe

Serves 4-6

2 tablespoons peanut oil

1 large onion, minced

2 pounds lamb stew meat, cut into 1 ½-inch pieces

½ cup creamy peanut butter

1 ½ cups cold water

1/3 cup tomato paste

2 cups hot water

4 large carrots, scraped and cut into 1-inch pieces

3 sprigs fresh thyme

2 bay leaves

salt and freshly ground black pepper, to taste

Heat the oil in a heavy saucepan, add the onion, and cook over medium heat until it is translucent. Add the meat and continue to cook, stirring occasionally, until it is lightly browned on all sides.

In a small bowl, mix the peanut butter with the cold water and pour it over the meat. Dilute the tomato paste with the hot water, pour the liquid over the stew, and stir well to make sure all the ingredients are well mixed. Add the remaining ingredients, lower the heat, cover, and cook, stirring occasionally, for 1 hour, or until the meat is tender. Remove the thyme sprigs and bay leaves. Serve hot over white rice.

A Taste of Ghana

Delving into African street food can bring great rewards.

People travel to Africa for history and for scenery but never the food. I don't get it.

I have found that Africa, with thousands of languages and cultures, each with its own cuisine, always rewards an adventurous eater.

Maybe the problem most travelers have is that finding good African food isn't always easy. Tourists are usually advised to stick to the hotel buffet. While a few countries, especially French-speaking ones like Ivory Coast and Togo, have developed an indigenous take on restaurant culture, many Africans prefer to eat at home. Barring that, they'd rather grab a bite on the fly. Although I travel frequently throughout Africa, I am not always lucky enough to snag an invitation to eat at someone's house, so my main source of authentic African food is on the street.

And few countries reward the sidewalk chowhound as well as Ghana. From rough-hewn sheds, women sell sharp wedges of starchy yam, perfectly fried in palm oil and slathered with a fiery sauce of pulverized Scotch bonnet peppers and garlic. From stainless steel bowls perched atop their heads, women dish out hearty bowls of perfectly spiced stew and rice, endlessly customizable with a plethora of condiments, from crunchy vegetables to a hard-boiled egg.

On a recent trip there, I sought out some of my old favorites and discovered some new ones. In both cases, to find good street food you have to go where Africans eat on the run: bus stations, markets, busy intersections, construction sites.

"You have to look where people stop and rest a minute," said Eddie Nelson, a Ghanaian businessman and fellow street food devotee I met over a fistful of *kelewele*, a delicious snack of cubed plantain tossed in hot pepper, ginger, and other spices, then fried until the sugar in the plantain caramelizes along the squared edges.

In the Kumasi market, I watched fou fou being made. A woman sat on her low stool next to a large metal basin set on the ground. Into it she tossed pieces of boiled yam as she peeled them. Two men, each with a stick, fatter at the bottom, and taller than themselves, stood on each side of the basin. As the woman added yam, they pounded—in rhythm—with their sticks, reducing the yams to a gluey mass. The woman had a second basin near her, this one of water, and as the men pounded, calling to each other, "A! B! A! B! A! B!" she scooped water from the basin and turned it into the yams. Timing her movements to the rhythm of the pounding, she folded the mass of yams over itself until it became a homogenous mass. She pinched off pieces occasionally to test its texture. Fou fou is eaten with the hands and a fat pillow of it will often be served in a bowl of soupy stew. It is worth the trip just to see it made. If you like—or don't mind—slightly gluey textures, you will also love the taste.

—Penelope Wisner, "Ghana: Fire and Water," Sally's Place.com

We were standing on a busy street just after sunset in Osu, a shopping district in Accra, next to Rosemary Nutsungah's *kelewele* shack. Ms. Nutsungah explained the secret to her snack.

"You got to have hot oil, that is No. 1," she said. "Then the plantain, it can't be too soft. It will drink the oil and become too oily. Also, you have to have very fresh ginger so it be sweet."

Mr. Nelson nodded approvingly, tossing cubes of plantain into his mouth from the crumpled newspaper in his hand. He then explained to me the finer points of selecting the right street food vendor.

"You have to look at the whole person," he said. "First, is her hair braided in neat rows, or does it go every which way? If it is neat, you are safe."

I put this wisdom to the test the next day on a trip to Kwame Nkrumah Circle, a roundabout at the heart of the city where thousands of minibuses converge, bringing commuters from across the sprawling metropolis.

Even in the chaos of honking horns and swirls of dust, it was evident that the street food business has a clear hierarchy and well-defined gender roles. At the top are the kebab sellers, always male, who sell a relatively high-end product because it contains meat, a prized addition to any meal. Ghanaian kebabs are a particular treat, called *kyinkyinga*. They are made of small, tender chunks of beef dusted with a spicy rub of peanut flour and hot pepper, dabbed with oil and then grilled over charcoal

Dairy products have similar status—cool bags of frozen yogurt and ice cream are sold exclusively by men.

Women sell any food that requires extensive preparation, usually from a container perched atop their heads. Fried yams, cassava, and sweet potato all require slaving over a hot stove and skillful timing to get just right. Selling rice and stew from a basin perched on your cranium means rising early to make the food, carefully wrapping it in layers of plastic bags as a kind of homemade insulation, then carrying it all the way to the bus station and serving it up in banana leaves to hungry commuters.

I tried to follow Mr. Nelson's rules, but after a few minutes I was not looking at hair, because I was distracted by the endless array of food. There were fritters made of plantain just this side of too ripe, mushed up with some hot pepper and then fried. There were balls of fried dough spiced with a bit of nutmeg, crunchy on the outside and tender on the inside. I had to stop after the fried wedges of cassava served with a pepper sauce called *shito*, made of tiny shrimp ground with hot pepper and oil.

Then there are some sidewalk meals you can't buy at any price. I found one such feast one day in Elmina, a coastal city west of Accra, where the oldest slave fort in the country bristles on a peninsula jutting out into the Atlantic Ocean, the portal through which countless Africans were shipped off as chattel to the New World.

Wandering the old fish market as the sun set, I stumbled upon Aba Theresa Mensah, a fishmonger who was winding down a long day of hawking octopus, snapper, and prawns by making a little dinner for herself and the other market women.

The customary "You are invited," was uttered as I eyed her glowing charcoal stove, and I eagerly plopped down on a simple wooden stool. I spoke only English and she mostly Fante, but we managed. On a stone she ground plum tomatoes and Scotch bonnet peppers, which she stirred into bubbling pot of blood-red palm oil. In went some bits of seafood culled from the catch of the day—a bit of octopus, a couple of plump red snapper fillets, a handful of prawns and, finally, the secret ingredient—a scoop of saltwater from the Atlantic.

"We go chop now," she said with some satisfaction, using the pidgin word for eat. She motioned to a young girl carrying *kenkey*, fermented gobs of cornmeal wrapped in leaves, a sort of African take on polenta that is the staple starch in this part of Ghana, and purchased a few balls.

She sliced the *kenkey* onto a plate, then ladled on the juicy bits of fish and octopus swimming in a fragrant bath of spicy stew.

"Chop," she commanded. I dug in, the *kenkey* sticking to my fingers and the sharp heat of the peppers warming my skin. It is called fanti fanti, and it is as simple and delicious a fisherman's stew as anything the Mediterranean has produced.

"It be sweet?" Ms. Mensah asked.

"Yes," I replied. "It be sweet."

Lydia Polgreen is a reporter with The New York Times.

I mprovisation is the key to survival in Africa. Here's a little tip for the serious campers among you. If you're ever in a bind and need a cooking contraption, nature provides one easily for you: deserted termite hills. Fashioned correctly, termite hills are a natural oven in the middle of the bush. Converting the termite hill to an oven is actually a simple task. Make a hole in the side of the mound, then make another hole in the top for ventilation. Add water to the soil you just removed and use it to create the oven's base. Once the base is dry, you can get the fire going with firewood—not hard to come by. Start your fire, and once that's ready, start cookin'! Apparently, termite mound ovens are not indigenous to Africa. South America also has a history of using them as well.

—Emilia Thiuri, "Extreme Camping"

PART FOUR

ASIA

First, the Mustard Seeds

A lavish wedding awakens a bride's taste buds.

*I*was on a plane trip that would last twenty-three hours. That's a long time to worry about meeting your new husband's family. Ashok and I had been married less than a month and were now going to India to have a full-blown, days-long, traditional Indian wedding. I was nineteen, he was thirty-two. He was a physician with a family full of physicians. I was barely out of high school.

When I met Ashok I was enrolled in nursing school, was a bit of a hippie, had two crazy roommates, and one devoted boyfriend. Five days later I moved out, postponed school, dumped the boyfriend, and Ashok and I were engaged. He was, and still is, eccentric, fascinating, and completely biased about Indian food "being the best in the world." I heard for weeks about his mother and what a wonderful person she was, as well as the only great cook he has ever known. I had twenty-three hours to fuss and fret and hope they wouldn't hate me.

We were met at the airport in Mumbai by dozens of relatives, food in hand. The heat waves off the airport pavement made the turquoise, yellows, and deep reds of my relatives' saris meld into a sort of LeRoy Neiman painting. There were excited greetings of "*Namaste,*" with prayer-hands and a nod of the head. I accepted the many snacks with bleary, jet-lagged eyes and a grateful empty belly. I found early on that not an hour goes by without an offer of tea, snacks, meals, or cooling drinks. Those first few days in India were filled with spice and heat, two things I love. I had left frigid Michigan weather in December, and my new family would constantly scold me for the next few weeks to get out of the sun.

My fears of getting along with my mother-in-law, Akka, disappeared as soon as she told me to follow her to the kitchen. She was called Akka by most everyone. It actually means "sister" in Kannada, my husband's mother tongue, but her little sibling had called her that as a child, and it stuck. I towered over her. I am five-six, she, four-nine. But my mother-in-law was the largest presence in the house. She was the first up, last to bed, and ran the entire household calmly and efficiently.

The house is in Bagalkot, a hot steamy area just south of the invisible line that separates the north and the south of India. The house is two stories, a pale peach wash on the outside, with a small yard out back with the ubiquitous red dust of India for a yard. Akka's kitchen in Bagalkot was not small, perhaps twelve-by-twelve feet. Everything she needed for cooking was low to the ground and within easy reach. There were wooden shelves and open cabinets for spices, pots, and utensils. Slightly higher was the sink, but the two-burner gas stove sat right on the floor. Akka would be flat-footed, resting back on her haunches, her pale cotton sari tucked between her knees, and have the vegetables, oil, and spices near the two gas burners, so she just twisted a bit to get whatever she needed. Her grey hair was tied neatly in a bun to stay out of her way.

The kitchen smelled clean, but earthy. Grass-green geckos scattered about the soft-white stucco walls occasionally, but my sister-in-law, Deepa, said they were welcome; they ate mosquitoes and other bugs. The floor in the kitchen wasn't the cement-like surface of the rest of the house. It was hard-packed, but had more give than the others. I asked what it was.

"Dung," said my sister-in-law.

"Dung?"

"Cow dung."

"Oh."

House shoes (non-leather) weren't even allowed in the kitchen as they weren't con-sidered clean enough; I could only be in the kitchen and on the dung floor with clean, bare feet. Apparently, cow patties become rather antiseptic when dry. Periodically, a fresh layer of dung mixed with mud is applied for cleanliness.

My first Indian cooking lessons began in that kitchen. I wasn't allowed to touch much in the beginning. But I watched in awe as Akka used her slicer, with its half-moon-shaped blade curving toward her. It was about eight inches long and was anchored to a block of wood. She would hold the vegetables gently with the first two fingers and thumb of each hand, and deftly move the vegetable into the blade until it was scattered on the block. There were neat little piles of sliced onion, or green pepper or chiles. A small eggplant would take seven or eight flicks of her wrists. She would pick up some pieces and dash them through again until every bit was of uniform size.

I watched and learned how to cook on high and move things quickly over a hot, hot fire. I learned the order of spices into the oil; first, the mustard seeds, then when

Imagine a pound of mustard seed. How many tiny yellow seeds, just three millimeters in diameter, does it take to make a handful, a cup, a pound? One pound of white mustard seed—the largest of the the three types—contains approximately 70,000 seeds, or 4,375 seeds per ounce. Just one of those seeds can produce several hundred new seeds during its growing cycle. One begins to understand why mustard seed has been used throughout history as a symbol of fertility.

The Hindu religion in particular identifies the seed as a symbol of fecundity. Early Christians, too, looked to the seed's symbolic possibilities, but used it to express other aspects of their tradition. There are numerous biblical references, most of which refer to its size and endurance. All the faith that one needs, Christians read, is as much as a grain of mustard seed. No doubt the seed was chosen in part because of its astonishing endurance, its innate ability to survive and transcend unfavorable conditions, waiting patiently in the ground until the rain comes in proper amounts and at the right time. Mustard can wait for decades, for as long as a hundred years or more, before sprouting. A mustard seed is full of remarkable power: all of mustard's potential—not just of the plant itself, but its heat and flavor—is contained within the small seed, a tiny miracle of which we avail ourselves with each squirt or spread or bite of mustard. It is no surprise that it has earned a place not only in our culinary history but in world mythology as well.

—Michele Anna Jordan, The Good Cook's Book of Mustard

they spatter, cumin seeds, *urad dal*, wait for more spatters and then *hing*, *masala*, and turmeric just before adding the vegetables, rice, or beans. She cooked quickly and deliciously, cleaning up as she went. I cook quickly and deliciously, but the kitchen looks like a war zone when I'm done, every pot used and abused. My mother-in-law could feed twenty people three meals a day with her two-burner stove. I want that Viking six-burner because I often run out of room, and pots.

We had a small wedding ceremony at the house in Bagalkot and then we were off to Bhantanur, the family farm, for a grander celebration. My husband's family had bought the house in town for the children to attend better schools years ago, but the farm was still considered the main residence. Several relatives and I piled into the small, non-air-conditioned car for the four-hour drive. Long garlands of flowers in yellows and whites draped the outside, cascading down on the windshield and up and over the back window in honor of the wedding. I wondered how the driver was going to see. We jostled and bounced and sweated, barely avoiding the scores of people, cattle, and vehicles careening down the tiny Indian roads.

We arrived in the village past dark. It was beyond dark, but as we turned from a small road onto an even smaller road, a lane really, I could see light from huge fires in the distance, and smaller, closer ones from handheld lanterns. There were people coming to meet us. The driver slowed to a crawl to allow the villagers to move aside, but still stay close enough for them to peer in the open window at me. I had been in India for three days.

There were dozens of people, or hundreds, I couldn't tell in the dark. They were there for our wedding reception. It was to take place in a few days, but the preparations had been going on for weeks. Marigolds were ordered, the priest was chosen, invitations had gone out all around India and the States, and one or two to Canada, or Britain, anywhere there were family or friends that needed to know about the marriage of a much-loved son. The son who was thirty-two and had become a doctor and moved to the States. They were invited to celebrate, even if the bride was only nineteen, blonde, American, and hadn't yet had time to go to college.

The darkness surrounded the car, the headlights spotting those directly in front of us. A few villagers spoke to Ashok, or the driver, and there was laughter all around after one of the conversations. The person peering in at me had started it.

"What's so funny?" I said.

"Many people think it is too bad that I am marrying someone so old," said Ashok.

"Old? Nineteen is old here?"

"No, it is not, but when I told them your age they said that it was most unfortunate that you had grey hair so early."

When I got out of the car I looked up and saw the blue-black sky lit by a billion stars. So many more than I had ever seen in the States. There were no streetlamps or city lights to dull their brilliance. But up on a hill in the distance, there were huge fires burning. There were tiny figures tending something above the fires, their outlines fuzzy from the rising smoke.

Everyone assumed I would go in and sleep after the dusty journey, but I asked Ashok to take me up the hill. As we got closer, I could hear singing. Groups of men were stirring massive pots of bubbling liquid, and singing a hypnotic tune that was passed from man to man. When one stopped singing, the next had already picked it up. Looping and moving, the song circled up and around the men, and the cook pots.

They quieted down a bit as we walked up, but the long night ahead, and their repetitive but important task, got them singing again. They were stirring huge iron cauldrons of sugar cane juice, boiling it down to make *jaggery*, Indian brown sugar. It has a melt-in-your-mouth texture

Barfi, halwa, ladoo, *and* kulfi *are just drops in the delicious ocean that is Indian sweets. In fact, Bengal is reputed to have over 2,000 distinct sweets. With milk usually serving as the main ingredient, these delectable goodies are an important thread in Indian life. Indian sweets, or* mithai, *are more than mere dessert, they are about sharing the good things in life. During the festival of Diwali, for example, Hindus exchange sweets with family and friends, and give them to the poor. Other occasions like passing an important exam, the birth of a child, or out-of-town relatives coming to visit all call for sharing sweets. Even new brides offer pounds upon pounds of sweets to their husband's family. Technically,* mithai *are not considered a dessert and many times will get served along with the main course. There is no consensus on the different of categories of sweets, but everyone agrees that making these delicacies takes a lot of time and patience, so sweet lovers mostly rely on professional sweetmakers for a fix.*

—Emilia Thiuri, "Priya's Wedding"

with a tone of molasses and sticky honey. It is wonderful and hard to come by in the States. The men were there throughout the night, and part of the next day, stirring and singing. Their songs and laughter in the darkness enveloped me in the ancient art of cooking, and the magic that takes place from good simple ingredients, attention, and heat.

There were four or five men standing around each cooking pot. They wore white sleeveless undershirts, banyans, and shorts or a *dhoti*, the wrapped yards-long fabric tucked around the waist and then up between the legs. One man would stir with a paddle for a bit, and then lean over and pass it to the man on his right. I never caught on if the song was supposed to move with the paddle.

India was still so new and noisy and vast in its ability to overwhelm me. Here on the hill, it was sweet-smelling, safe, and contained. I could only see what the light of the fires showed me. Above my head were the same moon and stars as home, they were more visible here, but they were the same. The soft singing, the repetitive movements, and the warmth of the fire made me calm. I left to go to bed when the sun was first showing red over the roof of Ashok's house in the distance. I woke late in the morning to the loud whispers of excited family bustling about the house.

I walked down the hall and wandered into the kitchen. It was an open room, flowing to a huge dining area. The room then narrowed slightly, opened to another room, turned a corner, and then opened into stalls and stable for the cattle. The house moved from a hallway for bedrooms to living spaces to barn to outside, with no doors. The ceilings were seven or eight feet tall. The walls were washed stucco with cubbies carved into them to hold utensils and pots, or gods and goddesses.

I loved the thick walls of the kitchen and the house, and the deep sounds the animals made. They were just around the corner and somehow it did not seem strange to have a resonant lowing drifting into the kitchen. I hated all the flies in the morning, but they were drugged from the night's cool temperatures and easily shooed away.

I feel at home in a kitchen. An onion is an onion, no matter where you go. My mother-in-law's kitchens were vastly different that what I was used to, but they were still places of cooking smells and cleanliness. I had been allowed to help a bit in the kitchen in Bagalkot, and wondered if it would be different here, with sisters-in-law, distant relatives, and more servants and crowds.

I was right; it was different. It was hectic in the village kitchen in Bhantanur. There were many more people to feed, and I was a novelty and a guest, so I was not allowed to work. Friends and relatives from nearby towns, as well as many states away, were showing up for the festivities. Each new arrival meant a round of sweet *masala* tea with *pakoras*, snacks made of vegetables deep-fried in chickpea batter, or *chewda*, a mix of pounded rice, peanuts, and raisins. I sat with the newcomers and gossiped and nibbled and stole glimpses of how they were managing in the kitchen to get it all done.

When Ashok and I were married back in town, in Bagalkot, the ceremony was private, immediate family only, with a small reception afterward. He told me that in the village there would be a bigger ceremony with more people attending. His family sort of was the village. Their farm needed many people to tend it, so they employed scores of families. My husband's father, Baba, had built schools and infirmaries and housing. The village had a compounder, or pharmacist, but when Ashok was home he was in high demand. He held mini-clinics to tend to the sick whenever he came to India.

The reception day came and my new family scurried around with last minute preparations. There were dozens of helpers making food.

"How many are coming to this anyway?" I asked, looking at a line of cooks sitting outside on the shaded porch.

"I'm not sure, perhaps two thousand or so," said Ashok.

"Ha! No...really, how many."

"Two thousand for dinner, then maybe more tonight for the fireworks. Why?"

"Two thousand peop...and fireworks? Oh...no reason."

That meant four thousand eyes looking at me. Wondering who I was and seeing if I did, indeed, have gray hair.

There were tents and more tents put up and mats laid down for the guests to sit. The tents were a glaring white against the bright sun of India. The gold of jewelry and the guests' best saris and wedding attire glittered madly. Under the tents it was calmer, shaded. People relaxed and waited for the food to be served.

After the first wave was seated, a big, deep-green banana leaf was placed in front of each person and the dishes came out and were served, one by one, by the helpers. The food was placed directly on the leaf. They had all been washed and dried earlier. A small mound of seasoned rice was surrounded by *raita*, yogurt and cucumbers, and *baingan bharta*, roasted eggplant, then came a yellow *dal*, lentils spiced with onions, and then a small serving of mango pickles. Each guest received a *ladoo*, a ping-pong ball shaped sweet of grains or nuts, held together with *jaggery*, white sugar, and cardamom. *Jalebis*, a deep-fried mound of squiggles, were placed on the leaf, dripping with syrup.

> There is no such thing as curry powder in India. Rather, the term "curry" refers to the overall spicing of the dish. Various combinations of spices result in a sweet, salty, bitter, astringent, sour, or pungent flavor—the six flavors around which Indian meals are based. These spices not only flavor and color the food, they are also used to stimulate appetite or digestion. Foods are also spiced depending on the season. I was in India during the winter, so I ate more "heating" foods, prepared with stimulating spices such as cloves, cinnamon, peppercorns, chiles, ginger, and cumin.
>
> —Deborah Fryer, "Food of the Gods,"
> *Her Fork in the Road*

There were chutneys and *chapatis*, unleavened wheat bread, added to the growing piles of food.

I had seen the *ladoos* being made the day before. An impossibly large steel bowl contained gallons of a pale yellow mixture while a man or woman would quickly scoop up a small, warm fistful, clamp it into a perfect round, and toss it onto a platter in about two and a half seconds. There were a dozen people doing the same thing, all in a row outside the house. I watched and tried to learn, but I have yet to master *ladoo*-making that does not result in half of them falling apart.

The reception was amazing and funny and probing. The younger girls ran up to me throughout the day and asked me my husband's name and I said "Ashok" and they would run away giggling, their arm and ankle bracelets making music as they dashed off. I was wondering why so many kids would be here if they didn't even know who the wedding was for…until it happened so many times I figured something was up. I asked my husband.

"A new bride is supposed to be so shy and happy, she can never say out loud the name of her groom," he said.

Whoops. Brazen me.

Before we left for the States, after the marriage was performed and the guests were fed and the fireworks died down and distant relatives went home, I could learn more about Indian cooking. I helped make several dishes like roasted eggplant with garlic, greens and *dal*, *dosas*, a fermented rice-and-lentil pancake, and *sambar*, a thin spicy soup. But mostly I learned my way around an Indian kitchen, and that it is a privilege to serve food to those you love, if it is done with love.

India and my mother-in-law taught me cooking by smell, taste, and touch. Akka taught me to feel or listen to a recipe. I learned how to wave my hand over the cooking pot toward my nose to see if a smell was just right. I can now ask my inner chef if a dish of *matar paneer*, peas and homemade cheese, is finished, or if it needs a few minutes more for the flavors to blend. Akka never measured a thing. I can now blindly pour salt into my hand, feel the heft of it, and know if it is too much or too little. I mix dough for *chapatis*, or *pooris*, deep-fried puffed bread, with my fingers, and can feel when the consistency is right. I listen for the deciding "pop" of the mustard seeds, and turn back to the pan from chopping onions to dash in the rest of the spices. I'm not as quick as Akka, but I pretend to have her skill and feel exotic and capable now that I know my way around Indian ingredients.

From the beginning, I shared Ashok's passion for good Indian food. I happily became vegetarian; I had been dabbling in it for years; and started buying vegetarian and Indian cookbooks. Cookbooks, however, would have been worthless to me without that first trip to India. That is where I watched and learned what happens in an Indian kitchen.

It could not have been easy for her, so many years ago, to watch a young foreigner marry her son, and know that it would keep him thousands of miles away. Perhaps she thought if she couldn't have him close, at least he might be well-fed. We ended up great friends, but in the beginning she did not know me. Despite that, she allowed me to learn from her. She allowed me to ask a thousand questions, and hover around her kitchen, and burn the *masala*, the hot oil and spices, a time or two.

The first time I burned the *masala* she didn't tell me what was wrong. She simply picked up the small pot of spices and *dal* and tossed it outside. The skinny farm dogs scrambled to eat it up. When I asked her why she had thrown it away she didn't scold, but said quietly in a blend of sign language, Kannada, and English, "the *masala* is burnt." I've since tasted burnt *masala*, and my mother-in-law was right in immediately getting it out of the kitchen, and knowing nothing could salvage it.

I have been back to India several times since then, learning more about Indian food each time, but the basics, and the honor of cooking well, I learned that first visit from my gracious mother-in-law. She died years ago, and I still miss her. I wish every summer I had asked her how to make green tomato chutney.

Eileen Hodges Sonnad has an MFA in Creative Nonfiction and teaches writing at Central Michigan University. She writes nonfiction "because real life is so wonderfully crazy, I could never make this stuff up."

Carrot, Cilantro and Mustard Seed Relish

Makes about 3 cups

1 tablespoon mild vegetable oil

2 teaspoons white mustard seeds

10 to 12 fresh kari leaves (see Note below)

2 pounds medium carrots, peeled and grated on a large blade

¼ cup cilantro leaves, minced

2 to 3 serrano peppers, minced

1 teaspoon fresh ginger, grated

2 tablespoons sugar

kosher salt

3 tablespoons fresh lemon juice

freshly ground black pepper

Pour the oil into a small sauté pan set over high heat. When it is hot carefully add the mustard seeds and kari leaves, cover the pan and cook for 45 seconds, or until the sizzling stops. Uncover, remove from the heat and let cool slightly.

Meanwhile, put the carrots, cilantro, and serranos in a bowl and toss gently. Put the ginger, sugar, and several generous pinches of kosher salt into a small bowl. Add the lemon juice and stir until the sugar and salt are dissolved. Pour the mixture over the carrots, add several turns of black pepper, and toss thoroughly. Add the mustard seed and kari leaf, toss again, tasting and adjusting the seasoning. Refrigerate, covered, for up to 4 hours before serving.

Note: Kari leaves, also known as sweet neem, are available in many Indian and Asian markets.

Japanese Salsa

Mexican cooking Japan-style.

Northern Japan hosts a very small population of *gaijin* (*foreigners* in Japanese) from the West, so as a local university student, I soon became rather well-known in my town. Because I could speak Japanese, people of all ages were happy to converse with me in the streets, in shops…basically wherever I went. Most wanted to practice their English on me, and would say things like: "You, Amelican? How old you are? You, married? Why no?" I wound up so annoyed at their innocent—yet prying—questions, that I just felt like crawling into my tiny apartment and hibernating. I wanted to hide from the locals who flocked over to me as soon as they saw my blond hair and white face looming above the crowds. "I'm not a walking English machine!" I'd swear to myself in frustration. "I'm here to study Japanese culture!" Other times, however, I'd feel lonely and was overjoyed to spend all afternoon sipping hot green tea with my elderly lady friends in their old wooden houses. I'd listen to these housewives exchange new recipes, laugh out loud as they covered their teeth, and chirped like tiny birds about the good old days in northern Japan.

After about a year, quite by accident, I ended up becoming a local radio celebrity, and thanks to this, I was asked to do a million off-the-wall things by City Hall. I was soon teaching French, English, and Spanish lessons, interpreting for bus trips, and one day,

I was asked to give a Mexican cooking class to young women in their twenties. "But I don't know how to cook!" I said, giggling into the phone, "and I'm not even Mexican!" It's true, I'm from the border of Mexico, but the other side. I started contemplating the invitation.... "I've probably eaten more Mexican food in my life than any other kind," I rationalized, "and I *do* speak Spanish. I guess I could fake it; they'd never know the difference." Besides, after a year of strictly consuming vegetables, seaweed, and raw fish, I was dying to dig into real Mexican fare again. The woman on the other end, my Japanese teacher's sister, pleaded: "Come on, Laura-san, they'll *love* you."

She briefed me on the situation. A local cultural center was offering a series of cooking classes for young women, to help prepare them for marriage. The director had heard of me, and thought it would be an advantage for these women to learn something about international cuisine. One of their major goals in life at this age was to learn to cook so they could find adequate husbands before they turned a certain age. According to tradition, if a Japanese woman is not married by thirty, she's considered by society to be a *kurisumasu keeki* (Christmas cake). Why a Christmas cake? Because that's what people throw out when it gets old and stale, after it's lost all its flavor. In fact, up until a few decades ago, these unfortunate young women had to move to distant cities to spare their families from disgrace. So after listening to this touching explanation, I accepted the challenge. Once again, I'd gotten talked into doing something I wasn't sure I wanted to do in Japan, but I felt sorry for these poor damsels in distress.

It was six o'clock on a Friday evening. Twenty-four sets of innocent dark eyes looked up at me, begging me, the exotic *gaijin*, to teach them how to bait a typical Japanese husband with *carne asada* and guacamole. Everything was perfect, the ovens were preheated, the ingredients were carefully laid out, we all had our dainty aprons on and our tiny pink plastic slippers. Mine didn't fit—they were *way* too small—and the director wouldn't let me wear the men's blue slippers, of course, because I wasn't a man. That's how things are in Japan. Women are women, so they get pink, and men are men, so they get blue. No exceptions are made, even if you're suffering. My heels hung so far over the back of the slippers, they practically rubbed the ground. I squealed. "Keep your heels up, Laura *sensei* (*professor* in Japanese), you'll lose weight this way," one of my new little protegés tried to encourage me. "Pretend they're *dietto suripa* (diet slippers), they'll keep you slim as you struggle to stay on your toes." With both calves cramping, I realized how silly I must look, perched on my toes in a starched white apron, hair pulled tightly back, and a gleaming chef's knife in my hand. Teetering in front of all the others, I was now in charge. The only problem was, I had no idea how to cook.

The director had placed a large mirror over my head, so everyone could see my fancy Mexican culinary maneuvers. I took a deep breath and started slicing a large red onion. After a second or two, a student cried out, "Oh no! Get that knife away from her!" I immediately stopped slicing and looked up, chuckling to myself. I wiped my hands on my apron and was just about to declare that I didn't know what the heck I was doing, when my eyes focused on a guy in the back, waving his hand in the air. Funny, I hadn't seen him come in. He came straight up to me and whispered something into my ear. He was a lanky, rather handsome young foreigner, with blond hair pulled back into an artistic-looking ponytail. He looked really cute in his plaid apron. I took a step back and looked right into his large grey eyes. I'd never seen him in our town before. I certainly hadn't expected someone like him in my Mexican cooking class for hopeful Japanese brides. Discreetly, he gave me a few pointers in English, which nobody could understand, and the students patiently let me continue cutting my onions. It turns out he was Italian, and used to help his father out in the kitchen during the summer. What luck!

Two hours later, the Japanese brides-to-be washed and dried all the cooking utensils so we could all finally sit down to enjoy our hot food. My Italian friend was happily surrounded by giggling, dark-haired female admirers. The long red-and-white tables were decorated lavishly, overflowing with *carne asada*, salad, guacamole, tortilla soup, and chips and salsa. It all smelled wonderful. Glorious memories of Baja California swept like waves into my ravenous nose. I realized it looked like I'd planned for forty, instead of twenty-five people. I'd forgotten that young Japanese women hardly eat; not so much out of politeness, but to stay skinny. I also realized I'd forgotten to prepare things to drink. It was a Friday night, and in Mexico, I know people would've been guzzling down ice-cold beers or tropical fruit juices or *sangria*…. Here we were with our tiny plastic cups filled with tap water. What a party pooper I was. Right then, I could've died for a Dos Equis beer, but nobody else seemed to care. We tapped our glasses together and pronounced "*salud*" (cheers in Spanish). I added: "*arriba, abajo, por fuera, por dentro*" (*up, down, outside, inside*) as I brought my cup above, below, then in front of my face and proceeded to drink down the tasteless liquid. My students all cheered and asked me to teach them this Spanish drinking expression, so I did.

We had just started picking into our food, with chopsticks, when one of the girls pulled out her instant camera. "*Shashin torimasho!*" she shouted as she jumped in front of the group. Everyone then got out their cameras—the Japanese don't go anywhere without them—and started flashing. After about ten minutes my cheeks hurt so much I couldn't smile anymore, and the food was already stone cold. Pictures are more important than food in Japan, I realized, as the same situation occurred time and time again. My stomach was grumbling and I wanted to attack my plate. To my surprise, since I followed the recipes I'd copied off the internet, everything turned out quite tasty. I was proud of myself. Everything, that is, except the salsa, which was so watery, I couldn't keep it on a tortilla chip long enough to get it into my mouth. It dripped all over my apron.

"What's wrong with the salsa?" I thought out loud, disappointed. "We did what you said, *sensei*, we chopped the onions into tiny bits..." offered the girl next to me. I inspected the sauce. You could drink this stuff without chewing it. "You cut the onions too finely," I blurted out, without meaning to scold them.

"Well, you know *sensei,* a woman must cut her onions *just so*, otherwise she'll never get a husband," the girl across from me rationalized. Then she added, not without a certain bit of mockery, "we all saw how you slice your onions, Laura *sensei*, and it's not surprising you haven't found a husband yet, at your advanced age." I looked at her, thinking she must be joking, but she was dead serious. The other students pursed their dainty red lips and looked down at their plates. Their uncomfortable silence confirmed my deplorable state. "So that's why I'm not married at such a ripe old age?" I laughed, wondering secretly if this might be the real reason. I was only thirty-three, but according to Japanese culture, I was already a Christmas cake.

Now, back in my country, whenever I slice my onions, I think back on that winter evening in Japan. What a fun learning experience that was. I'm careful to keep my fingers away from the blade, like my students showed me, by doubling up my left knuckles. I take great pride in my onion-slicing ability. Yet unfortunately, because of this, my salsa is often ruined. But I don't care. As I putter about my kitchen in my large blue slippers, I wonder if my young disciples ended up hooking Japanese husbands using my sumptuous *carne asada* as bait. I think about where my handsome Italian student ended up. He probably married one of them. I take a sip of my Dos Equis, smile, and crunch on some tortilla chips floating in my salsa.

Laura Kline is a Belgian-American creative writer, translator and interpreter, living happily in Brussels with her fuzzy Calico cat. She came back from Japan in 2003, after obtaining her Master's and Ph.D. degrees, and spends her free time jotting down anecdotes from her crazy traveling experiences abroad. Her dream is to write books and feature films (romantic comedies), and thus share her odd, yet true, international experiences to help make the world a playground for peace and love, instead of war. She is also currently taking cooking lessons, instead of giving them.

My first true overseas living experience was in Korea, where I moved to teach English in my mid-twenties. During my first few weeks in the country, I was so busy adjusting to the classroom and the rigors of living in a new culture that I didn't have much time to cook interesting or authentic meals. I ended up just preparing the Korean staple of bap (white rice) and eating it with a fried egg, soy sauce, and mandu meat dumplings that I'd purchase frozen at the supermarket. The dish suited both my Western tastes and my single-male instinct to keep things easy in the kitchen. Proud of my culinary creation, I named it "Mandu Rolf-bap," and told my college-aged students how to make it.

Several weeks later, I was much more knowledgeable about the wonders of Korean cuisine—bulgogi, bebim-bap, kalbi—and I'd nearly forgotten about "Mandu Rolf-bap." Then one day my evening class got onto the topic of food, and no less than five of my students confessed that they'd eaten bap with eggs, meat dumplings, and soy sauce that week. Upon further questioning, nearly every student in the class admitted to having eaten "Mandu Rolf-bap" multiple times since I first told them how to make it .

To this day, I tell people that the first thing I taught my students in Korea was how to eat like bachelors.

—Rolf Potts, "Mandu Rolf-Bap"

Uzbek Cornmeal

A cultural error creates a new delicacy.

I made an inadvertent contribution to Uzbek cuisine when I lived in Tashkent for about two years as a Peace Corps volunteer. One of the foods I missed a lot was homemade Southern cornbread, but I found it impossible to locate a local source for cornmeal. Although I lived in the largest city in the country and searched for cornmeal in every bazaar, I repeatedly returned home without success. Every time I went shopping, I checked and could never find any.

One day I happened upon a part of the huge Chorsu Bazaar that I hadn't seen before. There I saw sacks of all kinds of grains that weren't on display in the other sections of the bazaar—dried corn, mixed seeds, and in one sack, ground-up corn. To my American mind, a baker's supply place. This was not the kind of cornmeal I had used in America, but I thought the difference in texture might be from grinding the corn by hand rather than by machine. I promptly bought several kilos.

The next time I cooked an evening meal, I made the long-desired cornbread. Mashkura, my host mother, thought it was delicious.

"What kind of flour is this?" she wanted to know.

"That is the cornmeal I have been looking for," I answered. "It isn't exactly what we have in America, but I think it's O.K. It was really cheap."

"Where did you find this flour?" she asked.

"In Chorsu Bazaar, not on the main floor, but over to the side. There were big sacks of corn and other seeds near it."

An odd expression crossed her face and she asked to see the flour that I had bought. I got the cornmeal out of the cupboard and gave it to her. She sniffed it, ran her fingers through it, and began laughing. Through her laughter she said, "This is what we feed the animals." I had to laugh, too, but I made Mashkura promise that my mistaken ingredient would remain our secret. In exchange, I gave her the recipe.

The next day a woman who cleaned the stairwells and landings of the building we lived in was working near our apartment at lunchtime and Mashkura invited her in for lunch. She served some of the leftover cornbread to the cleaning woman, who loved it and wanted to know how it was made. Of course, Mashkura couldn't tell her without mentioning the secret ingredient.

In a few days the cleaning woman had some friends into her home and served them the cornbread she had made from my recipe. They also loved it and wanted to know how it was made. The recipe was passed on.

Now, thanks to my naiveté, there is a whole group of women who go to Chorsu Bazaar to buy cow chow, make cornbread, and think they are eating American food.

Ruby Long has traveled to many parts of the world. She writes about the adventures of travel, as well as her life in Oakland, California.

In frontier America, as in colonial America, any form of bread made with corn instead of wheat was a sad paste of despair. How sad is reflected in the lowliness of the names—pone, ashcakes, hoe-cakes, journey-cakes, johnny-cakes, slapjacks, spoonbreads, dodgers—all improvised in the scramble to translate one culture's tongue and palate into another's. Names got muddled by region and recipe as much as samp, hominy, and grits and for the same reason: the desperate attempt of a wheat culture to order by its own canon the enormous variety of pastes, batters, and doughs cooked by native grinders of corn.

For those who actually cooked the stuff, cornmeal was hard going. Not only was corn obdurately hard to pound even to coarse meal, but the meal refused to respond to yeast. No matter how they cooked it, in iron or on bark or stone, corn paste lay flat as mud pies. Heaviness was a constant colonial complaint, which cooks sought to remedy by mixing cornmeal with the more finely ground flours of rye or wheat—when they could get them.

—Betty Fussell, *The Story of Corn*

Chef for a Day

The tables are turned on a trip to the mountains of China.

For about fifty cents a man at the Rising Sun bike rental stand, located in front of the No. 2 Guesthouse in Dali, China, provides me with a sturdy mountain bike and a photocopy of a hand-drawn map detailing sights of interest which lay within a day's ride. It's a good thing the bike is built to take some rough terrain since that's exactly what I encounter. The narrow lanes leading east out of town turn into steep, bumpy paths that pass through cultivated fields before eventually arriving at the shore of Er Hai Lake. Having taken this cross-country route instead of the main road heading south, I get close-up views of people working in the fields and inadvertently startle a young couple making love in a haystack. My goodness, Dorothy, I think we are back in Kansas!

Stopping for a rest and a look at the local Kuan Yin Temple, I find that my visit coincides with two busloads of Chinese tourists. I wait nearly half an hour to take a picture of the temple as these folks block a clear shot by posing in every possible group configuration. My wait turns out to be entertaining, however, as I watch one particular old gentleman. He wears an obviously cherished though threadbare military uniform. Judging from his proud stance and the number of medals displayed on his chest, I imagine he's been defending China since the days of Genghis Khan.

Before setting out this morning my only breakfast had been a pint of yogurt I'd purchased from Tsho, an eight-year-old ethnic Tibetan girl who has befriended me. Previously, we had swapped some word translations, respectively telling each other the names for eye, nose, ear, tree, and the like. Therefore, I'm hot, tired, and hungry when I arrive in Xiaguan at one P.M. The road from Xiaguan to Dali is mostly uphill and I realize that the return ride is going to be much more strenuous.

By the light of the midday sun Xiaguan is devoid of the ghostly aura which had marked my semi-comatose, pre-dawn arrival from Kunming the previous morning by bus. It's a lively town situated along the banks of the Er Hai River where it flows from the lake with the same name. Er Hai Lake is in turn fed by snow melting from the Cong Shan mountain range and related springs. One notable spring in the area is known as Hudie Quan, or Butterfly Spring, after swarms of butterflies that converge here in late springtime. It's said that two ill-fated lovers attempting to escape persecution threw themselves into the spring, but since their love was pure, they were reincarnated as beautiful butterflies and begat the lineage that gathers here each year. Flowers abound in Xiaguan and children play in a well-designed but poorly maintained park at the river's edge. Old men, lost in deep contemplation, roost in a classic pagoda as their lives ebb away on the river's current.

Scouting the main street for a place to eat, I choose a café on the basis of the food I note being served and the relative cleanliness of the floor. When I have trouble deciphering the menu my perplexed waitress says "boss speak English" and goes to the kitchen to get Chuo Wen, the owner. Our communication falls short, too, and my clumsy attempt to covertly point at the meals of other patrons only adds to the confusion. At this point Chuo Wen offers to fetch a friend who also owns a restaurant. She says, "Liu Yu speak good English." Waiting patiently for her return, I invite myself into the kitchen where the cook hasn't any problem understanding my wishes as I point at selected items.

When Chuo Wen finally returns, I haven't any regrets for the wait. Her friend, Liu Yu, is most congenial and also quite attractive. However, her English skills are about on par with my grasp of Mandarin, which is too often sorely lacking. Since the cook has already started my lunch, we attempt to carry on a conversation with the help of my phrase book. Liu Yu finds the restaurant section in the book and starts writing down all the entrees in both Mandarin and English. She explains that she wants to create a bilingual menu to accommodate the Western tourists who have recently been coming to her restaurant in growing numbers. As she transcribes every menu item we practice, with mutual coaching, the phonetic pronunciation in each other's language. It becomes a far more involved process than I'd engaged in with Tsho.

Chuo Wen attentively hovers about our table. Presently, she and the waitress bring trays containing a few of the dishes Liu Yu and I have discussed, in addition to the entree the cook had prepared in response to my willful intrusion in the kitchen. Chuo Wen had misunderstood, apparently thinking that we were ordering the items as we practiced reciting their names. Fortunately, I'm very hungry, because I feel obliged to eat as much of the food as I can, and to pay for it, too. With chopsticks poised at every morsel, Liu Yu helps me eat the food as we become increasingly confident of our pronunciation.

With our prolonged lunch and linguistics tutoring completed, Liu Yu asks me for a special favor. She invites me to her restaurant for the purpose of teaching her how to prepare "American-style" ham omelet, beefsteak, and fried chicken. I find it ironic that she doesn't even ask if I know how to cook. However, having had some experience working as a professional chef years ago, I accept the challenge before even seeing her kitchen.

Liu Yu's restaurant seats about thirty-five people and has a big screen TV for after-dinner viewing with cocktails. Television is rarely available in private homes, so the restaurant also serves as a community gathering place. One large round table that seats up to ten people for family dining dominates the room. Whereas the dining room is comfortably modern with modest decor and a nice tile floor, the kitchen is downright primitive.

This smoke-darkened, rustic kitchen facility seems inconsistent with the fresh garden produce and savory cuisine served at Chuo Wen's restaurant. Liu Yu is an adept cook herself and is well aware of the need for separate chopping blocks for meats, poultry, and vegetables. This prevents contamination and possible poisoning, so she makes sure that these are at my disposal. Her wooden blocks look like family heirlooms, as they are deeply concave from many years of use.

Together we assemble all the necessary ingredients including fresh herbs and spices. Liu Yu takes careful notes throughout the preparations. I show her how to bread the chicken using egg whites, flour, spices, herbs, and crumbs derived from toasted flat bread. With all three entrees ready to be cooked, Liu Yu leads me to an outdoor courtyard where I'm disappointed to learn that the actual cooking is to be done on a dual-burner propane stove. I was actually beginning to look forward to the task of using the authentic, old-fashioned kitchen with its charcoal-fired stove. I guess I'll have to be satisfied with the prospect of cooking an omelet in a wok.

Liu Yu's mentally challenged younger brother joins us in the courtyard to watch the show. She has shooed him away a couple of times while we engaged in the sensual dance inherent in the preparation of food, but now allows his presence. I ask him to take a picture of us cooking and he gets so excited that he can barely hold my camera still for a shot.

Of course, once everything is cooked we must eat it as a taste test. Younger brother is a big help with this since Liu Yu and I have finished our huge lunch little more than two hours ago. She's very pleased with the way the dishes turn out, but I find them strangely foreign in this setting. If you ever eat at Liu Yu's restaurant you will now find "Bob's Home Fried Chicken" printed on the menu in both Chinese and English.

It's nearly four o'clock and Liu Yu's dinner chef, Yang Chen, arrives to begin preparing for the evening clientele. She invites him to join us for a glass of wine and a taste of the dishes we have been creating. He's skeptical about the beefsteak, but quickly warms up to the fried chicken and omelet. With a wink at Liu Yu, he asks if he will be cooking these items, or will "Mr. Bob" be staying around to do the job. She blushes deeply and chases him into the kitchen with playful admonishments to get to work and mind his own business.

Bob Rice lives, writes, and practices traditional Chinese medicine on the Oregon coast. From this idyllic home base, he has traveled extensively throughout the world logging seventy-nine countries to date. This story is an excerpt from his book manuscript On the Tail of a Dragon: A Sojourn in China. *In a series of articles published in* The Upper Left Edge, *he relates adventures encountered while crewing, for five months, from Vancouver B.C. to Wellington, New Zealand, on the replica of James Cook's nineteenth century ship H.M.S.* Endeavour. *He is the author of the novel* Box Canyon Sonata, *which is in search of a publisher.*

Fried chicken may be a quintessential American dish, but chicken itself is ubiquitous the world around, one of our most common sources of protein, and of flavor. In China, chicken is paired with pork (necks or ribs, butt or shoulder, and hamhocks), shallots, leeks, onions, fresh ginger root, and salt to make Strong Stock, or Superior Stock, an all-purpose ingredient in both home and restaurant kitchens that is the secret to flavorful soups, sauces, porridges, and stews. The stock is simmered for hours, often overnight, until it is rich, and concentrated. Learn to make good Strong Stock and you are on your way to making excellent Chinese cuisine. It is also an ingredient that crosses cultural boundaries—many chefs rely on Strong Stock for the depth of flavor it contributes to Italian, French, Spanish, and other cuisines far from Asia.

—MAJ

Kimchi Cravings

*Upon the author's return from Korea, his obsession had him
searching high and low for this addictive condiment.*

Kimchi, the national dish of Korea, is hot. Fiery hot. Hot like its colors, red, yellow, and green, producing a burn that swirls in the nose and sets eyes leaking before the first bite. Kimchi is hot on the lips and tongue, warms your mouth as you chew, and stokes your gullet as it glides toward the slow simmering cauldron formally known as your belly. It's everywhere in Korea, an obligatory side companion along with rice in any restaurant you visit, from the simplest country joint to the highbrow steakhouses of Seoul.

Koreans love a "*shiksa*," literally a "food feast," and kimchi, if not the focal point, remains at least the common denominator. There are dozens of different kimchies, over two hundred varieties by some counts, but the staple for generations, the "classic kimchi," has been the whole cabbage variety: heads cut in half, bathed in salty brine, thoroughly rinsed, then stuffed with varying mixtures of garlic, ginger, green onions, pickled fish, fresh oysters, and the kicker, red pepper paste, lovingly lathered and tucked into all folds of the cabbage. It sits to settle a couple days (or weeks), then per tradition gets stuffed in big earthenware pots and buried in the backyard for six months or so, to pickle, and ferment.

Kimchi is also delicious, and addictive as hell. Ask any Korean, they'll tell you kimchi is not just part of their diet but an essential component of their history, folklore, their very way of life. Chinese farmers first began pickling vegetables around 12 B.C. as a way to store perishables through the frozen winters. For the next thousand years, monks and other couriers helped spread the practice east, from China through Korea and eventually on to Japan. By the thirteenth century, Koreans were pickling like mad and had begun to discover different kinds of kimchi. The lineage of contemporary kimchi took a turn for the spicy in the late sixteenth century, when Japan invaded Korea. The Koreans repelled their attackers, but not before the Japanese introduced to Korean cuisine red pepper powder, an essential in today's kimchi.

Deny a Korean kimchi for a few days, he'll notice its absence, manifested in a sluggishness or an edge perhaps, or maybe his food just won't taste right. This sapping of energy can be attributed to vitamin loss, for kimchi has vitamin C like Florida has oranges; the lack of taste may result in imbalance or disharmony in the Korean meal: a main course of soup, pork, or beef surrounded by an army of side dishes: leafy vegetables, dried fish cut in strips, candied potatoes and sticky rice, and, of course, a handful of wildly different kimchis.

There's *kkaktugi*, hot radish kimchi, and *oi sobagi,* cucumber kimchi stuffed with radish strips. Wrapped-up kimchi is cabbage leaves rolled around combinations of fruit and nuts, seafood, and vegetables. Some seasons see pumpkin kimchi, others, wild leek-and-onion kimchi. There's young radish kimchi (especially nice when allowed to ferment in the same container as the *oi sobagi*) and crisp water kimchi. White kimchi, wet kimchi, kimchi with clams, or squid, or heavy on the onions, or tangy with sweet potatoes.

When many Westerners first see kimchi they tend to flip out at the sight (or smell) of it, and for quite a few, it's just too darn hot at first. But the key to kimchi consumption is to dig in and eat it, to weather the initial hot flash and keep going, for kimchi rewards with its savory bite and lip-smacking satisfaction both neophytes and veterans alike.

Spend a year in a foreign country and the nuances and extremities of its cuisine grow familiar over time, like bus routes in a new city or an alphabet of alien forms. One thing about Korea, the food is splendid. Koreans are fiercely proud people, with a strong sense of national identity and deep connection to the past. They can also be quite warm and giving, and in no area is this more apparent than with food. Koreans offer their food with pride and delight in sharing it with foreigners, in the restaurant and the home.

When Westerners sit down for a *shiksa* with Koreans the hosts pay them lavish attention, constantly refilling bowls, emerging from the kitchen to produce another side, a new flavor. And nothing rewards Korean hosts more than to see foreign guests munch kimchi with abandon.

During the course of a prolonged stay in Korea, not only did I grow to love the food and, in particular, the kimchi, I also grew to the point where like Koreans themselves, my body didn't just crave kimchi, it screamed for it. I lived at first in Haenam, a sleepy crossroads town of 20,000 people, deep in Chollanam-do, Korea's breadbasket.

I lived with my friend Mr. Cho and we'd meet back at home in the evening for our meals, which always began with kimchi. Those times when we'd open the fridge to find no kimchi or worse, just enough to tease, we'd react with sudden shock and quickly dash to the market, like frat boys who've just seen the last keg spit foam on a Friday night. We'd arrive at the market with its scents and clamor and watch the bustle of the *adjumas*, the older Korean women who prepare the food. Mr. Cho would glance at me with mirth and satisfaction and say, "Now we get some kimchi."

I returned from Korea in September and settled in San Francisco, that cosmopolitan jewel where devotees of any cuisine can find a fix on any night. It wasn't too long before I sussed out the *shiksa* spots, from the cheap soup and dumpling joints of Berkeley to the monstrous *bulgolgi* beefhouses, where you order mounds of marinated beef and fresh seafood then grill it at the table for that full-on meat buzz. I'd feast, suck my teeth, then kick back in reflection and digestion.

While these occasional quests for Korean food would stave off the demons for a short while, I still felt an absence in body, mind, and cupboard. Breakfasts were a drag and snacking on carrots didn't cut it; there was a void in my refrigerator. It was the absence of the kimchi. I missed it, like a bygone lover, with body and soul.

I consulted my Korean friend Jane and said, "Good God, girl, where's a body to get some kimchi in this here Bay Area?" With a glint of wisdom in her eye and a slight smile, she said to me "You miss it, don't you?" and I confessed it to her, right there— Yep, I said, I was hooked. A kimchi junkie, and not even thirty yet.

The first kimchi she brought me was from Oakland's Koreatown, a gallon-sized glass jar bursting with color, a day or so away from the optimum ripeness. I set it on the back porch and stared for two days in anticipation, then said to hell with it and cracked it open on the spot. I must have eaten a quarter of the jar that day, a binge that stained my chin with juices and left me leaned back against the door, belly bulging, mouth agape.

Eventually I refitted the lid and rolled to my room to sleep the sleep of a traveler just back from a long journey.

Soon after, I was headed with my friend Rebecca to her new place across town and discovered with joy she lived right around the corner from a small Korean grocery. Kaju Foods looks like a mom-and-pop store direct from Seoul, with crowded shelves and a glass case full of pre-made side dishes. "I've never seen half this stuff," Rebecca said but I wasn't there, I was somewhere else, letting memory flow through me. She got my attention, though, when she called from the back, "What on earth is this?" Something told me she'd found the motherload, and I was right. She was standing by a cooler full of kimchi.

My eyes lit up, and I grabbed a jar despite Rebecca's quizzical asides. The proprietor laughed heartily when he saw my impending purchase, and offered me some marinated

A careful observer might notice plump black pots lining the rooftops of apartment buildings and single-family homes, not only in the countryside of Korea but in its cities as well. These crocks, known as jahng dak, are an art in themselves, made by Korean potters for hundreds of years. Every year, thousands of jahng dak are filled with a flavorful fermenting stew of greens, chiles, garlic, fruits, spices, meat, and fish—the ubiquitous and essential kimchi, the cornerstone of Korean cuisine. The jahng dak are traditionally buried in the ground or packed in straw to age during the winter and lowered into wells or packed into cool caves in the summer, though these days most homes have a second refrigerator reserved for kimchi, and only kimchi.

In November, after winter sets in but before the first snow falls, markets overflow with both ingredients and customers as the annual kimchi-making season gets underway.

This winter kimchi is known as kimjang and it is the real thing, not the instant alternative that families make in the summer months when their winter supply is depleted.

Television news anchors include bulletins on the progress of kimchi-making in their nightly reports. Kimchi may be a family activity but it is a national ritual.

Whether kimchi is made in the winter or summer, it must include the seven traditional qualities: the taste of chiles, either sweet or hot; saltiness; sweetness; sourness; bitterness; astringency; and intensity, a characteristic contributed by toasted sesame seeds, seaweed, or that classic shortcut, MSG.

—MAJ

pork as a gift. The plan was I'd leave the kimchi at Rebecca's place that night, and she'd drive it to the store where she worked, where I'd pick it up the next afternoon. I got sidetracked and couldn't see her for a couple days, but when I went to the store, I walked in, took a whiff, and said, grinning, "Smells like kimchi in here." She glared at me and pointed to the back room, where my gallon jar sat in the corner encircled by a splatter of reddish goo I identified as the hot pepper powder, which had fermented itself straight out of the container. I wiped and apologized, realizing I'd no longer have this establishment as a halfway point for my pickled cabbage.

I became a regular at Kaju, making my way down there every couple weeks to replenish my gallon of goodies. But while the kimchi was great, the commute was not, what with two transfers each way and a heavy load of pungent, pickled vegetables on the return. Plus winter arrived, and in San Francisco that means rain accompanied by a wind blowing the wet at a 45-degree angle. During one such deluge, while lamenting the weather over the last of my kimchi with Jane, she looked in my eyes and said matter-of-factly, "You should just make your own kimchi."

At first, I was skeptical. I had seen those *adjumas* prepping the winter kimchi, and the workload seemed way too much for me. But Jane laughed at my doubt, and said it was different—those women were preparing a season's worth of kimchi, and for huge extended families at that. This making of the winter kimchi is known as the *kimjang*, she said, and a time-honored tradition in Korea. My project, she insisted, would be much more benign. After listening to her reasoning and looking at the empty glass jar, my confidence grew and my stomach growled its approval. Sure, I can make kimchi. Now where do I start?

A Korean Mother's Cooking Notes became my guidebook. This is a cookbook written by an *adjuma* from Seoul, "to my daughters-in-law" and anyone else who can't cook Korean food. I'd bought it in Seoul and showed it to Jane, who said the recipe for pre-cut cabbage kimchi looked good to her. This is the classic kimchi, as good a place to start as any. While each *adjuma* has her variations on the theme, I mostly stayed true to the guidebook, and made sure to include the requisite love.

Following are the recipe and the instructions I followed, and you can, too. Keep in mind I shopped at Asian markets, trying to duplicate the Seoul grocers as best I could.

I had a cooking partner, too, my friend Amy who also lived in Seoul and took over the kimchi mixing when my carpal tunnel began to set in.

Start with the cabbage, Korean preferably, six pounds worth, and fresh. A bulb of garlic, some ginger, and a bunch of green onions come next. Now head toward the condiment aisle, and gather ordinary sugar, red pepper powder, and coarse salt. Table salt won't work, because its too fine to rinse from the cabbage and throws the measurements off with its bitterness. Get a cup of fresh shrimp and some smelly fish sauce, which when mixed with red pepper powder creates a shiny paste. This gives the kimchi its bright red sheen.

Take the cabbage, rinse a couple times, then cut each head in half once, lengthwise. Place the halves into a tub of twelve cups water and two cups coarse salt for fifteen minutes of initial salting. After this quick soak, remove the cabbage and coat it with another cup of the salt, making sure to get between the folds and at the base, where the cabbage is thickest. After salting, resubmerge the halves in water and let stand for four hours, periodically rotating the cabbage to ensure even soaking. (Be aware larger heads may require a couple extra hours.) Your goal is a bunch of limp cabbage.

While the cabbage is soaking you can prepare the rest. Finely chop a tablespoon each of garlic and ginger and the shrimp. Cut three tablespoons worth of green onion, 1 1/2" lengths. At the four-hour mark, mix a cup of red pepper powder with 2/3 cup fish sauce, stir thoroughly, and let stand 45 minutes or so. Adjust accordingly for longer soak times.

Once the cabbage is limp and wilted, you need to wash it, several times, to remove the extra salt. This is important, for too much salt drowns out the other flavors. After its rinsed, chop the cabbage into 1 1/2" lengths, and rinse once again.

At this point, you're ready to mix. Roll up your sleeves, and no matter what, don't wear white! *Adjumas* in Korea are renown for their colorful clothing, and when you make kimchi once you'll know why.

In a large bowl, mix the cabbage with the fishy pepper paste. Don't be bashful—get your fingers in there and mush the stuff around. They say in Korea the kimchi gets its extra taste and nuance from the labor and love of the *adjuma's* hands; yours should have that extra effort, too.

Toss in the garlic, ginger, and shrimp and mix. Then add the onions and three tablespoons of sugar and swirl it all around. By this time your hands should resemble what's in your bowl, a sticky, wet, red and yellow mess. Fear not, though, this is normal. In fact, if your hands don't look this way, you just need to mix some more.

Now your kimchi is ready for jarring. The key to kimchi is the fermentation of its ingredients; after you've mixed it, your kimchi needs to settle, and ripen, and blend. Take the kimchi and stuff it into glass jars (these measurements yield about three quarts worth) and let it sit at room temperature for about three days. Every autumn in Korea *adjumas* stuff the kimchi into earthenware pots and then bury them, fully, in the backyard, not to be opened until spring. You can do this, too, especially if you like kimchi with your baseball.

These are the instructions I followed exactly, except for the burial. The kimchi sat in glass jars in my kitchen Sunday night, Monday and Tuesday. Wednesday came, and I woke up eager to sample. Carefully I cracked the lid, alert to potential expansion expulsions. I opened the jars, sniffed, then dug in with chopsticks.

Crunch, crunch. Tastes good so far! There's the pepper, and the garlic too. The heat hit my nose, slowly, not too thick, then swirled through my mouth as I vigorously chewed my first bite, and others. Then the ginger kicked in, subtle yet distant, and the realization hit me as my stomach began to warm that I'd done it, I'd made kimchi, this is the real stuff. Mr. Cho would be proud.

I invited some friends over, Jane and Amy and Rebecca among them, for a tasting party and some picture taking. Jane brought a treat, some *macchali*, Korean rice wine, traditionally drunk with friends over kimchi. We laughed, and we ate with chopsticks. The only problem was I didn't make enough! The kimchi was gone before the *macchali*, and Jane said with a smile to me "Now you need to make some more." I will, I told her, in bigger batches next time. Besides, I need to get back to the Asian markets soon. *Kkaktugi* is calling!

A travel, food and culture writer based in the San Francisco Bay Area, Jay Cooke always saves room for new spices and seasonings in his backpack. As Commissioning Editor at Lonely Planet Publications, he structures and develops travel guides including New York City, New Orleans, San Francisco, *and* Miami & the Keys. *As a freelance writer and editor he's contributed to* VIA, National Geographic Traveler, Business Traveler, Wired, *the* San Francisco Chronicle, *and the* Korea Times. *He also teaches travel and pitch writing classes and seminars for Media Bistro.*

JESSICA JACOBSON

Meat and Potatoes

A bloody transformation occurs in Siberia.

"I'm a meat-and-potatoes kind of guy," I used to hear both of my grandfathers say. This excused them from their reluctance to try the jelled, baked, sautéed, and marinated creations family members brought to reunions, preferring to stick with the time-worn and tested comfort foods; the stick-to-your-ribs kind of food that will load your arteries with fat and give you an extra dose of carbohydrates, but keep you full all night long.

I was never a meat-and-potatoes kind of girl. I had nothing against either meat or potatoes and would eat them gladly when they were set in front of me, but I had never prepared a steak in my ten years of independent living, much less a hamburger or a meatball. I had just about eliminated the good old bloody stuff from my diet...until I moved to the Aginsk Buryat Autonomous Region in southeastern Siberia. Populated by the descendants of Genghis Khan's Mongol hordes, this clan of Buryats in the midst of the Siberian steppe is a meat-and-potatoes nation.

On my first day living in the capital, Aginskoye, a small town of 14,000 nestled among stubby mountains, I met with the director of the school where I would be teaching. It was chilly mid-January and she wanted to make sure that the town's first Western resident survived the winter without incident. As we scrunched with three others in the closet-sized director's office, she scribbled a list of problems that needed to be resolved.

"We've got to get you some meat and potatoes," she said. "You can't even buy potatoes in the stores now, for everybody has their own stock. And while meat is available, it's too expensive."

"Actually, I don't eat all that much meat," I said.

"It is very cold here and both meat and potatoes are obligatory." She said this in the same caring but staccato tone in which she instructed me that I must wear boots and a fur hat every time I step out of my home. "You can't get through the winter without meat and potatoes."

I had dealt with much worse problems than a free supply of meat and potatoes when I resided in another area of Siberia and I was anxious to integrate into the local culture. *O.K., bring them on!* I thought. And she did.

But first, my roommate Ayuna, a twenty-eight-year-old Buryat administrator, built her own stockpile. Her parents pulled up in a puttering two-seater Moskvich and dragged a giant sack of red potatoes and several slabs of meat from their rural farm into our apartment. Ayuna placed the potatoes in the kitchen and initially stored the meat out of sight on our balcony, where the weather was cold enough to keep it frozen. A few days later, when I came home from work, I found the basin that I usually used for bathing (we didn't have hot water) on the kitchen counter.

Cooking meat is one of those activities that scientists say helped us evolve from our knuckle-dragging forebears. However, the business of cooking one's meat before consuming it apparently has nothing to do with palatability or killing germs. It simply makes the meat easier to chew and compresses calories, so we can consume more nutrition in shorter feedings. This frees up time for things like perfecting our Texas Hold'em strategies or perhaps opening a tanning salon (speaking of cooked meat).

—Carol Penn-Romine,
"Feeding My Inner Wolf"

Inside was a large pig's foot with the hoof still attached. It was thawing for dinner.

I was disgusted, but remained silent. We'd only been living together a few weeks and had developed a pattern of cooking dinner on alternate nights. Whatever was going to come of this foot, I knew it would appear on my dinner plate.

By the time I came to help cook later that evening, she had already removed the skin and hoof. She ground the meat, added some ground meat fat, and then we made *pelmeni*, small meat-and-fat-filled ravioli.

The soft dough was deceptive, for underneath, my teeth often became stuck on chewy tidbits that I couldn't swallow, little chunks of meat resembling plastic mauled by a dog. It was difficult to remove the image of that hoof from what I was eating. I carried on though, building up a small pile of what I found inedible at the side of my plate. Ayuna had no such pile.

One morning, I woke up late. As I opened the refrigerator to pull out a small carton of yogurt for a quick breakfast, I shrieked in horror. Everything was bathed in a sea of blood. Our poor electrical system meant that the slightest puff of air could interrupt the current and disconnect power. Somehow this happened to our refrigerator and everything from the freezer had melted.

Ayuna had stuffed the freezer with raw, unbagged beef and pork from her parents. The butter sat helplessly in a pool of viscous blood. The blood seeped into the honey jar, forming a sweet red conglomeration. My cheese dripped blood and all of the fruit and vegetables I'd carted from the city were dewy with droplets.

Disgusted and fearful of all the bacterial diseases we could contract, I pulled everything out and frantically tried to clean before I had to leave for work. Blood dripped onto our floor, our kitchen table, our counters.

I put everything into baggies to prevent such a catastrophe from occurring again, yet blood became a common sight. It could be a chunk of meat bathed in blood that would greet me when I came home, or the more innocuous, yet still disturbing spatters of blood that I'd come across everywhere, from the floor to the window sill.

One afternoon, my supply arrived. A wizened man sent by the school director appeared at my door with a sack of potatoes that reached my waist and several crimson prime cuts of meat. Leaving the potatoes by the door, I began the intimidating process of reducing the supply, day by day. Mashed potatoes, boiled potatoes, baked potatoes with mayonnaise (called potatoes *à la francaise*), even French fries. Even before I noticed any noticeable drop in the supply, I found that many of my potatoes were going bad.

"That's because we need an underground storage place, but we don't have one here," Ayuna said.

"We can't put them outside?"

"No, they'll freeze and won't be good any more."

So although we had rice and macaroni as well, I frantically tried to get through the bag of potatoes before they rotted. With the average local surviving on a salary of under $100 per month, I was loathe to let anything go to waste.

On the alternate nights when I cooked, I tried to make the most exotic things I could from local ingredients, supplemented by a few bottles of black bean sauce and spices that I had brought with me from overseas. Chicken-vegetable stir-fry was a favorite, as was homemade applesauce. Every night I cooked, Ayuna looked at my creations with wonder. "Wow, I've never seen that before," she said in simplified Russian to ensure I'd understand. "I've never thought of that!"

When she cooked, it was always a variation of meat and potatoes. There could be *pelmeni* or maybe it would be *buzi*, steamed meat-and-fat-filled dumplings that are the Buryats' national food. On other nights, I might find a soup made of meat, potatoes, fat, and noodles, or meat fried with potatoes, onions, and eggs. I wondered if she would ingest any vitamins at all if it weren't for the things I made.

As the weeks went by, I noticed that we were starting to incorporate the ideas we'd learned from each other into our own dishes. She began to add carrots and cheese to her fried eggs and meat. I learned how to cut meat and starting adding beef to my vegetable and potato dishes.

Recently, I was preparing to go three hours north, to the closest city to our village.

"Ayuna, can I pick up anything for you in Chita?"

"Yes. Could you please get some frozen broccoli or some of the green peppers you buy. When my boyfriend comes over, I'd like to make something unusual."

I added to my shopping list: vegetables for Ayuna and meat for me. I'm learning to be a meat-and-potatoes kind of girl.

Jessica Jacobson is a Lecturer of Public and International Affairs at Princeton University and the author of Roaming Russia: An Adventurer's Guide to Off-the-Beaten-Track Russia and Siberia. *Her work has appeared in* The Christian Science Monitor, The Moscow Times, Skirt! Magazine, *and* Student World Traveler, *among others.*

Pelmeni

Dough

2 cups all-purpose flour

1 egg

$1/8$ teaspoon salt

½ to ¾ cup water or skim milk

Filling

½ pound ground pork

½ pound ground beef

1 large onion, finely chopped

1 egg

½ teaspoon pepper

1 teaspoon salt

garlic to taste

½ cup finely shredded cabbage (optional)

Prepare filling by mixing all ingredients together.

For dough, mix flour, salt and egg together in a medium bowl. Add liquid, a little at a time, until dough is stiff. Knead dough for 2 to 4 minutes on a floured surface. (You will have to add more flour). Roll out dough to $1/8$-inch thickness with a rolling pin. Will a glass or cookie cutter, cut out rounds of dough 3 inches in diameter.

Put 1 tablespoon filling on one half of each circle. Moisten edges of dough with a little water. Fold dough over filling and press edges together first with your fingers, then with the tines of a fork.

Freeze to be cooked later or cook immediately by putting pelmeni in boiling salted water. Stir occasionally, until pelmeni rise to surface, approximately 8 to 10 minutes.

Serve with sour cream, mayonnaise, ketchup, or in broth.

Kaoru's Kitchen

High in the snowy mountains of Japan, a young traveler finds home.

I'm twenty-two and freshly graduated from college when I move to a small town in the mountains of central Japan. I am trying to find my way in the world and Japan seems as good a place as any. My country is in recession. I am told that my generation will be the first to be less prosperous than our parents. The job market is grim, and I am an art history major.

I am the only foreigner on a train that winds three hours into the mountains to my new home, a small town surrounded by snowcapped peaks. I am to live with a Japanese family for several months. The mother, Kaoru, meets me at the train station. She takes me to a tea house and tells me that I will be her American daughter. I don't know what to say, or how to say it, so I smile and nod.

That night at dinner I am lost in a flurry of Japanese. I am given special chopsticks with grooves carved into the shaft to keep the slippery fish cakes from falling from my uncertain grasp and back into the large stewpot in the center of the table that steams with carrots, potatoes, and eggs. I wonder if these chopsticks are for babies—the equivalent of Japanese culinary training wheels.

At breakfast the next morning I try to eat hot rice into which a raw egg has been broken. The grains are slippery in my mouth, the egg not fully congealed. When Kaoru leaves to go grocery shopping, I call the dog over and feed her the rest of my bowl. Even the dog likes the slimy rice; it's clear I am the only one who does not fit in.

That night, after another incomprehensible day and unrecognizable dinner, I cry myself to sleep under my thick futon blanket. What was I thinking to have come to a place so far away and so foreign?

The next day I slowly enter the kitchen, apprehensive, and am greeted by an unfamiliar smell. Kaoru is standing by the stove and smiles at me as I approach. "*Yaki nasu,*" she says, though the words mean nothing to me. On the stove in front of her are three long, purple Japanese eggplants, soft from grilling. I watch as she cuts a slit in the skin and spoons miso into the steaming cavity, mixing it into a paste that bubbles with the heat of the flame. The smell is intoxicating.

Kaoru shows me how to prepare the eggplant, pounding them on the countertop and rolling them between my hands to soften the flesh. With hesitant chopsticks I help her hold the cut vegetables open and spoon in the miso paste, carefully adding a bit of sugar. When the whole mess is bubbling and fragrant, we pour sesame oil over it all and take it off the flame of the stove. The taste of the *yaki nasu*, which we eat with bowls of steaming hot rice, is heavenly—sweet and piquant. I grin at Kaoru and she grins back.

Thus begin my days in the kitchen. At Kaoru's side I learn the proper way to prepare rice for steaming—wash it three times in the basin, careful not to lose any grains. She shares with me old Japanese proverbs: "If you waste rice, you will go blind." I learn to rinse *wakame* seaweed for our morning miso soup. I boil *daikon* and mix spinach with ground sesame seeds and soy sauce. I learn to make *dashi*, the stock on which all Japanese soups and sauces are based, and

A popular one-day class, readily available to foreigners, is the Nakano Udon School in Kotohira, Japan. The lesson teaches you the intricacies of making these delicious smooth and chewy noodles, from start to finish, which means cooking and eating them, as well. If you are really lucky, the instructor will blast some rock 'n' roll and the class will take turns dancing on the dough! Included in the course is a diploma, rolling pin, and a book of secrets on Sanuki udon-making.

—SB

one rainy day we make tempura, carefully dipping and frying the vegetables and seafood in hot oil.

In the course of these kitchen sessions I begin to learn the language. *Kuri* means cucumber, *gohan* means rice but also meal. *Shiru* is soup; *ninjin* is carrot. The first word I read in Japanese is *tamago*, egg. And at the market I recognize the sign for apple, *ringo*. By the end of my first month I can talk food, if nothing else.

Yet I still feel alone and lonely in this place filled with new scents and sounds, a culture so reserved there is no physical touch, not even a handshake. Every day is a lesson in accepting the different, the unfamiliar. In my trips to the market and through the town I am surrounded by the incomprehensible—a language spoken too fast for me to understand, customs and traditions I find counterintuitive. Kaoru's kitchen is the place I feel most comfortable. Amidst the warm steamy scent of fresh rice and the sharp tang of vinegar, my questions are answered simply and we slice cucumber in companionable silence.

After four months I leave my Japanese family to take a job on the other side of the mountains, in another small town. On my first trip to the grocery store I try to buy a package of miso and am stunned to find an entire row of miso, in various different colors. I attempt to match the shade of brown that looks most like Kaoru's miso but the array is bewildering. That night on the phone I explain my dilemma and Kaoru laughs, directing me to two different kinds—a sweet miso for *yaki nasu* and a strong miso for soup.

In my small apartment, on a two-burner stove, I make my own *dashi*, adding *wakame*, *daikon*, carrots, tofu, and miso for soup. With a grill pan I purchase at the market I make *yaki nasu*, carefully turning the eggplant with chopsticks that are now more confident, cutting open the softened flesh, and mixing miso, sugar, and sesame oil inside, until my whole apartment smells like Kaoru's kitchen.

At New Year's I return to Kaoru's home, returning like all Japanese children to their family home for this important holiday. The old house is cold in December, the kitchen the only warm room. Here we cook and conspire, carefully preparing the New Year's feast.

Kaoru tells me that the fish roe we will eat is said to bring many children, the *konbu* seaweed brings happiness, dry sardines promise a good rice crop, and *datemake*, a roll of cooked and sweetened egg, is said to bring wisdom and learning to those to eat it. We cook for several days, packing each item into a set of lacquered boxes that fit together in a stack, three boxes high. This is *osechi ryori*, the traditional New Year's feast that we will eat for three days.

On New Year's Eve we pray at the household altars: the large *butsudan* shrine with portraits of the ancestors gazing down, the smaller shrine in the tea-drinking room, and the kitchen shrine. We clap our hands three times and bow our heads to give thanks. I am thankful for finding a home so far from home and I wonder what the ancestors make of this blond-haired creature in their household, in their kitchen.

That night we feast on *osechi*. I fill my plate with *datemake* for wisdom, *konbu* for happiness, as well as *kurikinton*, a mixture of mashed sweet potato with chestnuts, and my favorite black beans glistening in a sweet sauce. They are Kaoru's favorite as well. We eat well and bundle up to go to the shrine. Even the dog comes with us, to get her New Year's blessings. We walk through crunching snow to pay our respects to the gods, then gather around a bonfire and drink hot sake.

For three days we eat *osechi* but on the fourth day, the day I am to return to my own apartment on the other side of the mountains, Kaoru makes *yaki nasu*. I wake to find her in the kitchen, rolling eggplant on the counter. Without a word I join her, preparing the vegetables, grilling and cutting them open, filling them with miso.

After breakfast she walks me to the train station and, for the first time, she hugs me. Her hug is stiff and awkward and she laughs at the same time, a sign of her discomfort. I realize this may be the only time she has ever hugged another adult; it is not customary here. From the train window I wave to her. She stands on the platform waving back until the train is out of sight, her small figure receding into a snowy landscape.

It is now eleven years since that New Year's, seven years since I left Japan. These days I live in San Francisco, a city in many ways Asian though not in Asia. Kaoru has become a name on my computer screen—short emails that sound like haiku—and a voice on the telephone when I call every New Year's. "When are you coming home?" she asks me. "I am waiting for you."

Though I cannot return to Japan as often as I'd like, sometimes, particularly in the fall, I go to Japantown. I head straight to the grocery store where I breathe deep the scent of fish flakes and soy sauce, seaweed and pickles. I finger the bags of lychee jellies, the cakes filled with bean paste, packages of buckwheat noodles, and bottles of *dashi*. But I leave with only two items: a bag of Japanese eggplant, purple and smooth, and a package of miso. It is all I need to bring me home.

Tara Austen Weaver is a freelance writer and developmental editor by day, food blogger by night (www.teaandcookies.blogspot.com). She has lived on three continents, in five countries, and brought back recipes from all of them. When not traveling or thinking up new ways to sauté and soufflé, she can be found in San Francisco where she is a founding partner in Creative Storefront (www.creativestorefront.com), an agency devoted to helping writers advance in their careers. Tara can be reached at www.taraweaver.com.

Yaki Nasu
Japanese Grilled Eggplant

Per person, multiply as needed:

1 Japanese eggplant

¾ tablespoons miso (see Note below)

1 ¼ teaspoon sugar

¼ teaspoon dark sesame oil

½ teaspoon chopped scallions, for garnish

Preheat the oven to 400°F. Begin by taking each eggplant and pounding against the kitchen counter, careful not to break the skin. Pound it evenly on all sides and along the full length, and roll it on the counter as well. You will begin to feel the insides loosen up as you roll. Place the eggplants onto a lightly oiled baking sheet and bake for about 10 minutes. Turn over and bake for another 10 minutes or so, until the eggplant feels soft along the entire length. The skin will turn brown as they bake.

In a small saucer mix the miso and sugar into a paste. Begin with ¾ tbs miso to 1 tsp sugar. Adjust sugar to taste.

Remove the eggplant from the oven and cut a slit down the length of the eggplant, stopping ¾ of an inch before you reach the tip. Carefully open the eggplant. With a spoon or chopsticks, spread the miso mixture into the cavity of the eggplant. Return to the oven for 5 minutes or so, until the miso begins to bubble. Remove and drizzle with ¼ tsp sesame oil. Garnish with finely chopped scallions and serve with hot rice and perhaps a nice piece of grilled fish.

Note: I use a mild or sweet miso, but it can be fun to experiment—different misos have different flavors.

PART FIVE

SOUTHEAST ASIA/ OCEANIA

Mama Rose's Coconut Bread

Her spirits rose with the dough.

Mama Rose impaled the coconut onto the wooden spike making a tear in the husk. Self-rolled cigarette hanging out the corner of her mouth, she continued with ease, lifting, turning, and thrusting the coconut on the spike till the husk fell away. Inside was a newborn white nut with brown hairs. Picking up a cleaver she motioned for me to come look. She sat on a coconut wood stool, placed a large bowl between her ankles and then pointed at the three eyes at the top of the coconut. She drew an imaginary line with the cleaver across the three eyes. She lifted the cleaver, lowered it gently to position, raised it again then *clack*! With one whack the coconut split in half, the water falling into the bowl.

In the Tuamotu atolls of French Polynesia everything is done from scratch. If you want dinner you have to go fishing; even for a glass of water, rain is collected since there are no mountains, rivers, valleys, or potable groundwater in the arid atolls. This day we were baking coconut bread and, in a land of some of the most capable people on Earth, I was learning from the master.

I had been living on Ahe atoll in French Polynesia for nearly two months. I had come in hopes of learning some lessons about hard work and self-sufficiency, to live with my Tahitian boyfriend Josh who was helping his father start a black pearl farm. Ahe was an isolated place: it was a two-day boat trip from Tahiti, had no roads, no phones, and only one store in the village. Our farm was on an islet that was a wet and bumpy half-hour boat ride from the village, which we rarely went to, and I was the only woman living among six work-obsessed men. Lacking the physical strength of a man, I had been unable to feel useful in the workplace, diving and hauling oysters. I had felt that my femininity was a hindrance to myself and to my co-workers. Although I had always considered myself a strong, capable person, the vastness of the lagoon, the starkness of the land, and the lack of female counterparts on the farm made me feel frail and lonely. Mama Rose, who sold oysters to Josh's father, seemed to sense my unease and had started inviting Josh and me to spend weekends with her at her house on an idyllic islet about ten minutes by boat from our farm. Slowly, she began teaching me how to survive in a predominantly male environment that, before I met her, had seemed devoid of softness.

So it was that I visited her on a Saturday morning after she promised to teach me to bake coconut bread. Rose met me on her dock while her husband, my boyfriend, and a few workers from our farm went back out onto the lagoon to go fishing. She was dressed in a faded purple pareu that was rolled at the waist so that the hem touched slightly above her coffee-colored knees. In a gesture of misunderstood religious prudishness, she wore a sexy black lace bra, at least one size too small, to cover her matronly breasts. Naked or in a nun's habit she would have maintained the same self-assured, natural manner in movement and attitude.

We walked along her white beach to her house: the bedroom, kitchen, and bathroom were constructed separately into three small, wooden structures with tin roofs. It was there that my lesson about coconuts began, culminating in the pitiless husking procedure.

Once we had husked and cracked several more coconuts (I managed to fumble through one), Mama Rose brought us to two coconut stools positioned at the blue lagoon's edge in the shade of a large leafy tree. A contraption that looked like a wooden cutting board with a round, serrated metal disk at the end was on each stool. She straddled hers.

"You, there," she said pointing at the other stool.

She spoke French, Tahitian, the local Paumotu dialect, and a little English. I spoke limited French. What we couldn't learn about each other through words became irrelevant as the time we passed together, always working towards the same goal, created a bond like I had never experienced in Western society. Our time and labor were being thrown in a bowl creating an unusual recipe for friendship that I was finding delicious.

As if, with the coconut carnage over, we could relax a little, she rolled another cigarette and smiled at me, exposing her perfect white teeth. They glinted in a sun ray and made me think that she blended perfectly into the sand and shimmering lagoon. I wondered how old she was; she could have been anywhere from thirty-five to fifty.

"Coco many work," she said.

"Yes," I said remembering that it had taken some time just to collect the coconuts along her palm-planted white sand beach. They needed to have fallen to the ground but not be rotted or sprouted. We had tested them by shaking them; if they were filled with water they were still fresh.

With another smile that made me feel like I had actually been helpful, Mama Rose picked up half a coconut and slowly, to show me, began to grate it against the serrated disk. Once I had more or less figured out the circular, two-handed grating technique, Rose picked up speed, eventually grating eight or more halves in the time it took me to grate two.

"Now my kitchen," she said lifting her bowl full of grated coconut while I picked up my nearly empty one.

Her kitchen was a small, square, plywood structure painted turquoise. The wood windows were propped open from the bottom letting in a slight breeze and a view of the lagoon. We put our bowls on the plastic table and Rose pulled out two gauzy dishrags and a smaller bowl. She put a large handful of grated coconut into one of the rags and squeezed it tight so the milk strained out into the small bowl. I tried mine, not getting out nearly as much milk but feeling a deep satisfaction of actually having produced coconut milk. It was almost like having learned how to turn water into wine.

Rose pulled out two boxes of Paradise-brand flour, a sack of instant yeast, some sugar, salt, and a bottle of oil. Making the rest of the morning's work look like a slow-motion scene in an action flick, she threw together these ingredients along with the coconut milk, some coconut water, and a few handfuls of unsqueezed grated coconut, making sure I could see how much of each she used.

She then turned the dough out onto a large coconut wood cutting board and began to knead. The billowing dough mimicked the soft fullness of Mama Rose's belly, arms, and breasts while its sallow cream color contrasted with her healthy bronze skin. She moved rhythmically in an ellipse, forward and down, back and up, her movements graceful and strong. After a few minutes she stepped aside offering me a try. I imagined myself as I had seen her, confidently pushing the dough, but instead it was sticky on my hands and I felt like I was out of time with the silent music that she had been danc-ing to. Still, I continued, closing my eyes and listening to the breeze and gentle waves on the nearby shore. When I opened my eyes, Mama Rose was looking at me with her brilliant smile.

"You make good cooking you," she said as if I had discovered some secret.

We finished kneading and let the dough rise in a bowl covered with a dishrag.

While waiting for the dough to rise, Rose made us some coffee and we tidied up her kitchen then put some rice and water in a pot to prepare for lunch. She was in constant movement; there was always work to be done but it never felt rushed or unpleasant, just natural. It was as if we should feel lucky to have such pleasant work at our disposal.

We shaped the dough into five loaves and set them aside for a second rise.

Rose handed me a rake and we raked the leaves around her kitchen. Then we went and took her laundry down from the line and folded it.

The bread had risen high and firm above the edge of the bread pans. We put them into her heated oven and then sat down to drink some water while Rose lit another cigarette. The perfume of sweet coconut and fresh bread filled the kitchen and made me feel hungry. From the window I could see the men coming in from the lagoon after fishing.

As the men approached the kitchen, the bread was just coming out of the oven. We had no idea how long they would be gone, but somehow Mama Rose had it timed per-fectly.

The look of delight on the shivering men's faces at the warm scent of the bread made Rose glow. It was then that I realized how important this "women's work" was, not just for the men but for the sanity of us all. Our bread was a jewel in the crown, the pillow under the head, the pleasure of life that was needed to keep the balance and make life on the island go on. Together with the men, we fried up the fish and set the table, starting our meal with the warm, soft, sweet bread.

Originally from the San Francisco Bay Area, Celeste Brash lived and worked as a cook on Kamoka Pearl farm on Ahe atoll for five years. She now lives on the island of Tahiti with Josh—now her husband—and their two children. She works as a Lonely Planet author and freelance writer and still bakes bread whenever she can find the time.

Coconut Bread

Makes 2 loaves

Instead of measurement, Mama Roses composes her dough using common sense; if it's too sticky she adds more flour, if she happens to have extra coconut she'll throw it in. I, on the other hand, improvise on a fixed recipe that is more or less the base of how I have seen Mama Rose mix her bread.

¾ cup coconut water or water

1 tablespoon instant yeast

1 ½ cups coconut milk

3 tablespoons melted butter or oil

3 tablespoons sugar

1 tablespoon salt

a handful or more grated coconut

6 to 6 ½ cups plain flour

In a large bowl add the instant yeast to the coconut water then add the rest of the liquid ingredients, the sugar and the salt. With a wooden spoon, mix in about 1 cup of the flour then add the grated coconut before slowly mixing in the next 4 ½ cups of the flour ½ cup at a time; you'll probably need to abandon the spoon and use your hands after the 4th of 5th cup of flour.

Turn the dough onto a lightly floured work surface and knead it while slowly adding the remaining flour as needed to prevent the dough from becoming too sticky. Continue to knead the dough till it is smooth and springy, about 5 minutes.

Place the dough in a lightly greased mixing bowl and let rise in a draft free place (a flash heated oven works great for this) till it has doubled in bulk, about 1 ½ to 2 hours.

Deflate the dough and roll it to fit into two buttered loaf pans. Let the dough rise in the pans until the dough has doubled in bulk again, about 45 minutes. About 25 minutes into the second rise, heat the oven to 375 degrees.

Slash a groove about ¼ inch deep, vertically down the tops of the loaves before placing them on the center rack of the oven. Bake for about 40 to 45 minutes or until the loaves are a golden brown.

Allow to cool at least 10 minutes before slicing.

360 Days a Year

It's a tough way to earn a living.

Competition is vicious. Margins are small. Working conditions are hot and close-quartered. And the hours are long, incredibly long. Running a neighborhood restaurant in Vietnam is not the easiest or quickest way to cash in on the country's economic boom.

The Phuong Anh restaurant, on Mai Hac De Street just around the corner from To Hien Thanh Street in Hanoi, isn't much to look at. From the curb, it's hardly different from the hundreds or thousands of small eating places that line the roads all over Asia. But over several days my wife and I had eaten lunch at Phuong Anh and each day the food had been marvelous. There were five or six different pork dishes. The same number of poultry and fish plates. There were a dozen delicious vegetable selections. There was no menu. We didn't know the names of anything. We simply pointed to dishes that looked tasty and ample servings piled onto small plates were brought to our table. With prices for everything in Hanoi shooting up, we were astonished each time we had a wonderful five- or six-course lunch for two—for never more than a few dollars.

"How does she make any money?" my wife asked. "How does she get everything ready?" was what I wondered. The restaurant itself was tiny, no more than a ten-by-twelve-foot room. At lunchtime it was jammed with up to twenty customers. The staff side-stepped in and around diners as Nguyen Thi Bich, the thirty-six-year-old owner, served up portions from an equally packed alcove at the front of the restaurant. One second she was serving, the next adding up a bill and making change, the next asking one of her ten workers for something. Every second she was on the go.

"Oh geez," Nina said, putting down her chopsticks. "Look at that." I followed her gaze to a corner of the room. An older, white-haired man was slowly climbing down through a small hole in the ceiling. From one metal rung embedded in the concrete walls to the next, he carefully lowered himself down, just above the customers' heads. Only Nina and I acted as though this was unusual behavior for a restaurant. The old man squeezed onto a wooden couch that was already crowded with four customers and lit up a smoke. "We've got to find out more about this place," Nina said.

I often work as a small business consultant. Nina is a wonderful cook. Yet both of us, watching the frenzy of activity in the tiny restaurant, were absolutely bewildered. With the help of a translator, I explained to Bich that I wanted to find out more about what it took to run a small cook shop like hers.

She told me that the secret of her success rested on three key factors: fresh food, low prices, and good service. If we wanted, we could follow her around for a day and she'd show us what was involved.

That day began the following morning at 6 A.M. Perhaps three-quarters of Bich's supplies come from bicycle-peddling vendors who roll up to the restaurant all day long with rice, salt, vegetables, roasted poultry, and frozen fish. But for the key ingredients, Bich goes to the market herself. She bicycled there. We trailed alongside on a motorcycle.

"She's so slim, " Nina remarked as we followed Bich through the empty streets of early morning Hanoi. Bich had the trim figure of an athlete. One would never know she was the mother of two teenage children.

At 6:30 in the morning the small market was surprisingly empty. We'd visited markets throughout Asia and the one common denominator shared by all was the overpowering, dank smell of animal blood and rotting vegetables stewing underfoot in the hot tropical weather. But at six in the morning, the meat and produce were still fresh. There was no smell but that of the cool morning. There were very few customers. Only restaurant and cook shop owners. They picked through the offerings like fur traders trying to select the best pelts. The variety of food before them was astonishing.

Live eels swam in basins next to still quivering, freshly skinned frogs. Thousands of small sand crabs tried to climb out of the metal basins that held them. Dozens of market women shaved the hair off the hides of slaughtered pigs and the skin of plucked chickens with double-edged razor blades held gingerly between thumb and index finger.

There were vegetables we had never seen before and the intestines of animals we wished we hadn't seen. Meanwhile Bich was selecting fresh meat and fish.

"Can you believe this?" Nina said as she watched Bich. "She's cutting her own meat." With the dexterity of a master butcher, Bich took a cleaver and pared the cuts she wanted from several large slabs of beef and pork. At stall after stall she selected just what she wanted. She trimmed away the bone and fat and paid only for the choice cuts she had made. "Try doing that at Safeway," Nina said.

When we returned to the restaurant at 7:30, the place was already buzzing. Bich's mother, father, aunt, and a variety of young relatives were all at work. The older women, also with razor blades, were slicing hundreds of scallions into what seemed to be thousands of thin green ribbons. They did this while squatting on the sidewalk, just inches from the street, where the earlier quiet of Hanoi had been drowned out by the continuous flow of cars, trucks, bicycles, and motorcycles. Across the street, construction on a new office building had begun. In and around the restaurant, Bich's employees quickly

Yen cooks in a room that could hardly be called a kitchen—a plank bed takes up most of it. In one corner, there's a two burner gas stove; in the other, an open cupboard for her few utensils and basic supplies. All she uses to cook are a wok, frying pan, and lidded pot; one mixing bowl and chopping board; a small sharp knife, scissors and ever versatile chopsticks for stirring, tossing, whisking eggs, levering the lid from her pot. Her only nod at technology is a rice cooker. Yet, in one hour she prepares at least five dishes: two of them meat- or tofu-based, one plate of cooked vegetables, soup and salad. On the floor beside the stove are bottles of oil, fish sauce, lemon vinegar, and a small sack of MSG. To travel in Vietnam and avoid MSG would be like going for a swim and keeping your swimsuit dry. My Vietnamese friends are amazed to learn it's unacceptable in the West. Yen prepares the ingredients either squatting in the garden or on the bed in the kitchen. She holds vegetables in her left hand, slices with her right. It looks terrifying but she's fast and sure.

—Pamela Payne, "In a Sa Pa Kitchen"

and methodically went about the dozens of tasks needed in a country where prepared foods have yet to hit the shelves.

In an alley alongside the restaurant, several girls tended two woks and several pots boiling with eggs and greens. An older woman squatted further down the sidewalk. She was washing dishes. For the next fifteen hours that is all she would do.

Bich's elderly parents had been at work since early morning. I asked Bich where they lived, wondering if they had to come from far away. She pointed to the space above the restaurant and the hole in the ceiling where we had seen the old man appear the day before. Turns out he is her father and the three-year-old restaurant is actually the parents' home. The dining area is their former living room. Their bedroom is the loft just above where we had eaten each day.

"How old is your father?" I asked her. "Eighty-three," she answered with a show of fingers. "How many eighty-three-year-old American men do you think are climbing up walls to get to their bedrooms?" Nina asked. I pointed to Bich's mother, who was squatting in the middle of the room slicing tree ear mushrooms paper thin, and asked how old she was. Bich held up seven then six fingers. Not too likely she'd be working a twelve-hour shift at Denny's in the States.

Soon after Bich's return from the market, all activity became centered in the middle of the living room. To be precise, on the floor. Twenty bowls and basins filled with meat, poultry, fish, mushrooms, spices, oils, fish sauce, and molasses sat in the center of a circle formed by Bich, her mother, her aunt, and a teenage relative. For the next three hours they hardly moved from their squatting position. I told Nina to try squatting with her knees tucked up in her shoulders the way the women were. She lasted less than a minute and then hobbled around for several more complaining she'd been crippled for life.

Basins of greens and boiled meats and fish came in from outside. The women quickly diced, sliced, mixed, kneaded, and rolled these together with other ingredients and spices. Bich's mother measured out molasses in the palm of her hand. Bich's fingers were the scoop used to measure sugar, salt, and pepper. Everything was measured by hand. No one sampled a thing. As quickly as the staff brought new items in, so went the now seasoned dish back outside for steaming, boiling, or deep-frying. It was an assembly line where there was little talk. Everything happened with the precision of a Japanese manufacturing plant. Except that it was all happening on the floor, in a tiny space, with only the light of two dim bulbs.

Watching the fluidity with which everything was happening, I asked if Bich made the same things every day. "No," she said. "It depends on what is fresh in the market." But I never saw her tell anyone that today they would be making this dish or that. Everyone just seemed to know.

Slowly, almost by slight of hand, finished dishes began to gather on the tables that had been pushed to the side of the small room. The place itself wasn't much on decor. Nothing more than a few outdated calendars and beer posters. Along one wall was the parents' large, mirrored wardrobe. High in a corner was a traditional altar, framed by Bich's two dead brothers, one killed in Hue in 1975, the other dead after an unsuccessful operation. The room was now a restaurant, but still had the soul of a Vietnamese living room.

Nina and I watched as tray after tray of complicated dishes of fried fish, steamed vegetables, boiled pork, and barbecued meats took shape. "The work they do, it's just amazing," Nina said as we watched the women working into their second and third hour of chopping, boiling, stirring, turning, flipping, and steaming, almost never rising from their crouches just inches from the floor.

Bich's fluency as a chef was very clear as she began making *van may* (cloud in the sky), a Vietnamese dish that is something like a stuffed crepe. Earlier, one of the younger workers had made dozens of yellow and white crepes from separated duck eggs. Now, Bich, with a cleaver in each hand, began mincing together the pork, garlic and other ingredients that she would roll inside the crepes before steaming them. For an hour, the small room reverberated with the rapid pace of a drum roll as Bich minced ingredients using only the two cleavers and a small chopping board that was nothing more than a round section cut from a tree.

"Do you know how fast you could do this with a Cuisinart?" Nina whispered to me. The only time Bich stopped work was when she quickly sharpened her knives and cleavers by dashing them back and forth against the bottom of a plate with the same practiced indifference as a barber sharpening a straight razor against a leather strap. She did this every few minutes.

"How often do we sharpen our knives?" I asked Nina.

"About once a year," she told me. "But we should do it more often."

"We'll have to buy some plates," I told her.

I asked Bich if she had ever tried using a machine to mince the stuffing for the *van may*. She said she had but the machine couldn't produce the fine blend she wanted and it quickly broke from wear and tear. She went back to the basics even though she wears out her cutting knives in a month's time and her cleavers in six.

After four hours of tossing, mixing, shaking, kneading, chopping, hacking, slicing, and cooking, it was time to move outside. Twenty different platters were ready for the lunchtime crowd. Spring rolls, shish kebabs and eight other entrees were still waiting their chance in the wok or over the brazier. Bich still hadn't taken a break, hadn't eaten, hadn't stopped moving since before sunrise. "I'm exhausted, " Nina said to me. "And I haven't done a thing."

We asked Bich how many hours she worked every day. "From six in the morning to ten or eleven at night," she said. How many days a year? "Three hundred sixty," she told us. She takes five days off during the Tet holiday when she mainly stays at home and tries not to think about food or cooking. She doesn't go out to other restaurants except to learn what they are doing. She told us she doesn't need to taste the food to know how it will turn out. She has the chef's equivalent of a musician's sense of perfect pitch.

As we chatted, the place was quickly swept clean. Tables were set out as were a dozen of the tiny stools the Vietnamese use for chairs. The thirty different dishes were stacked atop one another on the outside counter.

There were sea fish and river fish. Three different types of chicken. Six different types of pork. There was a shrimp dish and a squid plate. There were several varieties of small, broiled birds. She had salads of green beans, bean sprouts, pickled eggplant, and spinach. There was a fried tofu dish, something like a frittata. There were spring rolls and shish kabob. For the refined diner, there was a platter of butterfly larva.

Five hours earlier, when we met Bich outside her neighborhood home, nothing had been done, nothing had been prepped. Her brimming counter was a tour de force of Vietnamese cooking. Bich's mother lit a handful of joss sticks and placed them at the front edge of the counter. Perhaps this was to ward off evil spirits. Certainly it wasn't to cover up any unappetizing smells as everything Bich had made that morning was fresh, clean and wonderfully spiced.

The sign above the entrance to the Phuong Anh restaurant, which is named for Bich's daughter, says *Cac Mon An* and *Com Binh Dan* which translates to something like "All kinds of food" and "Everyday home cooking." Evidently, Bich needn't say anything more because soon after she had laid out the dishes lunchtime customers began to gather at the front of

Phuong Anh. For the next two hours, the small space was jammed with regulars. Bich stood at the doorway, now playing the roles of maitre d', cashier, hostess, and server. In the alley, the staff continued cooking, replenishing the most popular dishes.

Nina and I squeezed into a corner, my back jammed between the small refrigerator and the large wooden wardrobe. We had pointed to shish kabob, the *van may* cloud, freshwater fish, a green bean salad, and a deep-fried, minced squid dish that looked more like a potato pancake than seafood. Our drinks came to us warm. We fished hunks of ice from a bucket. Earlier we had watched Bich's mother as she hacked a large block of ice into the cubes we dropped in our glasses.

Everything was delicious. Bich had no time to attend to us as she was completely occupied making change, filling plates, adding up bills, squeezing in new customers, directing her staff, and laughing at jokes.

I took a break from eating to take in the incredibly crowded space. The walls were painted in what might be called a "distressed Jackson Pollack" style. A locked door had the weathered look of the faux finishing that is now the rage in the States. It was weathered from wear—not from the hand of an artist. A ceiling fan wobbled above the lunchtime crowd and provided a soft breeze but little cooling. A bunch of young men at one table took turns flirting with a table of young women. Like in every other small Vietnamese restaurant, bones and napkins were idly dropped on the floor to be swept into the street later on.

Outside Bich continued serving up new portions. In place of a serving spoon or fork she used a large tailor's shears to pick up the food and cut it into smaller portions. Our five-course lunch had filled us completely. It was so much better than meals we had eaten at many of Hanoi's more established and widely reviewed restaurants. When we got up to go, Bich quickly totalled up our bill. She tapped her pen on the figure: less than a double latte for lunch for two—including drinks.

By 1 P.M. lunchtime business was thinning. Bich stopped moving for the first time in seven hours. She leaned against a wall and lit up a 555. From two until five, the restaurant was closed—although several workers continued cooking. Another rush of diners filled Phuong Anh from 6 till 8:30 P.M. That's when we came back for dinner. Bich had set out two small tables on the sidewalk to handle the overflow crowd.

I went back to the restaurant around 11 P.M. The tables had been put away. The food was all eaten. The restaurant was again a living room. The father said goodnight and climbed up the iron rungs on the wall to the bedroom. Bich, her husband and children watched television. I don't know how long they stayed up. I never did get around to asking Bich if she makes any money. If she does, she certainly deserves it. For me, it was time for sleep. I had had a long day.

The next morning at 6 A.M., I went out for a run. Bich's mother was already slicing onions on the sidewalk in front of the restaurant. As I jogged past the market, I saw Bich haggling with the meat sellers. She didn't have time to waste. Lunch was only six hours away.

Robert Strauss, a three-time Lowell Thomas Award winner, has contributed to numerous Travelers' Tales publications. He's spent the last five years serving as Country Director for the Peace Corps in Cameroon and is looking forward to his next adventure.

During the Lunar New Year, or Tet as it is known in Vietnam, every family member and every visitor is given a piece of banh trung, a loaf of sweet rice, mung beans, and fatty pork wrapped in banana leaves, much as American southerners insist that guests eat a spoonful of greens and black-eye peas on New Year's Day. It's not about nourishment or taste—though a good banh trung is absolutely delicious—but rather about tradition and the good luck ceremonial dishes are said to convey.

According to Vietnamese lore, banh trung was developed by a boy who would be king. An ancient monarch, King Hung Vuong, knew that he must soon choose his successor. An old man with many wives, his choice would not be easy and so he issued a challenge to his sons: The boy who brings the best gift, the king declared, would take his place.

His sons brought gold, silver, silk and rare foods, luxuries the king did not need, for he was a wealthy man. Just one son, the poorest of them all, took a different approach. With the help of his mother, he devised the first banh trung, a loaf, he told the king, that could feed those who were poor and hungry.

You can guess the tale's conclusion. King Hung Vuong was impressed by his son's selflessness, who soon ascended to the throne.

Ever since, the story continues, Vietnamese people celebrate Tet with homemade banh trung.

—Michele Anna Jordan, "*Banh Trung: A Tet Tradition*"

A Cooking School in Bangkok

The story that ignited an editor's passion twelve years ago, and eventually begat this book.

Talk to anyone who has been in Thailand and invariably you will hear excited descriptions of the food, with virtual rhapsodies on the exotic flavors. But even though one of the most vivid pleasures of travel in Thailand is the cuisine, it is one of the most elusive memories.

Thanks to the foresight of The Oriental Hotel in Bangkok, travelers interested in returning home with some of the secrets of preparing Thai food can enroll in The Thai Cooking School run by the hotel. During a week-long course that combines lectures with demonstrations and some participation, I learned why Thai food tastes the way it does and how to achieve the balance of key flavors with what for many of us are new, exotic ingredients.

To be honest, a hotel-sponsored cooking program sounded at first like the ultimate tourist trap. Despite glowing reviews I'd heard about the school I had my doubts, but I should have known that The Oriental, with its reputation as one of the finest hotels in the world, would not get involved in anything that was not first rate. I left the school most impressed; I had gained more knowledge in one week at The Oriental than I had in much longer courses at other cooking schools, in both the United States and Europe.

The direction of the school and the man largely responsible for its excellence is Chalie Amatyakul. A native Thai, Chalie is a cosmopolitan fellow who studied literature in France and interior design in Vienna for several years after graduating with a degree in political science from Bangkok's prestigious Chulalongkorn University. He has traveled extensively around the world pursuing a career that has included stints as sales manager and food and beverage director for the Oriental. Successful as he's been in the hotel business, he seems to have found his real métier with the Thai Cooking School. A born teacher, Chalie is passionate about Thai food, and he shares that enthusiasm with an almost missionary zeal. He is both knowledgable and articulate on the subject, and not just in his native tongue. His fluency in English, French, and German has served him well in tutoring the large number of American and European students who have attended the school since it opened in June, 1986.

> *The Thai Cooking School at The Oriental has been in the capable hands of Sansern Gajaseni for more than ten years. The class is now held over a four-day period, rather than five, and covers the topics of snacks, salads, soups, condiments, steamed / fried / stir-fried / grilled dishes, and desserts. The facility remains largely unchanged and true to its innovative designer, Chalie Amatyakul.*
>
> —Susan Brady, "Dream Come True"

Thai cuisine conveniently falls into five general categories of dishes, giving a natural structure for the week's classes, beginning with snacks and salads and moving through soups and curries to stir-fried, steamed and grilled dishes before ending with desserts.

Despite its hotel connections, The Thai Cooking School is open to anyone, but the extras such as meals and tours are available only to guests at The Oriental. The complete course runs from Sunday night, with an introductory dinner at The Sala Rim Naam, through Friday noon and features such added amenities as breakfast every morning at The Oriental's Verandah restaurant and a lunchtime sampling of the hotel's other restaurants, including Lord Jim's. Also included in the tuition are a private tour guide for two afternoons of sightseeing and three dinners: a barbeque buffet at The Oriental's Riverside

Terrace; an elegant French respite from Thai food at The Normandie, and an interesting interpretation of what's been called "*nouvelle* Thai" at The Lemongrass, a local Bangkok favorite lodged in an antique-filled converted townhouse. There are clearly more than enough opportunities to eat during the week's course, and tastings of the dishes prepared in class each morning were so ample that I often skipped the hotel lunch.

The school can handle up to twenty people, but I was fortunate to have chosen a week when only one other student, a horticulturist from Greenwich, Connecticut, had signed up for the full course. Except for the two days when we were joined by an Australian homemaker and a New York-based book editor, my classmate and I had virtually private lessons. For someone visiting Bangkok for less than a week, it is possible to spend as little as one day at the school.

What I particularly liked about the classes is that they gave me a structure for my time in Bangkok. By steeping myself in Thai cooking each morning, my forays into the city streets each afternoon became more meaningful. Whether I was headed for a shopping spree or sightseeing, I was bombarded with the sights and smells of food, which were always exotic and often quite pungent.

Bangkok, among its other reputations, is clearly a city of gustatory pleasures. Never before had I seen so many stalls selling all manner of snacks and freshly sliced fruit, or wandered in so many street markets, or passed so many individual farmers who had staked out a square of sidewalk from which to sell their produce—all of them offering countless opportunities, if not to indulge then at least to view the incredible variety of raw ingredients and in many cases to watch them being cooked. Whatever questions I had about what I'd seen would be answered in class the next morning.

The school is housed—rather appropriately it seemed—in a nineteenth-century colonial teak structure that was formerly a riverside mansion. It stands next to the Sala Rim Naam restaurant, which is across the busy Chao Phraya river, directly opposite the modern River Wing tower of The Oriental. Each morning, after a breakfast of fresh papaya and toast, the latter serving purely as a vehicle for the dark and bittersweet pummelo marmalade made by The Oriental, I headed for the hotel dock to catch the private ferry. I looked forward to this ride, during which the ferry crossed the commercial lanes of traffic like a fearless jaywalker to the Thon Buri bank of the river. When The Oriental's boat wasn't immediately available, I'd spend the equivalent of a nickel to take the local ferry filled with Thais on their way to work. From the Thon Buri dock it was a short walk past lush greenery and through the veranda-like private dining rooms at the front of the building to the two classroms in the rear.

Despite the fact that both rooms were air-conditioned, Chalie, who helped design the school facility, left intact the natural ventilation that was ingeniously incorporated into the original building. The system takes the form of an open-air clerestory: decoratively shaped holes are cut out repeatedly along the top of all four walls, like a string of paper dolls. Hot air rises up and out of the rooms through the clerestory, and fresh breezes find their way in.

We reported each morning to a room filled with rows of mahogany desks facing a blackboard. Each desk was topped neatly with a stack of recipes, a small vase of orchids, and a cup and saucer for coffee—a far cry from the classrooms of my youth. On our first morning we opened our desk drawers to find an apron and sacks of Thai spices to take home as well as such staples as *naam pla*, the fermented fish sauce that is to the Thais what soy sauce is to the Chinese.

Each class began with a brief but by no means lightweight lecture on the background of the dishes to be demonstrated that day. Chalie made active use of the blackboard, which simplified our personal note taking. After about a half hour we would move to the demonstration room, which resembled a chemistry laboratory, with three long marble-topped teak units and an overhead mirror.

The ingredients for each dish, already pounded, chopped, or shredded, would be waiting in small bowls arranged on large platters, a welcome sight considering this labor-intensive cuisine. Chalie, with the help of his assistant, Sarnsern, performed a show-and-tell with the components of the recipes, encouraging us to smell and taste the raw ingredients to get a better understanding of their unique role in the complexity of flavor in Thai food.

For me it was my first encounter with certain exotic fruits, vegetables, herbs, and other seasonings that until then I'd only heard about or seen in their barely recognizable dried state. Here, at last, in the raw, was *kha*, or greater galanga, the ginger-like rhizome native to Indonesia. A sniff of greater galanga revealed its kinship to turmeric, itself another rhizome used fresh in Thai cooking; I was reminded instantly of ball-park mustard, which derives its characteristically bright yellow color from powdered turmeric.

Also new to me were kaffir limes and their leaves. Years before I'd seen dried kaffir lime leaves stuffed in little plastic bags in New York's Chinatown and never knew that they grow in pairs, almost piggyback style on the stem, the tip of one leaf barely overlapping the end of the one ahead of it. Infused with a citrus perfume, the bright green leaves were shredded fine and added at the last minute to soups and curries. The kaffir limes resembled the limes we are accustomed to in color only. In stark contrast to the smooth-skinned fruit we're familiar with, the kaffir limes were a mass of knobby little bumps, a curious trait that didn't prevent the rind from being grated and added as still another lemon-lime accent to Thai food.

As we were led through each step in the preparation of a dish, Chalie proved to be an overflowing font of information, suggesting all kinds of variations and substitutions. We often found ourselves scribbling down extra recipes and procedures Chalie rattled off from memory.

For the actual cooking we gathered around large, free-standing gas burners in the kitchen, which was separated from the demonstration room by glass doors. Although the classes were predominantly demonstration here we had the chance to try our own hand at certain techniques, sometimes quite literally as when we learned to drizzle beaten egg from our hands in a crosshatch pattern onto a skillet to make a woven-looking egg sheet.

The cooking equipment was unlike any I'd seen before, especially the striking brass woks, with their gleaming golden color and distinctive, unusual shape. Unlike Chinese-style woks, which feature narrow bottoms and sharply sloping sides, the Thai brass woks had wide, softly rounded bottoms and barely flaring sides. Originally designed for the preparation of desserts, the woks eventually proved their versatility as efficient vessels for stir-frying, deep-frying and the reduction of liquids. Although Chinese woks are used widely in Thailand, Chalie prefers the elegance of the brass version. The brass woks retain their shiny look even after long contact with flames on the stove, and so, frequent usage notwithstanding, the woks stay as beautiful to cook in as they are to serve from—the ideal kitchen-to-table-ware.

The mottled brown ladles and spatulas at the school were fashioned from coconut shells, a testament to both the ingenuity of the Thais and the profusion of coconuts. Made by the hill tribes near Chiang Mai in the northern part of Thailand, the coconut utensils are not readily found in Bangkok, but by sheer luck I happened upon a woman selling them at the sprawling weekend market just outside central Bangkok in Chatuchak Park. Whether one is interested in coconut utensils or not, the Chatuchak market is well worth the taxi ride to see the assortment of items—produce, jeans, dried fish, pets, plants, fabric, ceramics, counterfeit tapes, and the like—all being sold in one vast, tented area.

In designing the curriculum for the cooking school, Chalie researched recipes in many cookbooks, some of which were over a hundred years old. He tried several versions of a classic dish before determining the best one for the classes, keeping in mind not only what would translate easily to a typical Western kitchen. From his travels Chalie was aware of the limited availability of Thai ingredients in the West and kindly considered that fact when choosing recipes to demonstrate.

If I had to describe the classes in one word, it would be intensive. For a Westerner there is a great deal to learn about the raw materials even before commencing on the procedures for combining them in a recipe. Take coconut milk, for example, one of the most distinctive flavors in Thai food. Although a vessel of coconut milk is always on hand at the school, and freshly grated coconut is sold in all the markets, we had to learn to make it from scratch. That process alone involved cracking open a mature coconut, prying out the flesh, finely grating the meat, mixing it with water, and squeezing out the milky white liquid. The result was coconut milk in its simplest form.

But it didn't stop there. In some recipes the Thais make a distinction between coconut cream and coconut milk. The cream is a more concentrated extraction using half the amount of water used for coconut milk. This procedure can be followed by a second extraction, using more water and the same grated coconut to make a thin milk. In these coconut extractions the Thais have both a fat and a dairylike liquid. The cream, when boiled and reduced to release its oil, becomes the fat for cooking seasonings, and the milk becomes the liquid base for curries and soups.

Needless to say, making coconut milk is a time-consuming process, and the results depend on flavorful coconuts, which are often difficult to find in Western markets. Fortunately, good, unsweetened coconut milk is available either frozen or canned in Asian markets in major cities in the United States.

Thai food uses three varieties of fresh basil. The Thais are quite particular about their herbs. Each type of basil has its specific role.

Bai horapha is similar to the Italian basil that Americans and Europeans sprinkle over sliced tomatoes or blend into *pesto* as a sauce for pasta. In Thailand *bai horapha*, or basil-basil as it is also called, tends to be confined to the more refined, city-style of cooking, making frequent appearances in coconut milk-based dishes. When we prepared *panaeng nuea* (beef curry) in class, *bai horapha* leaves were stirred into the mixture at the last moment to wilt them and infuse the curry with their mild anise flavor.

Bai manglug, known elsewhere as sweet balsam or lime basil, has small, paler leaves reminiscent of our dwarf basil. In Thailand sweet balsam is usually added to soups, although it is sometimes sprinkled raw over salads and fish curries.

Most intriguing of all was *bai gaprow*, or holy basil, which derives its mysterious appellation from its Latin name, *ocimum sanctum*. Thai restaurant aficionados in the United States are probably familiar with this herb as the predominant flavor in what is fast becoming a ubiquitous classic, chicken with holy basil. Similar in appearance to Italian basil, holy basil is recognizable by its purple stems and green or reddish-purple leaves, which are slightly smaller and thicker than Italian basil leaves. Holy basil is treated by the Thais as a lusty herb, suitable for the robust chile dishes that have not been soothed with coconut milk. In the version of chicken with holy basil that we learned in the school, the fresh leaves were fried first, forming bright green crisps that tasted faintly of artichoke, before being added to the stir-fried chicken mixture.

Despite the subtle differences among the three basil varieties, fresh Italian basil can be substituted for the other two, and, in fact, it is preferable to the dried holy basil that is sold by some Asian markets and mail-order companies. Fresh holy basil is available sporadically in Thai markets in the United States, particularly in cities with a sizable Thai population such as Los Angeles, Houston, Washington, D.C., New York, Chicago, and Atlanta, and it is well worth the hunt to find it.

For many *farangs,* Thai food is synonymous with the incendiary heat of chiles, and one of the most frequent comments about the cuisine is that it's very hot, if not at times too hot. Chalie is sensitive to this complaint and insists that well-prepared Thai dishes should be balanced, so that the spiciness of hot peppers is offset by the sweetness of coconut milk or palm sugar, the pungency of fresh herbs, the sourness of lime juice or tamarind, or the saltiness of *naam pla*. Too often in Thai restaurants in the West that balance is out of whack. In traditional home-style cooking, Chalie explained, the mother spiced the dishes mildly and offered small bowls of hot sauce on the side so that each person could fire up his or her serving to taste. Only when she thought she didn't have enough food for a meal would the heat be increased to keep the family from eating too much.

We were surprised to learn that the chiles so loved by the Thais are not native to Thailand at all but were introduced to the country by Portuguese missionaries, who brought them from South America in the seventeenth century. Before that, the only peppers in Thailand were peppercorns, a fact reflected in their name, *prig Thai*. Peppercorns are still an important spice in Thai cooking, and the Thais are particularly fond of young, or green, peppercorns. In Bangkok markets the fresh green berries are sold still attached to their branches.

I marveled at how much more aromatic the fresh green peppercorns were than the brine-cured ones so loved by European and American chefs. What we consider an expensive specialty item in the United States, Chalie used with abandon, tossing clumps of peppercorns, twigs and all, into curries and soups. My favorite recipe utilizing green peppercorns, however, was for a concoction the Thais call a dip but that more closely resembles a relish or condiment. In this case the green peppercorns were mixed with garlic, sugar, dried shrimp, lime juice, and grated sour fruits. Chalie recommended it as an accompaniment for vegetables or grilled fish, but we found it addictive eaten straight with a spoon.

The Thais clearly took to the chiles that the Portuguese brought with them, and a myriad variety in different shapes, sizes, and colors overflow baskets in a riotous display in the markets. Although thin slices of fresh chiles appear frequently as a garnish, chiles are most often pounded into a paste with other aromatic seasonings. Depending on the type of dish it is headed for, the paste may include different combinations of such ingredients as the roots of fresh coriander plants, dried shrimp, shrimp paste, garlic lemongrass, and greater galanga. Chile pastes are the foundation of so many Thai dishes that it is no surprise to find huge conical mounds of them in the markets, in various shades of red, orange, and green. At least half the dishes we saw prepared in class, from curries to stir-fried noodles to soups, began with some form of chile paste.

"The secret to Thai chile or curry pastes is the pounding of the ingredients. You must break open the pores to bring out the flavors," explained Chalie to support his belief in the importance of the mortar and pestle. "A food processor does not do the same thing." Chalie was flexible on many other substitutions, but on this point he was adamant. He demonstrated the making of pastes with two different mortars and pestles. One was a deep, clay bisque bowl with a palm root for a pestle, and the other was carved from a solid piece of granite with a matching granite pestle. For those of us accustomed to modern, supposedly time-saving equipment, it was an eye-opener to watch the old fashioned mortar and pestle mash a mixture of garlic cloves, chiles, and lemongrass into an aromatic puree in no time.

What has long intrigued me about Thai food is its reflection of the unique way in which influences from neighboring countries have been adapted. As we tasted our way through five days of classes these culinary borrowings became clearer. From India came the curries, but, whereas Indian curries are based on spices, Thai curries are predominantly herbal, with the prevailing flavors of coriander root, lemongrass, chiles, and basil and only the occasional use of cumin, coriander seed, and cardamom. Reminiscent of Chinese cuisine are the stir-fried meats and poultry and the noodle dishes, but the addition of such seasonings as shrimp paste, lime juice, tamarind, and basil makes them distant relations. The Thais adopted *sates,* the skewers of grilled meats served with a peanut sauce, from the Malaysians, but instead of a dry marinade the Thais often combine the spices with coconut milk and let the meat marinate in the mixture before grilling it. The accompanying peanut sauce tends to be a touch sweeter and creamier with the addition of coconut milk than the typical Malaysian versions.

Thai cuisine was not new to me when I arrived in Bangkok, although the food I ate at the school and in the restaurants was far superior to anything I'd had before in the United States. Interestingly, I sampled my first Thai food at the New York World's Fair in 1964. I accompanied friends who had lived in Bangkok for several years, and we had lunch at the Thai Pavilion. I was eleven years old at the time, not a typically adventurous age when it comes to trying new foods, but I remember particularly liking the fried-noodle specialty, which I now realize was *mee grob,* sometimes referred to as the Thai national dish. Versions of *mee grob* I've had since then in New York City Thai restaurants have tasted overly sweet, a common problem due to the unfortunate belief that the American sweet tooth applies to savory foods as well as desserts, and so I was eager to learn the proper method of preparing it. Chalie confirmed that even in Thailand too much sugar gets added to *mee grob*, especially in the quick versions hawked in the markets. These simplified street concoctions bore no resemblance to the elaborate preparation we witnessed in the classroom.

Mee grob is a dish in which texture is crucial. Chalie explained that the noodles should be crisp and crumbly, not crunchy. To achieve this consistency he very briefly soaked the dried rice noodles in water to seal their pores so that they would not puff as they normally do when submerged in hot oil, then dipped them in beaten egg as a further sealant. When the egg coating had set, the noodles were deep-fried. The resulting tender-crisp noodles kept their consistency even after a later stir-frying with *naam pla*, rice vinegar, palm sugar, and a mixture of shrimp, pork, and chicken.

In a country blessed with a profusion of orchids, where people painstakingly string individual petals into elaborately patterned strands and necklaces and carve fruits and vegetables into a cornucopia of shapes, it is no surprise that aesthetics play an important role in the cuisine. "The Thais have always liked things to be pretty," explained Chalie. For novices and professional cooks alike, the inventive presentation of each dish made the classes especially worthwhile. For instance, to *gaeng rawn,* a simple bean thread noodle and vegetable soup, we added little bundles filled with the surprise of ground pork or vegetables and tied with a lily blossom. *Guay tiaw paad Thai,* a stir-fried noodle dish, was served enclosed in a thin egg sheet and decorated with red chiles. The monotone *mee grob* was mounded in an elegant and edible fried noodle basket, which looked impossibly complicated but was actually made easily with two metal bowls and a large deep-fryer in much the same way that French potato nests are formed. Delicate egg lace, created by drizzling beaten egg through a bamboo strainer into hot oil, was laid carefully over the *mee grob* and topped with red chiles and slices of pickled garlic and lime to create a spectacular-looking dish from humble ingredients.

In order to enhance our artistic appreciation of the cuisine, a skilled Thai fruit and vegetable carver led one afternoon session. We watched in awe as a lovely young woman with lightning-speed dexterity transformed a platter of fruits and vegetables into fanciful shapes and blossoms. A piece of rosy-red papaya took on the lines of a curvaceous leaf, a carrot metamorphosed into a partially shucked ear of corn, and a whole watermelon became a large blossom. The methods she used were simple, and yet the results were visually effective. I must admit that our first attempts to copy what we'd seen demonstrated were pathetic, proving that it wasn't as easy as it looked, but by the end of the morning we had made some passable creations. It was the most exciting class of the week for me. I saw so many new possibilities for garnishes that I couldn't wait to try the same tricks on other fruits and vegetables at home.

Given the exciting blend of flavors in Thai cooking and the artistry of its presentation, it is no wonder that European and American chefs are making a beeline to Thailand. There is much to be learned in this magical spot in Southeast Asia, whether one is interested in duplicating an exact dish or in using the delicate balance of spicy, sweet, sour, and salty flavors as a springboard for new creations. Considering how richly satisfying this cuisine is, the Thais, whose thin physiques belie their appreciation of good food, provide food for thought for all the Western world.

Kemp Miles Minifie, senior food editor of Gourmet *magazine, has been a fan of Southeast Asian food since her first bite in 1964.*

"*When in doubt," writes Kasma Loha-Unchit in her remarkable Thai cookbook,* It Rains Fishes, "*add fish sauce."*

Fish sauce is to Thai cooking—and to Vietnamese cooking, we can add—what soy sauce is to Chinese and Japanese cooking. If a dish is not coming together—and you know this only by tasting—add fish sauce until the flavors sing.

Known as nam plah *in Thai and* nuoc cham *in Vietnamese, fish sauce is a source of both flavor and nutrients, including salt, protein, B vitamins, and minerals. It is used during cooking, and again at the table, as a condiment. Fish sauce is made by fermenting very fresh anchovies in sea salt, a technique similar to one used in ancient Rome to produce a condiment known as* liquamen, *or* garum.

A Thai culinary expert, Kasma shares her talents teaching in Oakland, California, and by leading several culinary tours per year to Thailand. One of her favorite brands, Golden Boy, is from a small factory about 80 miles from Bangkok, where the same family has been producing fish sauce for nearly a century. It is rich yet mild, with a clean pure taste. You can recognize it by the picture on its label, a plump baby boy holding a bottle of fish sauce. Kasma also recommends Tra Chang, with a red label showing a scale and a fish. Both brands are available in Asian markets throughout the United States and through online sources.

—Michele Anna Jordan, The Magic Elixir of Southeast Asia"

Pla Nua Yaang Gub A-Ngoon
Spiced Salad of Grilled Beef with Grapes

Serves 6

2 cups sliced grilled flank or skirt steak (rare)

21 Thai chiles (prig khee nu)

5 cloves garlic

1 coriander root, 1 mint stem and 4 spearmint leaves

½ teaspoon salt

5 tablespoons fish sauce

5 tablespoons lime juice

½ teaspoon palm sugar

1 cup sliced lemongrass

½ cup kaffir lime leaves, sliced chiffonade

1 cup seedless red grapes, halved

1 cup mint leaves, chopped

romaine or red leaf lettuce

In mortar, pound chiles, garlic, coriander root, mint stem, mint and salt. Add fish sauce, lime juice, sugar and mix well. Pour dressing over grilled beef, adding lemongrass, lime leaves, mint leaves, and grapes. Toss well. Serve on a platter of lettuce. Garnish with mint leaves.

LUCY FRIEDLAND

The Slaying of the Yabbies

The author overcomes repulsion and trumps her fellow students.

I have no business being in culinary school. I'm slow, clumsy, uncoordinated. Not chef material. Here I am anyway, slogging through a Commercial Cookery course in Sydney, Australia. We've covered soup through dessert in just ten weeks, skipping over the main courses. But now the party's over. No more frilly stuff like canapés and Chantilly cream. We're in the throes of the Fish and Shellfish module. Crustaceans are on the menu, and we're staring down a tub-load of live yabbies.

So far, the seafood module has been less distressing than the previous one, Hot and Cold Desserts. By and large, fish dishes don't *collapse,* as do soufflés and Bavarian creams. The slumping mounds I presented as Bavarois Rubane didn't earn me top marks on the desserts exam. I have yet to master gelatin. Tricky stuff—gelatin.

For most of the modules, we've had no time to make anything more than once, but during the Fish and Shellfish module, we've practiced filleting in a few consecutive classes. I'm more skillful now, using the slender filleting knife to glide along a fish's skeleton, neatly separating flesh from bone.

I'm apprehensive, though, about the crustacean portion I've spent enough time around prawns to know I don't like them. After backpacking in Asia for a year, I found myself in Malaysia apprenticing with a Chinese chef. Grilled tiger prawns were one of his specialties. That apprenticeship lasted all of two months.

Prior to coming to Sydney, I had "volunteered" on and off at other restaurants in Malaysia. Mostly off. In order to get a decent—and legal—restaurant job, I would have to earn a chef's qualification. I visited a couple of Malaysian culinary schools. One of them wouldn't enroll a foreigner, and the other required non-Moslem cookery students to take a course in Moral Studies. I couldn't stomach that, so I decided on a culinary school in Sydney instead. Why a Sydney school? As they say in Malaysia, it was cheap and good.

The Australian yabby is the subject of today's shellfish class. Yabbies are a type of crayfish that grow to roughly six inches in length, with longish tails and claws. I'm hoping they'll be less nasty to prepare than prawns. After only five minutes of peeling prawns, my fingers start to itch. Mantis shrimp are another nightmare. They have grasping front legs that clasp at their chests, like praying mantises. In my book, prawns and shrimp are the roaches of the ocean, gobbling up refuse that more dignified sea creatures wouldn't touch. I've come to loathe their wiggling legs and waving tentacles. Live or dead, shrimp give me the willies.

The teacher, Chef Richard, begins the yabby demonstration as a dozen students in white jackets and toques gather around his stainless-steel worktable. He's standing beside a large plastic tub he just removed from the refrigerator. Reaching into the container, he grabs one of the critters by its back and holds it aloft.

"What we have here, class, are live yabbies. They're like miniature lobsters, but they live in fresh water. We are *not* going to drop them headfirst into a pot of boiling water. No, no, no. Some chefs kill them like that; they drop yabbies directly into boiling water. But if you do that, you lose all that good yabby flavor. No, no, no. Place your chef knife between their eyes and push down hard, one time. Slice neatly through their brains before cooking them. It's much more humane that way. They die a quicker death."

The chef puts four yabbies on his chopping board. *Snicker-snack*, he makes a quick cut through each of the heads and slices each body in half from head to tail. *Crunch, crunch.* He scoops out the guts with a spoon. Once all our yabby bodies are halved, we are to sauté them for a couple of minutes, extract the meat from the shells and use the shells to make a cream sauce.

"I don't want to see you boys torturing these animals," added Chef Richard. "If you do, it will make me *very* angry."

"Oh, no, Chef," I tell myself faintly, "the torture is all mine."

I'm thunderstruck. I had prepared for the day's events by reading carefully over my lesson, as I do for every class, but nowhere in the terse description does it say we have to *slay* the yabbies. The recipe merely reads, "Cut the yabbies in half and discard the sac from the carapace."

Despite my thorough investigation of the chef's profession, nothing prepares me for tasks such as these. It's dawning on me that just because I love to eat, it doesn't mean I love to cook. And if you want to be a chef, you have to *love* to cook. You're on your feet toiling away, for too many hours at a stretch, for too little pay to do it otherwise. In interviews, celebrity chefs claim to love what they do. At least the Western chefs do. All the Malaysian chefs I've met say they cook, not out of passion, but to survive. "Must *cari makan, lah*," they say, which literally means, "Must search for food," but with the broader sense of "earning a living." Whether or not you enjoy killing or cooking live animals is irrelevant. Your livelihood may depend on it.

Storing the yabbies in cold conditions had put them in a sedated state, but when Chef Richard took the tub out of the fridge, the beasts had awoken from their slumber. The yabbies remained tranquil for the chef, but by the time I come to collect my yabbies from the tub, they'd revived in the warm kitchen air. They're starting to panic. They're doing their yabby dance of fear, curling and uncurling their tails and flailing their claws. What a horror show. It's like a Chinese dragon dance; only these dragons are live and lunging for fingers, not pearls.

The chef gingerly picks up three and puts them on a plate for me. He starts reaching for more, but I say, "That's O.K. That's enough, Chef, thank you. That's *enough!*" I take the plate over to my chopping board and look down at the yabbies kicking and flopping. Suddenly, I start to scream. As soon as I hear the noise coming out of my mouth, I shut myself up. It's too late. I've humiliated myself.

I run the crawling plate back to the fridge and shove it inside. I slam the door shut so hard the fridge starts rocking. To steady the tall silver box, I spin around and push my back up against the door, my arms fully extending from both sides. I stand there quaking, drawing and expelling huge breaths. The fridge door is the sole barrier between those monsters and me.

Where did I get the crazy notion I could even be a chef? Somewhere in India. After a twenty-year career in publishing, I became restless and quit my job in the States to travel. During the trip, it had seemed that I wasn't traveling so much as *eating* my way around Asia. Sightseeing was secondary to finding good food. If I found something delicious to eat for lunch or dinner, then the day was a success. Food was my true calling. In India I met a couple of Western chefs who had it made. They were in demand. They could choose when and where to work and take time off to travel in between cooking gigs. They were happy and free.

Couldn't I do that, too? I had never shown the slightest predilection for cooking, but maybe I had never given it a fair shake. As a child, whenever I would wander into the kitchen to see what my mother was up to, she'd say, "Get out of here. Go read a book." So I would. The kitchen remained *terra incognita* to me.

I should have known early on that cooking isn't my forte. At age sixteen, I was fired from a deli for failing to cut the signature strawberry cheesecakes into twelve even pieces. When my first Malaysian chef stopped speaking to me, I found other, more patient chef-mentors. Even under their tutelage, I can't say I've improved much.

Now, it's halfway through the semester, and I still have grave doubts about my culinary aptitude. I don't advertise the fact that I have restaurant experience. If I did, my classmates would wonder why I'm so poky. I bring up the rear in nearly every class. During the exams at the end of each module, I complete my dishes a good fifteen minutes after everyone else. I sweat out my last presentation, racing back and forth between my stovetop and workbench, as the other whitecoats finish cleaning the kitchen *around* me and sashay out the door.

I imagine that the other students have the right stuff. They must've been cooking since they were old enough to peek over the edge of a chopping board. They probably wielded huge cleavers in their chubby little hands and mastered precision cuts quicker than most humans learn to use a remote. Before entering culinary school, they probably hosted gala garden parties for their families and friends. They would have heaved whole pigs onto spits to roast, while stirring great gallons of barbecue sauce in enormous pots. Their sated guests would have run their thumbs around uncomfortably tight waistbands, leaned back in their chairs and declared, in whatever language, "That kid sure has a bright future ahead of him."

Most of my classmates are from Asia and Europe. I'm the sole North American and twenty years older than almost everyone else. The largest contingent is the Chinese Indonesians. There are three of them. They break off into jovial huddles, cracking jokes in Indonesian. I envy their camaraderie. I can't relate to the sulky German woman who's the only woman in the class besides me. David—a Jewish, white South African—offers moral support when it's painfully obvious I'm lagging behind.

Unlike me, most of my classmates already have part-time restaurant jobs in Sydney. Robi, one of the Chinese Indonesians—and the tallest Chinese guy I've ever met—is the most accomplished cook. He's been apprenticing at an Italian restaurant for three years. Tareq, a Bangladeshi, works fast and smart. He's a commis cook for a yacht club. Pachi, from the Canary Islands, is working front-of-house, as a waiter and a maitre d', but he's a natural in the kitchen and *never* loses his cool in class.

As I stand there trembling, splayed across the refrigerator, I suddenly remember I'm not alone. How are these culinary prodigies handling *their* yabbies? I quickly scan the kitchen. Despite my outré behavior, no one is looking at me. Most of the whitecoats are looking down at their chopping boards with impassive expressions. Some are already at the stovetops with their extinguished yabbies, firing up their saucepans. No one is screaming or gesticulating wildly. No one is storming the exits. Peace prevails in the room.

Where the hell is Anica? Where is that miserable German girl? How is *she* coping? Recently, she announced that she *detests* commercial cookery and that next semester she's going to switch to Web design. She's only eighteen, but she has more sense than I have. *She's not here.* She's conveniently absent on Crustacean Day.

I can't get out of the slaughter. No one comes to my rescue. Chef Richard doesn't say, "That's O.K., Lucy, you don't have to do it. Ask one of the boys to kill them for you." I fight to regain my breath, realizing I have to go through with the deed. A real chef would not waver. A real chef would do it and do it fast. I push back my revulsion, turn and open the fridge door. I won't look at them. I just won't look. I grab the plate and rush it back to my cutting board. I had thought that if I put them back into the fridge, they would settle down. They're still riled, but a little less so than before.

I run over to the paper-towel dispenser, yank a few sheets and run back to my cutting board. I cover one of the bodies with a paper towel, leaving its head exposed. I pick up my chef knife. My hand is shaking so hard, I might as well be clutching a chainsaw. I bring the knife down over and over, until I make mincemeat of the head. Then I quickly cover the next body and whack at the next head. Then, the third. Paper towels off. I sever the remaining bodies in two while they're still convulsing. It takes the rest of my will power to keep from bursting into tears.

I'm way behind everyone else—as usual. I run the mutilated yabbies over to the stovetop, slap them into a pan with sizzling butter and fry their still twitching bodies until they turn pink and die for good.

The weekend comes and goes, and my composure returns. We're back to fish for the next couple of classes. At lunch break, I make a point of heading over to the canteen to find my classmates. Usually by the time I clean up my workbench, I don't have enough of a lunch break left to buy food at the canteen. I'll eat a sandwich I bring from home in the quiet of the women's locker room. But, today I have to find out if there's any fallout from the yabby debacle. Robi, Pachi, Jimmy, and a couple of the others are seated at a picnic table in the courtyard outside the canteen.

I join the table, unwrap my sandwich and ask as casually as possible, "Hey you guys, what did you think of Friday's class?"

"What was Friday's class?" asks John-Paul, the Dutch guy.

"You know...the yabbies." I look around at their faces. They glance at each other and shrug.

At last, David, the South African, turns to me and says, "Once you put those yabbies in the fridge, I never thought you'd take them out again. I don't blame you. Killing those things was distasteful. Then again, I don't like seafood, any seafood."

I check out Robi. "What about you, Robi? How'd you do?"

"No way, I had Pachi do mine." *Pachi?* How'd he get away with that? I look at Pachi. He purses his lips together and blows out a *pppfft* of air.

"Nada, No big thing."

"How many did you kill?" I wonder if he had killed the yabbies for all four students at his workstation without Chef Richard noticing.

"I don't know, lots of them."

I let it drop. Later, after class, I mull over Robi's confession. Astounding. A *Chinese* couldn't go through with the slaughter. Aren't the Chinese second only to the Japanese in their fetish for fresh seafood? Aren't Chinese chefs famous for yanking whole, live fish out of tanks and butchering them to order? A Chinese with three years restaurant experience—O.K., in an Italian restaurant—couldn't kill a puny yabby? At least I didn't hand off my yabbies to someone else to kill. Does this mean I have the mettle to be a chef, after all? If I do, then why am I such a nervous wreck in the kitchen? This whole cooking venture has been more harrowing than gratifying.

If I give up on being a chef—if I throw in my tea towel—I'll spare other living creatures, and myself, further torment. Maybe I can be a vegetarian chef someday. I have a better rapport with plants than animals, anyway. There's no chance of exploring that now. The Meat Butchery modules—beef, veal, pork, and lamb—follow in the wake of Fish and Shellfish. I've been dreading those meat modules. For lamb butchery, we have to hack apart a whole side of lamb.

I console myself that at least the lamb will already be dead.

Lucy Friedland abandoned her brilliant surfing career (see Travelers' Tales Australia*) for another dubious career as a cook. She did finally earn her Commercial Cookery Certificate I in Sydney, Australia. She returned to Malaysia and worked for three years at a South Indian vegetarian restaurant as a kitchen helper. She also assisted with the startup of Ecco Cafe in Penang, which specializes in homemade pasta and pizza. She has since quit the kitchen and spends her time writing, editing, and eating.*

Yabby, Rice and Lemon Soup

Serves 4

20 medium-sized live yabbies

¼ cup butter

1 leek, halved lengthways and thinly sliced

4 cloves garlic, finely minced

¾ cup vialone nano or arborio rice

1 quart stock (yabby, fish or chicken)

1 ½ tablespoons lemon juice

finely grated rind of 1 lemon

chervil sprigs, to serve

Place live yabbies in freezer for 1 hour or until cold but not frozen (see Note below). Remove and quickly plunge a sharp knife through the center of the head, just behind the eyes. Chop off claws and head and remove abdominal organs with a spoon. Cut tail in half, extract yabby meat. (Claws and shells can be used to make the stock for this dish. Discard head.)

Melt butter in a heavy-based saucepan and cook the leek, covered, over low heat for 6 to 8 minutes or until soft but not browned. Add yabby meat and garlic and sauté, uncovered, for another 2 to 3 minutes. Take out the yabby meat when half cooked and set aside.

Add rice and stock and season with sea salt and freshly ground black pepper. Cover and simmer soup gently for 20 minutes or until rice is tender, then stir in lemon juice, lemon rind, and yabby meat and cook for another 1 to 2 minutes or until yabbies are just cooked through. Check seasoning. Ladle soup into warm bowls, scatter with chervil sprigs and serve immediately.

Note: Make sure the yabbies you buy are live, since dead uncooked yabbies will deteriorate very quickly. Placing the yabbies in the freezer puts them to sleep, so when they are killed they will not suffer as much and the flesh will remain tender. If yabbies are unavailable, fresh jumbo prawns may be substituted.

Souvenir

Memories can last longer than any tchotchke.

We had been in Bali nearly two weeks and I didn't have one souvenir to show for it. We had crossed oceans to be married and spend our honeymoon on this tiny little island in a beautiful corner of the planet, and I had no tangible memories to bring home with me. Home is a cozy thirty-six-foot sailboat, so we are selective in the items that share our precious square footage. But this was ridiculous. Every time I saw something I wanted to bring home, my groom would squawk that it was touristy junk and a waste of money, and would ask what would we do with it on a boat. I selected little things, unique things, handmade things, soft things, and still he debated me into closing my wallet and walking away. Here we were, just two days from departure and I had nothing to remember my trip by except our wedding photos, an Indonesian marriage certificate, and some heated newlywed squabbles. So on the morning of our second to last day, when the travel alarm clock buzzed unnaturally at me, all I could think was, "I want to go shopping." Instead we were planning to spend the day doing something completely foreign to both my new husband and me: cooking.

The sun gently kissed the Balinese landscape into consciousness. The roosters started the animal orchestra with their powerful trumpeting, followed by a percussion of wild

My pantry is home to culinary treasures I seize while roaming the world. It is very difficult to find the typical tins of tuna or boxes of dried pasta nestled in this treasured cupboard. Peek at her shelves and she'll reveal to you mole mustard and smoked salmon farfalle from LaJolla, cone sushi wrappers from Hawaii, herbs de Provence, lavender sugar and moutarde au cassis de Dijon from Paris, and Kilkenny black-currant rum jam as well as Guinness stout-flavored chocolate bars from Ireland.

Surveying the shelves of my pantry is as satisfying as thumbing through a photo album containing pictures of Paris, Dublin, and Honolulu. It comforts me when I am suffering from the post-vacation blues, to remember the shop on the hidden street in Killarney where I found the mango chutney spiked with good Irish whiskey and I know that one savored spoonful of jam has the power to transport me back to the craggy, mountainous, sheep strewn vistas of south western Ireland.

—Jill Delehanty, "A Traveler's Pantry"

dogs, and the gentle bass of ancient cows. As I sleepily inhaled the moist, warm air permeated by incense from the morning offerings, a minivan sped up to our hillside inn, wheezing and snorting at the incline. Heinz, an Austrian expat, exploded out of the driver's seat in a way that made me wince in my pre-coffee haze.

"Ah, are we ready? Very good, let's go then!"

The minivan rolled down the steep hill until Heinz swerved off to the side of the road and stopped suddenly. Within seconds he was on the edge of the hill overlooking the vast countryside below. He took a deep, cleansing breath normally reserved for yoga instructors.

"Isn't it beautiful?!" he demanded. "Ah, where is my camera?"

We listened in sleepy amazement as our driver-cum-chef waxed poetic about a landscape he's called home for thirteen years now. The fact that after all these years he would stop and notice, let alone photograph, the soft silhouettes of temples and volcanoes against the pastel dawn was telling of Heinz von Holzen's love for Bali. Love is what brought him here from Europe when he married a Balinese woman. Leaving the five-star world of upper-crust European cuisine behind, the gourmet chef moved to Indonesia and opened a restaurant and cooking school. Today we were his only pupils. Heinz snapped a few photographs and corralled us back into the minivan.

A few turns later and we were whisked onto the back streets of Denpasar. I watched as the sarong stalls and *satay* stands of the main strip blurred away, quickly forming a shopping list in my mind for later. A sharp turn through a crowd of motorbikes and suddenly the tourist shops were replaced by a local farmer's market of sorts. The sun wasn't even high enough to start scorching my pasty skin, and yet the market was pulsing with activity.

Heinz shot out of the van and plunged in on foot. We did all we could to keep up as his soaring, lean physique maneuvered through the Lilliputian brown bodies. Around us a potpourri of new shapes and smells and colors were on display. Heinz halted and whipped around with a gnarly root in his hand resembling the fingers of a troll.

"What is it?" He queried thrusting it towards our blank faces. This was Lesson Number One of the Bumbu Bali Cooking School.

He sliced the root with a pocketknife and the fresh aroma raced to my nostrils, trying to give me a hint. Inside was a brilliant orange flesh, but we still couldn't recognize it.

"Turmeric!" he exalted.

Of course, having only ever seen it ground and powdered and in a neat little jar, we would never have guessed it. It was the first of many spices, herbs, and foods we would encounter in their natural states.

The market was alive, literally. The chatter of chickens blended with the frenzy of human bargaining. Mystery fruits still clinging to whole branches lay in piles next to makeshift stalls. A circle of buckets around a heavy central table caught blood and excess carnage from the show-and-smell butcher shop. And dense stacks of diminutive packages filled with kernels, powders, and spices that our Western sensibilities could not categorize were everywhere. Heinz told us that "mama Bali," his global term for Balinese women, usually only bought what she needed for that day's meal, hence the bite-sized plastic baggies with seven or eight peppercorns inside. The "mama Bali" expression is rooted in tradition. The market is the woman's domain. She goes every morning, has a little snack at a food stall, and shops to feed her family for the day. Meals are a private affair, left in the kitchen for everyone to help themselves when they please. Solo, no-fuss consumption is favored over Western family-style productions. The "ladies only" aspect made Heinz quite the spectacle at the market, but one that he and the women were now used to after many years. He spoke the local dialect flawlessly, and the teasing remarks and smiles flew faster than the men outside on their motor scooters. One ancient matriarch fiendishly tickled Heinz with a banana leaf from afar and he was quick to lunge back at her with a startled live chicken aroused from its nap. Squawks and laughter exploded through the stalls.

"If I were not with you," he warned, "they would eat you alive." It was certainly a scene we were glad to witness, but happy to be guided through. But still nothing around me looked like souvenir material.

Heinz bargained and purchased while we watched and carried sacks full of ingredients. Then it was a short jaunt to the beach to rummage the fish market. The pungent smell of the ocean's bounty, still flopping on tables, was overwhelming. Scales and slime and salt water coated our shoes as we inspected the stalls. A heated exchange ensued between Heinz and a vendor. He explained to us that this particular pile of fish was no good.

"Look at the eyes. They are blank, clouded." He held up a specimen. "These have been here for days, maybe longer. No ice. These are no good. Remember when you go to buy, look at the eyes."

I didn't have the nerve to tell him that where I buy fish I just look at the expiration date on a hermetically sealed fillet.

The Bumbu Bali Restaurant looked like something out of a Southeast Asian dream scene. The sound of gurgling water accented by wind chimes lured us into a cool courtyard adorned with equal parts natural and manmade eye candy. Meticulous local carvings graced every door and post while willowy bamboo and dripping vines flirted with the rare breeze. Eleven chefs and thirty-six employees kept the established restaurant and growing inn churning with a pleasant equilibrium of European efficiency and Balinese peacefulness. Every person we encountered greeted us with a cheery and heartfelt, "Good morning, *selemat pagi.*"

Breakfast was as beautiful as it was delicious. An assortment of local fruits was complemented by black rice pudding and other tasty sweets. Over strong coffee we learned that Bumbu Bali is actually one of the few authentic Balinese restaurant in Bali. The others are Indonesian. Indonesia is an archipelago of more than seventeen thousand islets. Spread over 2 million square kilometers, these islands range from specks on the maps like Nusa Lembongan to substantial land posts like Java. The waters of the Indian Ocean separate the islands physically and culturally, but the dictates of modern governing call them one united Indonesia. Bali has always marched to the beat of its own drum. Indonesia is largely Muslim. Bali is Hindu. Bali has its own dances, traditional dress, ceremonies, legends, and character.

It also has its own food, but naturally never sought to capitalize on it. Heinz combined his unique culinary radar honed through years of professional training with access to authentic local life from marrying into a Balinese family. He was amazed to find out that there was no formal written record of traditional Balinese food. It became a quest and a challenge to collect these gastronomic gems. He spent years talking to cooks and chefs, from common folk to honored village elders. Gathered around a table, he had them rattle off the ingredients and processes while taking notes. The challenge was getting everyone to agree. One may sauté in coconut oil while the other insists it must be done in vegetable oil. One region says to chop the *kencur* root while the folks from the neighboring village counter that it must be sliced. Heinz slaved at consensus and came up with an extensive and authentically Balinese menu.

Aprons were tied around our midsections as my husband, Doug, and I were ushered into the open air kitchen. A thick, bound collection of recipes were waiting as Heinz left us in the hands of his sous chef Joko. After quick introductions, Heinz excused himself for a few hours, and Joko began to cook. Doug and I didn't have the chance, or the guts, to tell them that they were dealing with two American yuppies whose idea of cuisine focused on which take-out menu was on top of the junk drawer. I thumbed through the twenty-six recipes in amazement, wondering which simple dishes would be chosen for us to tackle that day. But as Joko began sorting mountains of peppers and forests of lemongrass, explaining the order of operations, it dawned on me that we were cooking everything—every recipe in the book!

"Yes, we have sixty-four guests reserved for tonight, we have a lot to cook. Must get going!" Joko ordered. "First, we do spice paste!"

The fact that we were helping to cook for paying customers made us sweat from more than the equatorial humidity. Joko started weighing the ingredients for the spice paste on an old fashioned scale and pouring them into a hand-cranked meat grinder that worked better than any food processor I've ever seen. He explained that the various spice pastes—basic, poultry, seafood, and beef—were the foundation of nearly every Balinese dish. Large portions can be prepared and frozen for later use. For the culinary challenged like us, it was pure miracle to watch shallots, hot peppers, nuts, herbs, and spices fall into a meat grinder and come out the other end a brilliant ocher-colored paste.

With the spice pastes finished, we began a frenzy of sautéing, boiling, slicing, grinding, and baking. Doug and I were concentrating like teenagers taking the SAT as we whizzed through the recipes. We began to get into the rhythm of things, handing over ingredients and stirring boiling cauldrons at Joko's command. Doug read the next step aloud to me.

"Add sixteen cloves to the sautéing fish."

"Perfect," I declared. "We have exactly sixteen cloves."

I lifted the bowl into which I counted carefully sixteen zesty smelling kernels of clove spice and ceremoniously dumped them into the fish dish. Joko's chef radar switched on and he whipped around from the other side of the kitchen.

"What did you add to the fish," he queried.

"Cloves," I said.

His nose instinctively twitched and he peered into the bubbling fish sauté. The little black bobbing nubs gave us away. His hands went to work before the words made their way out of his mouth.

"No," he gasped. "Garlic cloves. GARLIC. Did you look at the recipe?"

We simultaneously glanced over at the book and realized our error. Without saying a word Doug started working on the garlic as I stood half-laughing, half-dying inside as Joko feverishly fished the clove spice from the pot.

As the heat of the day began to melt into the velvety Balinese evening, the air smelled of spice paste and sweet rice. We tossed off our aprons and joined the paying customers for an authentic Balinese dinner. Giddiness overcame us as we ordered, realizing we had intimate knowledge of each dish. And as other people's food arrived it was all we could do not to rubberneck and watch for reactions as they tasted the fruits of our labor. I couldn't help but look at their plump, sunburned faces and think about what they had done that day. Tour a temple? Lay on the beach? Go for a snorkel trip? Shop for sarongs? Did these innocent travelers realize we helped cook what they were eating? I wanted to get up and announce to everyone, "Hey I smashed those chile peppers while you were ordering your third beer from the cabana boy." I realized then that we actually spent the day doing something, I mean really *doing* something. We learned about Balinese culture and food. We learned that we'll never be gourmets like Heinz and Joko. But with careful guidance and patient hand-holding we *can* make something exotic and tasty, and it doesn't have to include a trip to the prepared foods counter at the gourmet grocery store.

Our dinner finally arrived. It sat before us on the plate with an air of familiarity I have never felt before sitting in a restaurant. It tasted like accomplishment. Granted, if we were genuinely responsible for the meal Doug would still be smoldering in the kitchen with a pasty pile of spicy fish goo and I'd be slumped over a sarong stall in a shopping coma. But following your food from raw market ingredients to refined restaurant dish gives the meal a whole new meaning.

As a perfect *pièce de résistance* Heinz gifted us with a Balinese cookbook that he wrote. Heinz styled and photographed the food for his cookbook and it was as beautiful as the food was succulent. *Finally*, something to take home.

Fast forward eighteen months. Our neighbors decide it would be fun to cook a different international meal together every Sunday night. We had been through Mexico, India, Cuba, Italy, France, Jamaica, Japan, and the Bahamas. It was technically "our" night to arrange the meal and we were stumped. Frankly, the others had always done most of the cooking and organizing and we just sort of helped eat and clean. Under a pile of well-used take-out menus I came across my Balinese cookbook, dusty, but shiny and new and un-creased. Guilty as charged: we never opened the thing.

The memories flooded back as we chopped and grinded and sautéed. We read the recipes carefully, minded our "cloves," and burned some incense to conjure the Balinese cooking gods. We needed them to smile upon us to spare our friends an unsavory evening. The chicken gurgled in the spice paste with knots of lemon grass floating by and everything actually started to smell right. Looking anxiously at each other, we took a taste. It was actually not bad. We felt confident we could serve it to our friends without calling poison control.

Later that night we feasted, talked about our memories of Heinz and Joko, and looked at pictures from our trip. With no carvings or textiles to show off, I grumbled that the class and gifted cookbook were meager substitutes for exotic souvenirs.

"But you did get a souvenir," our friend Lisa said. "*Souvenir* is French for *remember*."

Much to the horror of her hippie-no-TV-allowed parents, Cindy Wallach makes her living as a TV producer and writer. She has worked for Home & Garden Television, A&E, Food TV, Fox, CBS, and countless others. When people ask her what she does though, she says sail. She and her husband have lived aboard a catamaran for eight years with their dog and now two-year-old son. They have traversed the U.S. East Coast, the Florida Keys, the Bahamas, and Cuba. Currently she is living on the boat in Annapolis, Maryland, working towards their next sailing adventure.

Sate Lilit
Minced Seafood Satay

Serves 6 to 8 as an appetizer

Spice Paste (recipe follows)

2 tablespoons peanut oil, palm oil or other mild oil

1 pound fresh boneless firm white fish fillets, such as snapper, mahimahi or catfish

10 ounces fresh shrimp, peeled and deveined

½ cup canned coconut milk

1 egg white

2 tablespoons fresh lime juice

3 kaffir lime leaves, cut into very thin slivers

4 teaspoons palm sugar or firmly packed brown sugar

kosher salt

24 fresh lemongrass stalks, outer leaves removed or wooden skewers soaked in cold water for 1 hour

1 large bunch cilantro, rinsed

Prepare the spice paste. (seee recipe on next page.)

Pour the oil into a heavy sauté pan set over medium heat, add the spice paste and sauté, stirring continuously, until dark and fragrant, about 5 minutes. Transfer to a bowl and set aside to cool.

Meanwhile, use a very sharp knife to mince the fish and the shrimp. Alternately, cut the fish into chunks and put it, along with the shrimp, into the work bowl of a food processor and pulse until almost smooth. Transfer to a bowl. Fold in the cooled spice paste, the coconut milk, egg white, 1 tablespoon of the lime juice, kaffir lime leaves and sugar.

Set a clean sauté pan over medium heat, add a small amount of the fish mixture and sauté for 1 or 2 minutes, until just done. Cool slightly and taste; it should be full flavored and slightly tangy. If it is flat, add more salt to the fish mixture; if it needs acid, add the remaining lime juice. Cover the fish mixture and chill it for at least two hours and as long as overnight.

To form the satay, line a baking sheet with parchment or wax paper. Divide the fish mixture into 24 equal portions. With your hands wet, take one portion of the mixture in one hand and hold a skewer (lemongrass stalk or wooden one) in the other. Mold the mixture around the skewer, so that it looks like a sausage about 3-inches long. Press it firmly in place and set on the lined baking sheet. Continue until all 24 satays have been made. Cover with plastic wrap and refrigerate until ready to cook but no longer than four hours.

To cook, heat a stovetop grill to high or prepare a fire in an outdoor grill. Make sure the grill or grill rack is clean and brush it lightly with a mild oil. Cook the satays until they golden brown all over, rotating them a quarter turn about every 2 minutes. Use a thin metal spatula to loosen the satays before turning them.

Spread the cilantro over a serving platter and set the cooked satays on top. Serve immediately.

Spice Paste

4 large shallots, thinly sliced

6 garlic cloves, thinly sliced

3 Thai or serrano chiles, thinly sliced

4 macadamia nuts

1-inch piece fresh ginger, grated

1-inch piece fresh galangal, minced

2 teaspoons ground coriander

½ teaspoon ground turmeric

black pepper in a mill

1 tablespoon Thai fish sauce

kosher salt

To prepare the spice paste, put the sliced shallots in a large mortar and use a wooden or granite pestle to grind nearly to a paste. Add the garlic and crush until smooth. Crush the chiles into the mixture, add the nuts and grind them until they are mixed in finely with the other ingredients. Add the ginger, galangal, coriander, and turmeric and mix until smooth. Season with several generous turns of black pepper. Stir in the fish sauce and 3 or 4 generous pinches of kosher salt. Set aside until ready to use.

Trin Diem Vy

The author learns what it means to eat with his eyes.

T rin Diem Vy, or Miss Vy as she is known to everyone, is the third-generation owner and chef de cuisine at what is now called the Mermaid restaurant in Hoi An. It began as a market stall operated by her grandparents when they were young. "I still use the same recipes my grandmother and my mother used," she says in her Australian-accented English. "Mine is the home cooking of the central region of Vietnam."

"My kitchen is not a commercial or an industrial restaurant kitchen. It's a traditional home kitchen. It's larger than most, but it's the same as you would find in any traditional home in my country. When you come into my kitchen, you come into my home."

Besides operating the restaurant, Vy teaches what she cooks. She offers three programs for the English-speaking traveler—each lasting either one hour, four hours, or eight hours. It is amazing how much knowledge and skill she can impart in that time.

And so Vy admits us into her home, into her hearth, into the focus of her days and nights. We are reminded that the Latin word for hearth is *focus*. At the center of her kitchen is the ancient source of all Vietnamese cuisine: the earthenware charcoal brazier, with three little nubs that represent the kitchen gods at its rim. Those telltale deities report to the creator all the goings-on within a family, because all the goings-on that matter within a family occur within their earshot.

Vy has three braziers, and the walls next to them are blackened with years of cooking. The heat rising vertically from the fires is intense, but that radiating outward towards us is tempered, warm, and reassuring. The few simple implements that such a kitchen requires hang or lie within easy reach: a ladle, tongs, a curved spatula. Some pots, a couple of sauté pans, wire racks for grilling complete the setting.

"No woks?" we ask.

"Some people like to use them. But they aren't necessary. We don't fry in quite the same way as the Chinese, and not at the same temperature."

At a remove from the braziers is a modern gas cooker (no oven), plenty of counter space, and heaps of fresh herbs, vegetables, and other foodstuffs. She picks up a handful of greenery and says, "This is your first lesson: good food from fresh ingredients. If you forget this, you cannot cook Vietnamese. In this country we don't keep perishable foods at home. We go to the market every day, sometimes two or three times in a day."

For some students, it is surprising how satisfying it is to cook without the modern appliances and conveniences many are used to. When we are fortunate enough to have the time to cook in this hands-on way, there is great pleasure in clutching a bundle of fresh herbs. We find aubergines not only beautiful to look at, but to touch. There is a soothing mantra in the steady slicing of delicate spring onions, and the prayer-like working of mortar and pestle. We feel we have come home.

And so we begin. We learn how to fold rice paper in triangles around a stuffing of carrot, rice vermicelli, and mushrooms, with a tasty pink shrimp on top. We are to let the tail stick out of the little package. It serves as a handle, and provides the name for this little treasure, *tom phi tien*, flying shrimp spring roll. We have to wrap it tightly and neatly so that it will not fall apart while frying.

We learn the fine points of cabbage leaves stuffed with carrot, manually mixing sugar with grated carrot, macerating it until the sugar has been fully incorporated. Then we add crushed garlic. Dip the cabbage leaves in boiling water for a moment to soften them and remove any bitterness. Roll the leaves into tight little bundles and cut them into colourful slices.

"We don't use as much sugar as they do in the south," Vy says. "And we use less coconut.

We use more spice than the north, and we are more concerned than either north or south with the dish's appearance. We like to say that you must 'eat with your eyes' as well as your mouth."

Vy shows us what seems a simple dish, but is more challenging than most—stuffed squid, one of the most eye-appealing in her culinary canon. We suspect the influence of a confectioner, so pretty is it to look at. With the tentacles removed and set aside for garnish, the squid tubes are stuffed with a mixture of pork that has been "ground" for several minutes with a mortar and pestle so that its texture is silky smooth, and rice vermicelli with a few spices. "Always use fresh spices when you can," Vy tells us. "Dry spices can produce a floury texture." The squid tubes and tentacles are braised in their own juices with a little *nuoc mam,* and cut into thin circular slices and served with the tentacles with other garnishes.

"In cooking this dish, and in grilling with leaves, you will see the essence of the Vietnamese cooking technique: you have to

It is a curious aspect of Cambodian restaurant culture that in all but the swankiest places, it's perfectly normal for hawkers to come in and sell you all manner of things, other food included. Today's delicacy was tarantula. My host offered me an arachnid, after picking off several legs for himself first. He told me how the people of Skuon had long used the local tarantulas in traditional medicine; they were thought to be good for the heart, throat, and lungs. The practice of using them as a foodstuff started in the years of terror under the Khmer Rouge. Across Cambodia, starvation was rife and people ate anything they could get their hands on, including insects. When Pol Pot's murderous regime came to an end, most Cambodians were happy to stop eating bugs, but the Skuonese decided that they'd developed a taste for the local tarantulas.

—Rhymer Rigby,
"The Spider Women of Skuon"

be there every minute and be in control of the whole process. You can't put something on the fire and leave it. You have to cut everything to the proper size for the cooking method you'll be using. You have to know the temperature of the dish at all times so that it cooks quickly enough but not too quickly. You have to know exactly when to put the lid on the pot so that the squid will not get tough. In cooking with leaves, if the fire is too hot it will burn through to the food, so you have to raise it up from the fire. If it's not hot enough you have to fan it to make it burn hotter. You have to be in control."

And so Vy has taken us to the heart of the matter. We exercise control of each process for another hour. We slice vegetables with precision. We blanch them with watchful eye. We bring dying fires back to life with lumps of charcoal and brisk fanning. We fry some vegetables in peanut oil infused with garlic rather than use fresh garlic, because we will fry so hot that fresh garlic would burn. Members of Vy's family run to the market for more supplies. We are intensely aware of what we are doing, and how, and why. And we are intensely satisfied.

We sit down, triumphantly, to dine in traditional Vietnamese family style with Vy and members of her clan. The convivial table reminds us that eating in Vietnam is no lonely task, but a ritual of sharing. It reaffirms our bonds of kinship, friendship, and of ourselves to the natural world. Before us is a large pot of steaming rice, a tureen of corn and crab soup, and a plate of aromatic leaves that we wrap around a spring roll and dip into *nuoc cham*. We have tuna with fresh turmeric presented in the leaves in which we cooked it. We have the stuffed squid, looking like a Japanese flower arrangement. And we have heaps of delicious fresh vegetables, without which no meal can be called Vietnamese. This meal is a special experience for us. We have worked closely together to produce it. Now we will consume it, closely together.

Richard Sterling has been dubbed "The Indiana Jones of Gastronomy" by his admirers, and "Conan of the Kitchen" by others. He is the editor of the award winning Travelers Tales Food: A Taste of the Road, *and of* The Adventure of Food: True Stories of Eating Everything. *He is also the principal author of Lonely Planet's World Food series, which was proclaimed "Best Food Book Series in the World" by the International Gourmand Cookbook Awards.*

Operation Kitchen

The gauntlet is thrown. Is he up to the challenge?

Something is going on in the kitchen at the little bungalow hotel on the island of Koh Pha Ngan in Thailand where I am staying. The aroma of frying fish and simmering curry drifts from the kitchen. I can hear foods sizzling in hot oil but I can't see a thing. A sign above the kitchen doors states "Hotel Staff Only" in English.

In the open-air dining room, waiters take orders from the *farang* seated at picnic tables and return soon with buttered toast, burgers, fries, spaghetti Bolognese, and bottles of Coca-Cola and Gatorade.

Later in the afternoon, while guests are at the beach, the hotel staff eats. I stay behind, lingering on the periphery of the dining room, looking with both envy and expectation at a whole steamed fish topped with purple shallots, garlic, and bright red chiles, duck in green curry, minced pork with basil and green peppercorns, colorful fruit shakes.

I feel like a dog waiting for a scrap to fall to the floor.

"Do you like Thai food, Mr. Tummy?" Miss Miaw, the hotel's accountant, asks.

Thais often introduce themselves by their nicknames, so I've used mine, too.

I consider her question an invitation and shuffle over to the table. She gives me a spoonful of minced pork.

Ambrosia. Fresh green peppercorns, unlike the pickled kind I use in the states. Holy basil, from the garden behind the kitchen. I feel like a kid at a high school dance but I try not to show too much enthusiasm.

"We made something similar at a class on Samui," I say, casually, referring to a two-week course I took on a nearby island.

"I have some photos of the food we made if you are interested," I add quietly.

"You really like Thai food?" Miss Miaw asks, somewhat incredulously.

She asks to see the photos and the staff quickly crowds around the two-inch screen of my digital camera as I move through pictures of omelets stuffed with pork and vegetables, pineapple stuffed with chicken and raisins, baked pumpkin filled with custard.

A Massaman curry is met with cries of "*arroy jung who*," which means "delicious" in the dialect of southern Thailand, the source of the curry.

Someone summons Chef Som, a tiny dark-skinned woman and twenty-year culinary veteran who works in the hotel's kitchen. She asks to see the photos and so I page through them again. Chef Som corrects my pronunciation as I struggle to identify each dish in Thai. More employees join us.

Not convinced that I actually know how to cook these dishes, Chef Som challenges me to cook for the staff. As a *farang*—a white foreigner—she declares, I could not have made these dishes myself.

I am not one to shrink from a challenge, especially one made by a woman, a very short woman, who is teasing me about my ability as a cook.

I volunteer to make *hor mak pla*, a terrine of fish, coconut cream, and red chile paste.

Chef Som smiles and makes a remark in Thai as she walks, laughing all the while, to the kitchen.

"Chef looks forward to your cooking and will watch carefully to see what she can learn from you," Miss Miaw translates.

The gauntlet has been thrown down.

The next morning I sit in my beachside brick bungalow, preparing. I take out my Thai food dictionary and my notebook, where I write the ingredients in English in one column and in Thai in another column. I will need fish filets, red chile paste, coconut cream, kaffir lime leaves, and fish sauce.

I was never very good in penmanship in grammar school and so I work extra slowly, carefully copying the loops and lines of the Thai words and hoping that I don't transpose letters and accidentally spell out "poison" or "dog hair" or something else equally inappropriate, or insulting.

Satisfied that my list is accurate, I walk across the sand to the kitchen and hand Miss Miaw my list. She looks surprised and compliments me on my writing, as if I am a precocious pre-schooler.

So far, so good.

Hor mak pla translates literally to "fish wrapped and hidden." The classic recipe calls for a mixture of fish, coconut cream, and chile paste to be wrapped in a banana leaf and then set inside another banana leaf, which is then secured with a bamboo skewer.

Instead of following the traditional version, Miss Miaw suggests we simplify the process by folding banana leaves into cups and stapling the sides together. I defer to her judgment.

Soon I am given a barracuda tail, not a filet. No problem, I think to myself.

Using a cleaver Chef Som sharpened on the bottom of an overturned clay bowl, I shave the scales and skin off the fish and discover that it is filled with sinew.

I attempt to shred the flesh but worry I am getting too many fibers and that they will interfere with the smooth texture the terrine requires.

Chef Som watches me with an amused smile. Finally, after she and her assistant have stopped laughing, she shows me how to use a spoon to scrape out the sinews from the flesh. It takes two minutes.

I mix the fish with the coconut cream and two tablespoons of red chile paste, just as I had learned in cooking school. Chef Som sticks her finger in the mixture, tastes it and then adds more chile paste. I stir and she tastes again. She adds more chile paste. I stir. She tastes.

She reaches for a mortar and pestle and quickly makes more chile paste, grinding bright red *prik khi nuu*—Thai bird chiles—with purple and white shallots, garlic and pungent gray fermented shrimp paste that smells like a seaweed-covered beach at low tide. She adds two tablespoons of the paste to my fish, which has now turned reddish brown, like *café au lait*.

Once Chef Som is satisfied that the seasoning is balanced, we pour the mixture into the banana leaf cups. We set three thin strips of red *chee faa* chiles—fresh cayenne—

and three cilantro leaves on top of each terrine, a traditional garnish in Thailand that symbolizes the three gems of Buddhism: the Buddha, dharma, his teachings and *sangha*, the community.

Half an hour later we remove the banana leaf packets from the steamer. Miss Miaw helps me arrange them on a large round metal platter.

We open each leaf and top the terrines with a tablespoon of fresh coconut milk, strips of red chiles, and wild lime leaves cut into very thin slices. Chef Som gives me a knife with a wavy blade so I can cut rings of carrots and cucumbers, which I use to decorate the platter. After adding cilantro sprigs and red chiles, the tray looks beautiful.

I am proud of my creation.

Now for the tasting.

I take a bite. It is heart-stoppingly spicy but luscious and rich. I take another bite.

As I mop the sweat from my face, I declare the creation that Chef Som has supervised the best I have ever tasted, thanks to her guidance.

One by one, employees taste the terrine. I await their judgment.

Always polite, they claim to be impressed with my effort, but if I want it to be perfect, like the terrines their grandmothers make, I should add more chile paste.

That night, Chef Som invites me to watch her cook dinner. I have passed the audition.

I smile as I walk through the kitchen door.

Chef Tummy (William P. Pitts) is exploring Thailand by motorcycle, train, bus, and elephant to gather cooking tips and recipes from chefs and grandmothers he meets.

I can feel an unbridled charge of energy in the air as we, the makers of red hot curry paste, pulverize. A solo voice enters: "Add the kaffir lime leaves." The voice—alto, tonal, staccato—belongs to Chef Roongfa Sringam. She shouts out instructions above the clatter: "And the mixture of lemongrass, galangal, and coriander roots. Add and blend." In unison, ten hands ferret out small bowls of condiments, dump and grind. A new aroma blasts through the room—zesty, citrus fragrances now predominate.

I and my ingredient-chopping, chile-mashing, wok-stirring companions are in the throes of a Thai cooking lesson. In lieu of spending another afternoon sun-worshipping and sipping fruity tropical drinks on the restful white powder sand beach, I have enrolled in this class for exposure to Thai culture and arts. Acquiring new culinary skills to take back home comes as a bonus. In England, I immersed myself in plays and musicals. In France, I visited art galleries and attended jazz concerts. In Ireland, it was dance shows and pub music. Now in Thailand, I am getting to experience Thai culinary arts from a closer vantage point than a restaurant menu. Many tourists sample local fare as part of the travel experience, but the real culinary adventure begins before food reaches the taste buds. In short, I am on a sensory thrill ride exploring Thai cuisine, whose dishes catapult from safely pleasing to tongue-scorching.

—Mary Hughes, "A Culinary Jam Session"

Hor Mak Pla
Thai Steamed Terrine of Fish

Serves 8

The Thai name for this dish means "fish hidden with wrapping", because the fish is traditionally steamed in banana leaves folded to make wrapper. If you don't have banana leaves in your larder (and most of us don't), I recommend you steam the fish in small 3-inch ramekins. I've also made this in teacups and the teacup handle makes it easy for your guests to hold the aromatic fish terrine while digging in with a spoon.

1 ½ cups white fish filets chopped finely (red snapper, cod,
    and catfish all work well)

1 tablespoon Thai red curry paste

½ cup coconut cream

6 kaffir lime leaves sliced finely

1 cup white cabbage sliced finely

1 fresh red chile, seeded and sliced finely (reserve 12
    small chile rings for garnish)

1 egg

½ cup sweet basil leaves

2 teaspoons fish sauce

2 teaspoons oyster sauce

½ teaspoon sugar

¼ teaspoon black pepper to taste

⅛ cup cilantro leaves for decoration

In a quart mixing bowl, add the fish with the curry paste, kaffir lime leaves, sugar, oyster sauce, fish sauce, pepper, egg, and coconut cream. Mix well.

Sprinkle the cabbage and sweet basil in the bottom of your ramekins, and then place a several large spoonfuls of the fish mixture to fill the ramekin 7/8 of the way to the top. Top each ramekin with red chiles slices and cilantro leaves lime leaves for color. Add a teaspoon of coconut milk around the edges of the terrine.

Steam the filled ramekins in a closed steamer for 20 minutes. Check for doneness by inserting a toothpick in the fish mixture; if the toothpick come out clean and the top of the mixture is firm to the touch, the fish terrine is cooked. The oil from the coconut milk will separate out and float to the top, but don't be alarmed. After the terrine is cooled the oil will harden again and the top of the terrine will show off the colorful garnish. Serve warm or at room temperature.

Pie on Ice

Learning to cook on an Antarctic glacier.

November, 2005 found me on a glacier in Antarctica, where I was researching an upcoming novel in my forensic geology mystery series. Karl Kreutz's remote field camp was nothing more than an array of little tents, completely dwarfed by the immense expanse of ice on which it rested, and the ragged peaks of the mighty Olympus Range, on which our glacier sat like a saddle on a horse's back.

The men who comprised Karl's team—Bruce, Toby, Terry, and Mike—cared dearly about food but didn't have much time to cook. They were busy drilling into the ice to retrieve a long cylinder to be analyzed for indicators of climate change. It was up and at 'em in the mornings, lunch was a hurried affair, and in the evenings, they just wanted to stuff their faces and head off towards the warmth of their sleeping bags. Their biggest discussions centered around which package of cookies to open next. Toby was keen on Chips Ahoy, while Mike had more subtle tastes and tended to ferret out a genteel brand of ginger snaps from New Zealand.

Food is of critical importance to the success of any project in Antarctica. It's wildly beautiful and everybody who goes there already adores being in such places, but the stresses of hard work and being so far separated from loved ones are not to be trifled with, and, need I mention, it is *cold* out there! The National Science Foundation's U.S.

Antarctic Program, which supported the project, takes pains to teach participants that food equals fuel, and we are the furnace. Eat, eat, eat, they tell us. And they supply the best foods they can.

Refrigeration is no problem, and there are no vermin to protect against, either. When I arrived at the camp, the men had been there for several weeks already, and they had fallen into a routine around food, selecting items that were quick to cook and easy to find in the jumble of boxes that doubled as anchors for the cook tent. We took turns preparing meals on two propane-fired Coleman stoves. Halfway

Antarctica covers 5.4 million square miles and is comprised of 90 percent of the world's ice. Although the lowest recorded temperature in history (-128.5°F) was recorded there, it is considered a desert due to its lack of precipitation (roughly the same as the Sahara Desert). There is no arable land on Antarctica, and all food (other than local fish) must be brought in by boat or plane to one of the 60+ research stations located on the continent.

—SB

through my week with them, a pair of helicopters arrived to move us and all of our equipment to a second mountain-top glacier, and brought a resupply of food. In our new home, Mike and Terry got out the chain saw and cut a deep freeze for the meats, while Bruce, Karl, and Toby again threw the rest of the boxes around the skirts of the cook tent to keep the rig from blowing away with the wind.

A few "freshies" had been sent out with the load: Three oranges and two bananas. Fresh foods are rare in Antarctica. They have to be flown in from New Zealand on the military transports, space permitting, and too often bad weather develops on the ice and the planes have to "boomerang" back to Christchurch, where all fresh foods soon perish in the summer heat while they wait for the storm to blow out. Six weeks total on the continent gave me a whole new appreciation for the succulence of lettuce, which in that time I saw exactly twice, and the miracles of apples, which I had once. I enjoyed these in the galley at McMurdo Station, which is where the planes make their landing. It's even rarer for any such frost-tender delectables to make it out into the remoteness of a field camp.

Terry parsed the bananas among those interested quick before they turned black in the cold, and, as an after-dinner treat, cut the oranges into quadrants, making two apiece. They ate each bit of their wedges, and Terry set his skins aside to dry on a toasting plate to flavor some other dish. I ate only one of my quarters and left the other on the edge of the table. I've never been fond of eating oranges that way; the fibers stick in my teeth. At length, I noticed that people were staring at the remaining wedge. They were trying to be polite, but it was clearly a strain. Karl, who was sitting closest, observed it with something approaching religious devotion.

"That's up for grabs," I said.

Karl's hand shot out faster than a gecko's tongue, snatching it into the cover of his palm. Then, with consummate restraint, he cut the quarter in half and offered one of the bits to Bruce. Bruce sighed, gazing on it with a humility that mirrored the immense courtesy of Karl's gesture. "That's a mighty kind offer," he said, and took it in his hand lovingly.

To make myself useful—and in gastronomic self-defense—I took it upon myself to inventory the food. The boxes had been packed in interest of conserving space, with no consideration for grouping like items. It soon became clear that the guys didn't really know what they had. And one of their Coleman stoves had a grill. And stuffed underneath the aluminum cook table, amongst a very miscellaneous collection of cooking pots, I found a Coleman oven. They'd been eating ramen noodles when they could have had steak!

I began to sort the foods, and found condiments, spices, herbs, and dried mushrooms. There was a four-kilogram sack of scallops at the bottom of one box, and the pork chops, steaks, and fish cutlets were scattered across three, a few here and a few there. There were more bricks of cheese than the men seemed to know about, and there were bags of frozen vegetables and berries that were being all but ignored.

I re-sorted the stores and then got out a marking pen and labeled all the boxes, but on Sunday, when the men took the time to make pancakes rather than just toasting frozen bagels and chugging coffee for breakfast, they sprinkled small handfuls of the berries on top of the cakes after they came out of the pan, still frozen! I was appalled.

My maternal instincts came to the fore. I began to assert myself, starting with a nice prawn-and-scallop stir-fry with shitake mushrooms, green beans, and carrots over brown rice, with gingerbread for dessert. This last came from a packaged mix which is not my preference, but any port in the storm, and just like Mike I have a thing for ginger. When he saw what I was making, he hovered over that oven, anxious that I might burn it, but by some miracle it came out just right. As he plunged the first forkful into his mouth, he closed his eyes, and after he opened them again, gave me a look that was worth every instant of the time I had spent cooking.

On my last morning in camp, my seventh day on the ice, I rose early and dug from the food stores all the ingredients of a thank-you present for these kind men who had supported me in my splendid visit to the ice wilds: Flour, butter, salt, strawberries, blackberries, sugar, and cornstarch. I poured the berries into a bowl and sprinkled on the sugar and cornstarch, then turned to the flour. Someone in the food storehouse had packaged it in small zip-lock bags, pre-measured. Dredging a pie crust recipe from memory, I cut the butter into the flour and salt and reached for water from the big pot on the stove. As first up that morning, I had started the daily process of melting enough snow for drinking water. For the first time ever in my career in pie making, I had to add hot water to get the ingredients properly mixed. Quick before the men began to arrive for their morning bagel-thawing ceremony, I put lids on both bowls and hid them at the end of the tent. It wasn't any problem keeping them chilled. The floor of that tent sat directly on the ice, and even the top inch of the enclosure seldom rose above forty degrees with both stoves running full blast.

After the men had gone to work, I put the Coleman oven on one of the stoves, fired it up, and reached for the pie crust, which was now properly rested. Here I ran into a snag: The cook kit was remarkably detailed, but there was no rolling pin. No worry, I borrowed their vodka bottle and rolled it out. The freezing cold aluminum cook table made this a snap. Having cracked into the liquor stores, I sprinkled a little Grand Marnier over the berries as I loaded them into the crust to give my pie a little extra yum.

The next problem was that the oven just wouldn't come up to 425 degrees. At full blast in that environment, it topped out at about 325. Nothing daunted, I just left it in longer—an hour and a half, to be exact—watching carefully for the first bubbles of juice to appear through the slits in the crust. In the meantime I rolled out the leftover strips of crust just as my grandmother had taught me and laid them out in a separate pan to be baked up for a mid-morning snack. I thawed out a jar of raspberry jam to spread over most of them before I placed them in the oven, but for Mike's strips, I mixed up a combination of brown sugar and ground ginger.

When the crust strips were ready, I carried them down the slope to the drilling tent, and walked first to the position where Mike knelt sharpening the dill bits. I bent down and pointed to his, saying only, "These two are brown sugar and ginger."

Very delicately, he lifted one from the pan and placed it in his mouth. "Sarah," he said, "you have been hiding your talents."

It was a sunny day with no wind, so at lunchtime when the pie was finally ready, the men arranged their chairs outside the cook tent where they could overlook the dancing peaks of the St. John's Range. I emerged triumphantly through the tent flap carrying my gift, a big knife, and six plates and forks. Mike insisted on taking my portrait with the pie, and then assisted in cutting it into sixths. Bright red juice leaked out onto the ice, and we scrambled to gather it up, both because we didn't want to waste it and because on this environmentally protected continent, this was considered an unauthorized release.

I ceremoniously disbursed these treasures with four-ounce slabs of cheddar cheese, no need for anything else on the luncheon menu that day. Then I took my seat and lifted the first forkful to my mouth. I thought it was maybe not my best but given the circumstances pretty good, and the scenery and company just couldn't be beat.

There was silence for several moments, just long enough that I began to wonder if my new friends might not quite like the meal I had prepared for them. Then Toby said, "Crap. This is the most flavorful thing I've had in my mouth in four weeks!"

Cupboard love can be the adventure of a lifetime.

Sarah Andrews is a geologist who writes mystery novels because scientists are really detectives in disguise. She visited Antarctica in November and December of 2005 on a grant from the National Science Foundation's Antarctic Artists and Writers Grant. She thought the food there was pretty darned good considering that there were hardly any fresh fruits or vegetables to be found anywhere on the continent.

RESOURCES AND REFERENCES

Research Tips

*T*he world has a lot to offer when it comes to cooking schools, classes, and culinary tours. The choices are myriad and research can be exhausting. The goal of this Resource Section is to provide you with a starting point to investigate the world of culinary travel. Specifically, the following topics are covered:

◆ Cooking Schools/Classes: We have endeavored to include only classes which include hands-on training. While there may be demonstrations with some of the programs and schools listed, these would be in addition to the hands-on aspect of the class. Organized in 5 sections and covering the Americas, Europe, Africa/Middle East, Asia, and Southeast Asia/Oceania.

◆ Culinary Tours: Similarly organized to schools and classes, there is quite a variety here in tour type, cost, and amenities included. Check out the website, read the fine print, and make sure you call and talk to a tour representative prior to booking, so you know exactly what you are getting.

◆ Internet Resources/Clearinghouses: There are a large number of web sites that contain extensive listings of schools, classes, and tours. This can be a good place to start if you are unsure of what you want or where to go.

◆ Recommended Reading: In addition to reference books dedicated to listings of cooking schools and classes, there are guides to culinary vacations, reference books on food terminology and ethnic food, and some basic kitchen dictionaries. Magazine listings are strictly food related and have web sites for reference, stories, and ordering subscriptions.

Because schools, classes, and culinary tours change regularly in scope, offerings, and prices, only those with web sites were included. This allows you to get the most up-to-date information, as well as being universally accessible. You may live in Mexico, but you can sign up with a British culinary tour to go to Spain. It also allows you to get a better idea of content, from class size, instructor credentials, actual tour itinerary, a visual look at lodgings and classrooms, and cost breakdown.

The book is dedicated to learning about culture through food, so we have tried to stay true to limiting the schools/classes/tours to those that were indigenous (a French cooking class in France, rather than a French cooking school in Cincinnati). In particular, the United States was a difficult territory to cover. While there are an enormous number of recreational schools and classes available in the United States, we list those that focused on regional American cuisines, such as Tex-Mex, Creole/Cajun, or even California Fresh.

The variety offered in schools, classes, and culinary tours can be very intimidating. It can be helpful to start by asking yourself a few questions to help narrow down your search. To aid you, we have provided a list of the typical considerations you should weigh before booking that travel itinerary.

Cost: How much do you want to spend? Expensive doesn't always mean the best. Many high-priced, popular classes are fully booked, not allowing individual attention that a student might need with a new cuisine and ingredients. Alternatively, many small home-based classes use only what is affordable and may not be able to offer as full a range of dishes that a more traditional class would offer.

Length of Class or Tour: How long do you want to spend in a classroom or gone from home on holiday? While there are a few classes out there for half-day, typically the shortest term would be a one-day class. Most schools and classes offer a range of classes, lasting from one day to one week. Culinary tours generally last 7–14 days.

Size of Class: How much individual attention do you need? Do you learn well in a quiet or livelier environment? A small class allows more individual attention and works well for the neophyte and anyone reticent about asking questions in a large group format. A medium-sized class allows for a more convivial atmosphere and the opportunity to meet more people and compare notes. A large class will be noisier and you may find yourself sharing in making recipes, which can be a good thing.

Type of Class: This is where it gets a little trickier. Casual environments include homes, as well as kitchens in B&Bs, villas, and other small lodgings. Classes held in cooking schools, restaurants, and hotels are professional kitchens, completely outfitted with all the latest gadgetry. A free-standing class is one where accommodations are not included. Resorts, cruises, B&Bs, and villas are examples of all-inclusive tours, where your food, accommodation, and class are all part of the price. And what do you want the price to include? Just cooking lessons? Trips to local producers, markets, growers, wineries? Non-food related cultural tours?

Type of Food / Destination: What kind of food are you interested in learning about? Tapas in Spain, gumbo in New Orleans, curries in India? If you can narrow your focus, to at least a region, your research will be substantially narrowed.

Level of Difficulty: What kind of cook are you? A dedicated foodie who cooks international food regularly and is familiar with obscure ingredients might opt for a higher level of difficulty, while a recent college graduate on intimate terms with a microwave might be looking to learn the basics of French pastry. Think of how comfortable you would be with the cuisine choice, and let that be your guide.

No matter your budget, interest, or level of knowledge, we are sure you will be able to find something to fill your culinary travel requirements in one or more of the resources listed here. We sincerely hope that you enjoy learning something new, both culturally and gastronomically.

Culinary Schools/Classes

The Americas

Cooking Cajun
www.cookingcajun.com
Located in the Riverwalk Marketplace in New Orleans, this school has over 15,000 students per year.

Cooper's Cove Guesthouse & B&B
www.cooperscove.com
World-renowned guesthouse in British Columbia featuring Chef Angelo Prosperi-Porta and his cooking school. Packages include room, breakfast, cooking class, plus 5-course dinner.

Copia: The American Center for Wine, Food & the Arts
www.copia.org/content/food_programs
Interactive food center located in the Napa Valley, which offers daily food classes and regularly scheduled food programs.

Cordon Bleu
www.cordonbleu.net
Offering short courses and gourmet sessions. Programs vary by locations.

Culinary Institute of America
www.ciachef.edu/enthusiasts/programs
The prestigious CIA offers a variety of programs to food enthusiasts at several of their campuses.

A Culinary Journey of Hawaii Regional Cuising at Sugar House
www.bevgannon.com
Week-long culinary adventures and cooking classes at Sugar House, a traditional Hawaiian plantation house that now operates as a B&B and event center. Led by Bev Gannon of the famous Hali'imaile general store, on the flank of Maui's famous volcano, Haleakala.

Gourmet Retreats

www.gourmetretreats.com

Cooking adventures in the heart of the Napa Valley.

Greenbrier Gourmet Culinary School

www.greenbrier.com

One of America's oldest and premier resorts offers a continuing list of classes for its guests, including such culinary gems as BBQ University with the author of *The Barbecue Bible*.

La Villa Bonita School of Mexican Cuisine

www.lavillabonita.com

Cooking school and relaxing culinary vacation with noted chef Ana Garcia in Cuernavaca, Mexico.

Louisiana School of Cooking

www.louisianaschoolofcooking.com

Run by Chef Patrick Mould, this school focuses on regional cuisine and also offers online cooking classes.

Mardi Gras School of Cooking

www.mardigrasworld.com/cooking/classes/html

Cooking school offering guest houses along with classes on authentic Creole and Cajun cuisine.

Mexican Home Cooking School

http://mexicanhomecooking.com

This school is set in a B&B retreat environment and teaches traditional Mexican cuisine, highlighting its Spanish, French and indigenous influences.

New Orleans Cooking Experience

www.neworleanscookingexperience.com

Authentic Creole and Cajun cuisine taught in an 18th-century plantation house that also serves as a B&B.

Polanco Tours

www.internetsanmiguel.com/polanco/

One-day Mexican cooking classes in San Miguel de Allende, Mexico.

Ramekins Sonoma Valley Cooking School
www.ramekins.com
A combination cooking school and B&B offering demonstrations and hands-on classes.

Santa Fe School of Cooking
www.santafeschoolofcooking.com
Offering classes in Southwestern cuisine.

Seasons of My Heart
www.seasonsofmyheart.com
Chef and cookbook author Susanna Trilling runs a cooking school, B&B, as well as culinary tours in Oaxaca, Mexico.

Tante Marie's Cooking School
www.tantemarie.com
A small private cooking school in San Francisco, they offer one-week vacation courses and weekend workshops.

Wine Country Cooking
www.winecountrycooking.com
Located on an estate near Niagara-on-the-Lake, this is Canada's first winery cooking school. Cooking classes, culinary weekends, and culinary vacations are all offered, using fresh local products and exploring the relationship between wine and food.

Europe

A La Bonne Cocotte
www.lydiemarshall.com
Cookbook author Lydie Marshall offers cooking classes at her home, a medieval fortress, an hour north of Avignon. Students may stay at the Chateau.

Aldeburgh Cookery School
www.aldeburghcookeryschool.com
Located in Suffolk, England, this school offers full-day, hands-on courses using fresh, local products.

At Home with Patricia Wells
www.patriciawells.com
Popular cooking classes in Paris or Provence with well-known cookbook author Patricia Wells. Classes in 2006 and 2007 are booked, but you can get on a waiting list.

Badia a Coltibuono
http://coltibuono.com
A B&B offering courses in classical Tuscan cuisine, focusing on the fresh products of the region.

Ballymaloe Cookery School
www.cookingisfun.ie/schoolcourses/courseindex.htm
Half-day, full-day, 2-day and 4-day courses on traditional Irish cuisine.

Belle Isle School of Cookery
www.irishcookeryschool.com
Located in Northern Ireland, this school offers hands-on courses to introduce you to the local bounty and national cuisine.

Berry Lodge Cookery School
www.berrylodge.com
Located in County Clare, Ireland, this country house/B&B offers cooking holidays and culinary courses such as A Taste of Irish Cooking and Creative Pub Cookery.

Betty's Cookery School
www.bettyscookeryschool.co.uk/
Proprietors of the Craft Bakery and Betty's Café Tea Rooms in Harrogate, England offer bread-making courses, specialty chocolate courses, and their popular Yorkshire and Swiss courses.

Casa Caponetti
http://caponetti.com
A cooking school in Tuscany, Italy offering all-inclusive packages (airport transfer, accommodations, meals, tours, and classes).

Catacurian Culinary Vacations
www.catacurian.com
Alicia Juanpere teaches traditional Catalan cuisine in her family home hear El Priorat, Spain. Students stay in recently remodeled upstairs rooms.

Confident Cooking
www.confidentcooking.com
Residential weekend courses, day courses, and demonstrations at Manor House in a small Wiltshire village (England).

Cook in France
www.cookinfrance.com
Offering a relaxed hands-on cooking holiday in Dordogne, France.

Cooking with Friends in France
www.cookingwithfriends.com
One-week all inclusive class on the French Riviera featuring culinary history, hands-on classes, and gourmet dining in a foodie's paradise.

Cordon Bleu
www.cordonbleu.net
Offering short courses and gourmet sessions. Programs vary by locations.

Cours de Cuisine with Francoise Meunier
www.fmeunier.com/concept.html
Three-hour course includes preparation of 3 dishes. Also offers demonstrations and private lessons.

Cuisine et Tradition School of Provencale Cuisine
www.cuisineprovencale.com
Vacation getaways combining a B&B and Provencal cooking school in Arles.

Dunbrody Abbey Cookery Centre
www.dunbrodyhouse.com/html-files/school.htm
Culinary courses that emphasize fresh Irish ingredients and specializing in regional and national cuisines of Ireland.

Ecco la Cucina: The Italian Culinary Experience
www.eccolacucina.com
Intimate cooking classes at an estate in Tuscany. One-day seminars, or week-long vacations which include meals, accommodations, and day trips to cheesemakers, wineries, olive oil mills, and more.

Ecole de Cuisine du Domaine d'Esperance
www.esperance.fr
A French cooking school located in an 18th-century house in Gascony. One-week seminars are held six times per year, with transportation, lodging and meals included.

Fontana del Papa
www.cookitaly.it/
Learn Italian cuisine in a small family-run, secluded, 16th-century farmhouse.

Food Artisans Culinary Workshops in Italy
www.foodartisans.com/workshops/
Week-long culinary programs exploring the backroads of Italian food culture. Located in Campania, Tuscany, Piemonte, and Emilia-Romagna.

Good Tastes of Tuscany
www.tuscany-cooking-class.com
Hands-on cooking classes held at 13th-century Villa Pandolfini, as well as wine tours throughout Tuscany.

Giuliano Bugialli's Foods of Italy
www.bugialli.com
Located in Florence, and one of the first Italian cooking schools to teach in English, this school combines cooking instruction with full immersion in local life and culture.

Helsinki Culinary Institute
www.kulinaarineninstituutti.com
Half-day and full-day courses and workshops on Finnish cooking.

Hotel Pelops Cooking Courses
www.greekconnections.gr/cookery_classes.html
Five-day Greek cooking courses.

Institut Paul Bocuse
www.institutpaulbocuse.com
Week-long courses in the foundations of French cooking are offered to recreational cooks at this famed school located in a 19th-century chateau in Lyon.

Italian Cookery Course
www.italiancookerycourse.com
Selected as one of the Top 10 Cooking Schools in Europe by *The Observer*, this school at Casa Ombuto offers courses in Tuscan and Italian Mediterranean cooking.

La Cuisine de Marie Blanche
www.cuisinemb.com
Located in France, this school offers a wide variety of classes, including cooking, pastry, tasting, as well as longer term courses awarding a Grand Diplome.

La Divina Cucina
www.divinacucina.com
One-, two-, and three-day sessions, as well as tours. Located in Florence, Italy.

La Cachette Culinary Academy
www.lacachette.net/
An eight-day culinary journey with master chef Karl-Heniz Dickheiwer.

La Combe en Perigord
www.lacombe-perigord.com
Culinary vacations set in the heart of France. Guest chef programs, week-long classes, and the Un-Programmed Program, where you create your own schedule.

La Divina Cucina
www.divinacucina.com
One-, two-, and three-day sessions are offered in Italian cuisine, along with special culinary tours to Chianti.

La Manoir de L'Aufragere Cookery School
www.laufragere.com
Set in an 18th-century manor house in Normany, France, La Manoir offers Cordon Bleu gastronomic cooking courses, as well as accommodations.

La Varenne
www.lavarenne.com
Bilingual weeklong classes are held in the summer and fall at the Chateau du Fey in the heart of Burgundy.

Leith's School of Food and Wine
www.leiths.com
In addition to professional training, this London school offers evening, Saturday, and special interest cooking courses.

Manoir aux Quat' Saisons/Raymond Blanc Cookery School
www.manoir.com/web/olem/olem_a2a_home.jsp
One- two-, and four-day classes, which can include a 7-course dinner, luxury accommodations, breakfast and lunch, as well as the opportunity to watch and learn in the kitchens of a two-Michelin Star restaurant.

Manoir de Bellerive
www.cookery-in-dordogne.com
Located on the banks of the Dordogne, courses are offered in 3- and 6-day increments, and include visits to the area's castles, caves, villages, and prehistoric sites.

Nick Nairn Cook School
www.nairnscookschool.com
Located in Menteith, TV chef Nick Nairn offers one- to five-day courses focusing on New Scottish cuisine.

Padstow Seafood School
www.rickstein.com/padstowseafoodschool.htm
Led by chef Rick Stein, the courses endeavor to cover every aspect of seafood cookery. One of the few of its kind in the world, it is located on the coast of England.

Promenades Gourmandes with Paule Caillat
www.promenadesgourmandes.com
An intimate cooking school offering full-day classes. Operated in the Paris apartment of Chef Caillat.

A Question of Taste
www.aqot.com
Excursions, cooking lessons, and wine tasting in Seville, Spain.

Rhodes School of Cuisine
www.rhodesschoolofcuisine.com
Offering luxury vacations at their three cooking schools in France, Morocco, and Italy.

Ritz-Escoffier Ecole de la Gastronomie Francaise
www.ritzparis.com
One-week certificate courses open to professionals and amateurs at this famed school.

Scuola di Arte Culinaria
www.gestionecupido.com
Dedicated to promoting the culinary culture of Umbria, this school is located on a modern estate and offers a variety of courses.

A Taste of Provence
www.tasteofprovence.com
Culinary adventures set in a Provencal farmhouse. Limited to six guests, this all-inclusive program shops the local markets, provides hands-on classes, and local tours.

Tenuta di Capezzana Wine and Culinary Center
www.capezzana.it/
An estate producing wine and olive oil, they also offer cooking workshops in the estate kitchen in the hills overlooking Florence.

Toscana in Bocca
www.toscanainbocca.it/html/index.html
Culinary school focusing on history, tradition, and the rich variety of products available in the Tuscan region.

Toscana Saporita Cooking School
www.toscanasaporita.com
Italian cooking school offering small hands-on classes as well as tours throughout Tuscany.

Umberto Cooking School/Villa Delia Cooking School
www.umberto.com
Umberto Menghi runs the Villa Delia Cooking School in Tuscany, offering both all-inclusive cooking school packages, as well as stand-alone classes.

Walnut Grove Cookery School
www.walnutgrovecookery.com
Five-day all-inclusive cookery courses in the Loire Valley, featuring contemporary Continental cuisine with elegant presentation.

Africa/Middle East

Atami Hotel
www.atamihotel.com/Culinary-Tours-Turkey.htm
A small boutique hotel in Turkey offering culinary classes and tours.

Cooking Alaturka
www.sarnichotel.com/turkishcookingcourse.html
Held in the Sarnic Hotel in Istanbul, students prepare authentic regional Turkish and Ottoman dishes in a half-day class.

Cordon Bleu
www.cordonbleu.net
Offering short courses and gourmet sessions. Programs vary by locations.

Culinary Magic School
www.culinary-magic.com
South African and game cooking courses are offered at this school run by Celeste Labistour in Cape Town.

Rhode School of Cuisine
www.rhodeschoolofcuisine.com
Offering luxury vacations at their three cooking schools (France, Morocco, or Italy).

Asia

Chinese Cuisine Training Institute
www.vtc.edu.hk/~ccti/eng/all.htm
Half-day course with demonstration and hands-on cooking in Hong Kong.

Chopsticks Cooking Centre
www.discoverhongkong.com/eng/touring/experiences/ta_expe_1384981l.jhtml
Located in Hong Kong, this school offers 1-week cooking courses in Chinese cuisine. Half-day tourist classes are also available on a drop-in basis.

Cordon Bleu
www.cordonbleu.net
Offering short courses and gourmet sessions. Programs vary by locations.

Haritha Farms
www.harithafarms.com/cookinghollidays.htm
Weeklong course in basic Keralan cooking on an eco-friendly farm.

Konishi Japanese Cooking Class
www.seiko-osp.com/private/sekigu/kjcc
With over thirty years offering Japanese cooking courses, the school offers day as well as long term courses.

A Taste of Culture
www.tasteofculture.com
Located in Tokyo, food journalist Elizabeth Andoh offers traditional Japanese cooking courses, as well as such themed courses as "A Taste of Miso" and "Temple Vegetarian."

Yangshuo Cooking School
www.yanshuocookingschool.com
One- or two-day courses of regional Chinese cooking.

Southeast Asia/Oceania

Accoutrement Cooking School and Epicurean
www.accoutrement.com.au
Offering a large variety of classes onsite in New South Wales, Australia.

Baipai Thai Cooking School
www.baipai.com
Conducted in a home-style environment in Bangkok, half-day classes are offered Tuesday through Saturday. In addition to traditional Thai cooking, fruit- and vegetable-carving and personalized, private classes are also available.

The Blue Elephant
www.blueelephant.com/school/index.html
Classes in traditional Thai cuisine are taught in a century-old mansion in the heart of Bangkok.

Chiang Mai Thai Cookery School
www.thaicookeryschool.com
The oldest cooking school in Chiang Mai, classes are offered at two locations in 1, 2, 3, 4, and 5-day increments.

Cookery Magic
http://pachome1.pacific.net.sg/~ruk/
Singaporean cuisine taught in a traditional home atmosphere.

Cordon Bleu
www.cordonbleu.net
Offering short courses and gourmet sessions. Programs vary by locations.

Duck Under the Table
www.duckunder.com
Offers a wide variety of classes at their modern school in New South Wales, Australia.

Lanna Cooking School
www.fourseasons.com/chiangmai/special_features.html
Located in the Four Seasons Resort in Chiang Mai, this cooking school offers an introduction to Thai cuisine.

Mom Tri's Boathouse
www.boathousephuket.com/culinary.php
Located in Phuket, Thailand, Chef Punchun offers weekend courses on the secrets of great Thai cooking. Ten recipes are taught over the two-day period at the hotel overlooking Kata Noi Beach.

Puri Ganesha Villas
www.puriganeshabali.com
A Balinese hideaway offers a week-long course titled "Rice and Spice Adventure." Includes cooking, market and farm visits, and cultural and colonial history.

Royal Thai School of Culinary Arts
www.gourmetthailand.com
One- to fifteen-week courses in traditional Thai food, Southeast Asian cooking, vegetarian dishes, and regional cuisines.

Raffles Culinary Academy
www.raffleshotel.com/culinary.htm
Classes in Singaporean and Asian cuisine are led by award-winning chefs at the famous Singapore hotel.

Ruth Pretty Cooking School
www.ruthpretty.co.nz
Set in rural Te Horo, New Zealand, a wide range of full-day classes are taught by food personality Ruth Pretty as well as guest chefs.

Samui Institute of Thai Culinary Arts
www.sitca.net
Offering ½ day classes which include learning one curry paste and three different dishes. Classes rotate each day, Monday–Saturday, so that you can take 6 classes without repetition.

Snowball & Pemberton Food Workshop
www.spfoodworkshop.com.au
Hands-on cooking classes and 3-day tours of Sydney, Australia.

Sydney Seafood School
www.sydneyfishmarket.com.au
Located at the Sydney, Australia fish market, this school teaches locals and overseas "foodies" how to utilize seafood in a variety of cuisines. Twenty to twenty-five evening, half-day and full-day classes are offered each month.

The Thai Cooking School at the Oriental Hotel
www.mandarinoriental.com/hotel/510000256.asp
One of the premier urban Thai cooking schools. Located on the Chao Phraya, classes are offered 4 days per week.

Time for Lime
www.timeforlime.net
Professional Thai cooking courses on the beach in Ko Lanta.

Culinary Tours

Note: Travel and tour companies are listed multiple times if they have offerings to more than one continent/destination.

The Americas

Absolute Caribbean
www.absolutecaribbean.com/cuisine.html
Cuisine travel packages to such places as Curacao and Aruba.

APL International Cooking Schools
www.foodvacation.com
Tours to Costa Rica and Canada.

Central Market Culinary Travel
www.centralmarket.com/cm/cmCulinaryTravel.jsp
Travel adventures in San Francisco, California Wine Country, Mexico, and Alaska.

Cooks and Books and Corks
www.cooksbookscorks.com
Culinary excursions to California wine country.

Cook Sonoma
www.cooksonoma.com
California wine country cooking classes.

A Cook's Tour
www.acookstour.com
Food and wine hands-on culinary adventures to Mexico.

Costa Rica Culinary & Gastronomic Vacations
www.cerrocoyote.com/id11.html
Combining a 5-star luxury hotel and eco-lodge with a vacation cooking school. Guests learn to cook gourmet cuisine and about sustainable and organic agriculture.

Culinary Vacations
www.culinaryvacationsinc.com
Chef John Wilson offers culinary vacations to North Carolina.

Cuisine International
http://cuisineinternational.com
Provides culinary tours and vacations at specific schools in Brazil.

Epiculinary: Distinctive Cooking Journeys
www.epiculinary.com
One of the leading providers of culinary vacations, specializing in North America.

Five Senses Culinary Tours
www.5sensesculinarytours.com
Unique culinary experiences in California, as well as cruises and custom tours.

Food & Wine Trails
www.foodandwinetrails.com/index.html
Expertly led cruises and small-group trips throughout the world's best culinary regions.

Gap Adventures
www.gapadventures.com
Offering culinary tours to Chile and Argentina.

Gourmet Getaways
www.gourmetget.com
Vacations which combine luxury accommodations and small unique cooking classes led by master chefs.

Gourmet on Tour: Culinary Adventures
www.gourmetontour.com/index.html
Glossy high-profile company offering cooking courses, gourmet vacations and wine tasting throughout the world.

Jane Butel's Culinary Tours
www.janebutel.com/culinary.html
Culinary adventures to Mexico.

Les Liaisons Delicieuses
www.cookfrance.com/pages/home.php
Gastronomic adventures to Canada.

On the Menu Holidays
www.holidayonthemenu.com
Culinary tours to Mexico.

Savory Sojourns
www.savorysojourns.com
Offers exclusive and customized tours of New York's culinary destinations.

To Grandmother's House We Go Cooking Tours
http://tograndmothershousewego.com
Culinary and cultural tours focusing on legacy cooking in Oaxaca, Mexico.

Trout Point Lodge of Nova Scotia
www.troutpoint.com
An eco-lodge and wilderness inn located in a UNESCO Biosphere Preserve that offers culinary vacations. Focus is on the use and preparation of local seafood.

Worlds of Flavor
www.prochef.com/wof_travel/index.html
Operated by the Culinary Institute of America at Greystone, Worlds of Flavor leads culinary educational programs to Mexico, Memphis and the Mississippi Delta.

Europe

Active Gourmet Holidays
www.activegourmetholidays.com
Providing getaways in France and Italy that provide culinary instruction.

APL International Cooking Schools
www.foodvacation.com
Focusing on Italy, Spain and France.

Arblaster & Clarke
www.winetours.co.uk/gourmet-italy.htm
Italian wine and culinary tours to Piemonte, Naples, Istria and Tuscany.

Artisans of Leisure
www.artisansofleisure.com
A high-end tour company offering private and highly-personalized tours, including hands-on cooking classes in Spain and Italy.

A Taste of Vienna
www.herzerltours.com/culifr.html
All-inclusive tour that includes four-star accommodations and classes at Vienna's leading professional cooking school.

Bon Air Travel
www.kwik-link.com/database/tours.html
Full-service travel agency offering customized itineraries and food, wine and cooking school tours in France, Italy, and England.

Cantalupo Tours
www.cantalupotours.com/sicily.shtml
Offers a "Sicily's Culinary Splendors" tour with cookbook author Michele Scicolone.

Central Market Culinary Travel
www.centralmarket.com/cm/cmCulinaryTravel.jsp
Travel adventures in France and Greece,

Chocolate Lovers Paradise Tours
www.intrend.com/clpt/fs_index.html
Escorted tours in Belgium for chocoholics which include tastings and hands-on participation.

Classic Journeys
www.classicjourneys.com
Gourmet cooking tours to Provence, Tuscany, and the Amalfi Coast.

CookEuro
www.cookeuro.com
Personally escorted cooking programs to Tuscany, Umbria, Romagna, Provence. Also offering Kosher cooking programs to Tuscany, Romagna, and Provence.

Cook Italy
www.cookitaly.com
Cooking holidays and food market tours throughout Italy.

A Cook's Tour
www.acookstour.com
Food and wine hands-on culinary adventures to Italy and France.

CST Tours:What's Cooking on the Amalfi Coast
www.csttours.com/amalfi.asp
Tour includes accommodations, cooking classes, excursions and meals.

Cucina Casalinga
www.cucinacasalingua.com
A regional cooking school in Connecticut that offers group and private tours to Italy.

Cuisine International
http://cuisineinternational.com
Provides culinary tours and vacations at specific schools in England, France, Greece, Italy, Portugal, and Spain.

Culinary Communion
www.culinarycommunion.com/travel.html
Food worship in the form of cooking tours. Provence is the main destination, but additional destinations will soon be available.

Culinary Spain
www.culinaryspain.com
Specializes in exclusive gourmet food & wine tours and cooking vacations throughout Spain.

Culinary Vacations
www.culinaryvacationsinc.com
Chef John Wilson offers culinary vacations in France, Italy, and Spain.

Cumbria on a Plate
www.cumbriaoonaplate.co.uk
Gourmet tours through the Lake District of England led by food writer Annette Gibbons.

Deborah Krasner's Culinary Vacations
www.deborahkrasnersvermont.com
This Vermont cooking school offers week-long culinary vacations to Umbria. Includes meals, accommodations, excursions, and classes.

Diane Seed's Culinary Adventures
www.italiangourmet.com
Italian cookbook author Diane Seed leads culinary tours to Rome, the Amalfi Coast and in Puglia.

Discover France
www.discoverfrance.com/Getaways/tours/winetravel.html
Selections of cooking, wine and walking tours in France.

Discover Friuli
www.discoverfriuli.com/eng/wine/culinary.html
Exclusive culinary tours throughout the Friuli-Venezia region of Italy.

Epiculinary: Distinctive Cooking Journeys
www.epiculinary.com
One of the leading providers of culinary vacations, specializing in Europe.

Everyday Gourmet Traveler
http://gourmetravel.com
Personalized culinary tours of Europe's best destinations.

Flavours of Italy Ltd
www.flavoursholidays.com
Italian cooking holidays to Lazio, Bolgna, and Puglia.

Food & Wine Trails
www.foodandwinetrails.com/index.html
Expertly led cruises and small-group trips throughout the world's best culinary regions.

Gap Adventures
www.gapadventures.com
Offering culinary tours to Italy and France,

Georgeanne Brennan Culinary Vacations
www.georgeannebrennan.com/culinary_vacations.php
Award-winning food writer Georgeanne Brennan leads one-week long programs to Provence.

Gourmet Getaways
www.gourmetget.com
Vacations which combine luxury accommodations and small unique cooking classes led by master chefs.

Gourmet on Tour: Culinary Adventures
www.gourmetontour.com/index.html
Upscale company offering cooking courses, gourmet vacations and wine tasting throughout the world.

Gourmet Safaris
www.gourmetsafaris.com.au
Food and indulgence tours in Greece.

Herzerl Tours
www.herzerltours.com
All-inclusive "A Taste of Vienna" tour that includes four-star accommodations and classes at Vienna's leading professional cooking school.

The International Kitchen
www.theinternationalkitchen.com
Cooking vacations throughout France, Italy, and Spain.

Italian Connection
www.italian-connection.com
Tours offered in Umbria and Sicily, as well as customized culinary tours for small groups.

Italian Cooking and Living
www.italiancookingandliving.com
Unique itineraries throughout Italy comprised of visits to local food producers and wineries, tasting seminars, and cooking lessons.

Italy Cooking Schools
www.italycookingschools.com
Mama Margaret offers cooking, wine, and walking tours of Italy.

Jane Butel's Culinary Tours
www.janebutel.com/culinary.html
Culinary adventures to Mexico and Spain.

Joanne Weir Culinary Tours
www.joanneweir.com/tours
Cookbook author and on-air personality Joanne Weir leads culinary tours to Tuscany, Piedmont, Provence and Veneto.

Laguna Culinary Arts
www.lagunaculinaryarts.com/pages/vacations.php
Offering culinary vacations both domestically and abroad.

L'Arte di Cucinare
www.cucinare.com/html/italytours/italytours.html
Eight-day Sicilian tours featuring cuisine, scenery, and culture.

Les Liaisons Delicieuses
www.cookfrance.com/pages/home.php
Gastronomic adventures to France.

Li Tour: Culture Tours in Bulgaria
www.li-tour.com
One of the rare companies offering culinary tours to Bulgaria.

Mallorca Cooking Holidays
www.cooking-holidays.com
Hands-on cooking workshops in Mallorca, Spain.

My Croatia Ltd.
www.responsibletravel.com/Wholesaler/Wholesaler100418.htm
Offering two weeklong tours in Croatia: Cuisine and Spa holiday and Gourmet and Culture holiday. Includes accommodations, meals, classes, excursions, and guides.

Off the Beaten Path
www.traveloffthebeatenpath.com
Tour company specializing in fully guided, small group gourmet, wine, and cultural tours throughout France and Italy.

On the Menu Holidays
www.holidayonthemenu.com
Culinary tours to France, Italy, and Spain.

O Sole Mio
www.osolemiotour.com/tours.htm
Food and wine tours of Italy.

Papillon Select Tours
http://papillonselect.com/default.htm
Classroom, cruise and barge culinary tours in France and Italy.

Peggy Markel's Culinary Adventures
www.peggymarkel.com
Handcrafted, personal culinary tours to Tuscany, Morocco, Sicily, and Elba.

A Question of Taste
www.aqot.com
Offering food and wine tours throughout Spain.

ResponsibleTravel.com
www.responsibletravel.com
Culinary, cultural, and cooking tours to Greece, Croatia, Crete, England, Italy, and Spain.

Rhode School of Cuisine
www.rhodeschoolofcuisine.com
Luxury vacations for the gourmet traveler to French and Italian cooking schools.

Rosemary Barron's Greece
www.rosemarybarronsgreece.com
Cookery courses and tailor-made tours are available from Rosemary in Greece, including "Ancient Wisdom, Modern Tables" course, named one of the Top 10 Cooking Courses by CondeNastTraveler.com

Rustico Cooking
www.rusticocooking.com/tours.htm
Tours throughout Italy with the opportunity to cook with some of the country's top chefs.

Saranjan Tours
www.saranjan.com
Custom tour design and private guided services to Spain and Portugal.

A Taste of Spain Culinary Adventures
www.atasteofspain.com
Customized and scheduled gourmet food and wine tours throughout Spain.

Tasting Places
www.tastingplaces.com
Offering both cooking holidays worldwide, as well as master classes with famous chefs at their restaurants in London.

To Grandmother's House We Go Cooking Tours
http://tograndmothershousewego.com
Culinary and cultural tours focusing on legacy cooking in Sicily, Italy.

Toscana Mia
www.welcometuscany.com/en/index.php
Offering hands-on Italian cooking lessons in Italian countryside homes in Florence and Chianti.

Tour de Forks
www.tourdeforks.com
Uncommon epicurean adventures to Sicily.

Travel as a Second Language
www.spaincooks.com
Cooking and wine-tasting tours in Spain.

Tuscan Way
www.tuscanway.com
Offering courses in traditional environments, including a country house: Casa Caponetti, medieval home: Casa Innocenti, country estate: Villa Gaia, and upscale estate: Villa Poggiarello in Tuscany. All-inclusive.

The Juicy Chef: Tuscany Cooking Classes
www.tuscany-cooking-classes.com
Culinary programs in Tuscany including cooking classes, wine appreciation, and gastronomic tours.

Vallicorte
www.vallicorte.com
Tailor-made gourmet classes and weekend retreats in Tuscany.

Vantaggio Tours
www.vantaggio.com
One-week travel programs, including cooking classes, to Italy.

Venice and Veneto Gourmet
www.venicevenetogourmet.com
Teaching traditional Venetian cuisine in a local palazzo apartment near the Rialto market.

Worlds of Flavor
www.prochef.com/wof_travel/index.html
Operated by the Culinary Institute of America at Greystone, Worlds of Flavor leads culinary educational programs to Spain and Italy.

Africa/Middle East

APL International Cooking Schools
Vacation Cooking Schools Guide, Culinary Travel & Cooking Vacations
www.foodvacation.com
Focusing on Istanbul.

A Cook's Tour
www.acookstour.com
Food and wine hands-on culinary adventures to South Africa.

Cuisine International
http://cuisineinternational.com
Provides culinary tours and vacations at specific schools in Morocco.

Go2Africa.com
www.go2africa.com/activities/
A variety of tour offerings, some of which include culinary elements.

Gourmet on Tour: Culinary Adventures
www.gourmetontour.com/index.html
Glossy high-profile company offering cooking courses, gourmet vacations and wine tasting throughout the world.

Indus Tours
www.industours.co.uk
Culinary holidays to Tunisia and Morocco.

The International Kitchen
www.theinternationalkitchen.com
Cooking vacations throughout Morocco.

Joan Peterson's Culinary Tours
www.ginkgopress.com
Hands-on culinary adventures to Morocco and Turkey.

Kitty Morse
www.kittymorse.com
Cookbook author Kitty Morse leads culinary and gastronomic tours to her native Morocco.
Laguna Culinary Arts
www.lagunaculinaryarts.com/pages/vacations.php
Offering culinary vacations both domestically and abroad.

Les Liaisons Delicieuses
www.cookfrance.com/pages/home.php
Gastronomic adventures to Morocco.

On the Menu Holidays
www.holidayonthemenu.com
Culinary tours to Jordan and Morocco.

Peggy Markel's Culinary Adventures
www.peggymarkel.com
Handcrafted, personal culinary tours to Morocco.

Rhode School of Cuisine
www.rhodeschoolofcuisine.com
Luxury vacations for the gourmet traveler to Moroccan cooking schools.

Asia

Absolute Asia
www.absoluteasia.com/vie/vietnam_tours_asia_travel_culinary.asp
Culinary tours of Philippines, India, as well as other parts of Asia.

Artisans of Leisure
www.artisansofleisure.com
A high-end tour company offering private and highly-personalized tours, including hands-on cooking classes in Japan.

Eastern Journeys
www.easternjourneys.com
Offering 8- to 15-day "Tastes of Asia" culinary journeys to Hong Kong, China, and India.
Gap Adventures
www.gapadventures.com
Offering culinary tours to China, Japan, and India.

Gourmet on Tour: Culinary Adventures
www.gourmetontour.com/index.html
Glossy high-profile company offering cooking courses, gourmet vacations and wine tasting throughout the world.

Imperial Tours
www.imperialtours.net/culinary_tour.htm
One of the few tour companies to offer culinary tours to China. Includes banquets, lectures, demonstrations, hands-on lessons, and visits to tea and food markets.

Joan Peterson's Culinary Tours
www.ginkopress.com
Hands-on culinary adventures to India.

ResponsibleTravel.com
www.responsibletravel.com
Culinary, cultural, and cooking tours to China and Japan.

A Taste of Culture
www.tasteofculture.com
Located in Tokyo, food journalist Elizabeth Andoh offers traditional Japanese cooking courses, as well as such themed courses as "A Taste of Miso" and "Temple Vegetarian."

Southeast Asia & Oceania

Absolute Asia
www.absoluteasia.com/vie/vietnam_tours_asia_travel_culinary.asp
Culinary tours of Vietnam, as well as other parts of Asia.

Adventures in Thai Cooking and Travel
www.thaifoodandtravel.com
Based out of San Francisco, cookbook author Kasma Loha-unchit offers local cooking classes as
well as Thailand travel adventures.

Artisans of Leisure
www.artisansofleisure.com
A high-end tour company offering private and highly-personalized tours, including hands-on
cooking classes in Southeast Asia.

Eastern Journeys
www.easternjourneys.com
Offering 8- to 15-day "Tastes of Asia" culinary journeys to Vietnam and Thailand.

Food & Wine Trails
www.foodandwinetrails.com/index.html
Expertly led cruises and small-group trips throughout the world's best culinary regions.

Gap Adventures
www.gapadventures.com
Offering culinary tours to Malaysia, Thailand, and Vietnam.

The Globetrotting Gourmet
www.globetrottinggourmet.com
Culinary adventures to Vietnam. Burma, Singapore, Cambodia, and Thailand.

Gourmet on Tour: Culinary Adventures
www.gourmetontour.com/index.html
Glossy high-profile company offering cooking courses, gourmet vacations and wine tasting throughout the world.

Gourmet Safaris
www.gourmetsafaris.com.au/
Food and indulgence tours in Vietnam and Australia.

Howqua Dale Gourmet Retreats and Tours
www.gtoa.com.au
Luxury gourmet tours, cooking classes, and weekend retreats in Australia.

The Inside Route
www.insideroute.com
Culinary tours to Myanmar (Burma) with Michael Coon (CIA at Greystone) and his wife Valarie Brown.

Lemongrass Tours
www.lemongrasstours.com
Providing culinary tours to Southeast Asia including Thailand, Cambodia, and Vietnam.

On the Menu Holidays
www.holidayonthemenu.com
Culinary tours to Australia, Thailand, Indonesia, and Vietnam.

Responsible Travel.com
www.responsibletravel.com
Culinary, cultural, and cooking tours to Malaysia, Thailand and Vietnam.

Sri Lankan Flavours Cooking School and Tours
www.srilankanflavours.com.au/
Located out of Melbourne, Australia, this school offers classes on Sri Lankan cuisine, as well as cooking tours to Sri Lanka.

ThaiFocus Tours
www.thaifocus.com/tour/cookery.htm
Three full-day Thai cookery courses, each offering a different menu. You can take one or all three in Chiang Mai.

Tour de Forks
www.tourdeforks.com
Uncommon epicurean adventures to Sydney, Melbourne, and Tasmania.

Travel Indochina
www.travelindochina.com.au/
Culinary Discovery tours to Vietnam and Thailand.

Worlds of Flavor
www.prochef.com/wof_travel/index.html
Operated by the Culinary Institute of America at Greystone, Worlds of Flavor leads culinary educational programs to Vietnam.

Online Clearinghouses

Asia Food
www.asiafood.org/cooking_schools.cfm
Resource for finding cooking courses on Asian cuisine throughout the world.

Australia Gourmet Pages
www.classic.com.au/wizard/schools.htm
Selection of cooking chools available in Australia.

Bed & Breakfast Inns Online
www.bbonline.com/cooking.html
Listings of cooking schools and workshops at B&Bs in the U.S.

Best Cooking Sites.com
www.bestcookingsites.com/cooking_schools.html
Listing of cooking schools, classes, and culinary vacations.

Cooking and Culinary Arts Schools
www.cooking-culinary-arts-schools.com
Online resource guide to cooking and culinary arts schools in the U.S.

Cooking 'n' Pleasures
www.cookingnpleasures.com
Listings of culinary colleges, cooking lessons, cooking classes, and other related sites.

Cooking Schools.com
www.cookingschools.com
A comprehensive directory of cooking schools in the U.S. and 30 countries worldwide.

Cooking Schools Worldwide
www.cookingschoolguide.com/cooking_schools/
A guide to cooking school and culinary programs throughout the world. Listed by location or by area of study.

Foodreference.com
www.foodreference.com/html/culinary-tours-gourmet-tours.html
Education Resources section has a listing of Food Tours-Culinary, Cooking and Wine Tours.

Food Vacation.com
www.foodvacation.com
Listing of culinary tours and classes around the world.

GoNomad.com
www.gonomad.com
Special section on culinary tours and schools throughout the world.

Gorp Travel
http://gorptravel.away.com/xnet/one-product.tcl?product_id=115071
Clearinghouse for tour operators with a special section on Cooking Schools. Offering tours in Singapore, Thailand, Alaska, Italy, France, Japan, India, Argentina, Chile, and Canada. Constantly updated.

Gumbo Pages
www.gumbopages.com/la-chefs.html
Listing of Louisiana cooking schools for Cajun and Creole cuisine.

The Guide to Recreational Cooking & Wine Schools
http://cookforfun.shawguides.com
A free online directory provided by the Shaw Guides.

Peterson's Culinary Schools
www.petersons.com/culinary/
A listing of top cooking and restaurant management schools around the world.

The Recipe Link
www.kitchenlink.com/schools.html
Listing of cooking schools and culinary institutes.

ResponsibleTravel.com
www.responsibletravel.com
Specializing in unique travel holidays "that give the world a break," including a variety of culinary tours.

Sally's Place
www.sallys-place.com/food/chefs-corner/schools.htm
A review of cooking schools both in the U.S. and abroad, as well as fun learning experiences throughout the world.

The Splendid Table
http://splendidtable.publicradio.org/whereweeat/travel_italyschools.html
Lynne's recommended cooking schools in Italy.

TouristClick.com
www.touristclick.com/SpecialtyTravel_Culinary.html
Links to cooking school and additional clearinghouses.

Travel Wizard
www.travelwizard.com/culinary-vacations.html
Listings of culinary tours, wine tours, and cooking vacations.

Whispy Directory
http://whispy.com/culinary-travel-resources.html
Culinary travel resources.

Bibliography

Blum, Daniel. *Pocket Dictionary of Ethnic Foods.* Washington, DC: Word Craft Publishing, 2005. A handy reference guide to take on culinary tours abroad and to help decipher recipes at home.

Carucci, Linda. *Cooking School Secrets for RealWorld Chefs.* San Francisco: Chronicle Books, 2005. A basic book for cooks with technique illustrations, charts, cooking tips, and recipes.

Cooking Club of America. *Culinary Resource Directory: Cooking Schools & Tours (7th ed.).* Minnetonka, Minn.: Cooking Club of America, 2005. A directory of culinary and wince courses, culinary tours, in-home cooking classes, and various resources.

Culinary Travel Journal. Berkeley, California: Ten Speed Press, 2000. A Planning tool, resource and memory book to record your culinary journeys.

Damico, Serge. *The Visual Food Encyclopedia: The Definitive Practical Guide to Food and Cooking.* New York: John Wiley & Sons. 1996. This is a cook's companion to the markets and kitchens of the world, with helpful explanations and preparations of more than 1,000 ingredients.

Foster, Dereck and Richard Tripp. *Food and Drink in Argentina: A Guide for Tourists and Residents.* Argentina: Aromas y Sabores Publishing; US: Beagle Bay Books. Complete rundown of the food and wine of Argentina.

McGee, Harold. *On Food and Cooking: The Science and Lore of the Kitchen.* New York: Scribner, 2004. The updated version of the classic on gastronomic science and lore.

Montagne, Prosper (ed.). *Larousse Gastronomique*. New York: Clarkson Potter, 2001. The original culinary encyclopedia, this book is considered by many as a "must have."

Morris, Sallie. *Cook's Encyclopedia of Spices*. London: Lorenz Books, 2003. An expert kitchen reference book to the herbs and spices of the world.

Muir, Jenni. *Cooking School Holidays: In the World's Most Exceptional Places*. New York: Abbeville Press, 2004. Comprehensive description of 25 of the world's top places to take culinary classes. Includes beautiful full color photography and recipes.

Naftali, Joel and Lee. *Cooking in Paradise: Culinary Vacations Around the World*. New York: St. Martin's Griffin, 2001. Over 150 listings of international courses.

Norton, Gail and Diane Thuna. *Cooks in My Kitchen: Tales and Recipes from a Cooking School*. British Columbia: Whitecap Books, 2003. Originating out of The Cookbook Co. Cooks cooking school program, this book is filled with personal commentary on learning to cook, along with some great recipes and photos.

Peterson, James. *Essentials of Cooking*. New York: Artisan Publishers, 2003. One hundred essential coking techniques proffered by one of America's most widely respected cookbook writers.

Peterson, Joan. *Eat Smart Culinary Travel Guides* (Brazil, India, Indonesia, Mexico, Morocco, Peru, Poland, Turkey). Wisconsin: Ginkgo Press. Guidebooks focusing on local cuisine which help the traveler make the most of a culinary adventure.

Rolland, Jacques L. *The Cook's Essential Kitchen Dictionary: A Complete Culinary Resource*. Toronto, Canada: Robert Rose, 2004. Defining 4500 key food words, along with historical and cultural backgrounds.

Saulnier, Lewis. *Le Repertoire de la Cuisine: A Guide to Fine Foods*. New York: Barron's Educational Series, 1977. A standard reference book for the culinary world, it is also accessible to the average home cook.

Shaw Guides. *The Guide to Cooking Schools 2005* (17th edition). New York: Shaw Guides, Inc. 2005. Regularly updated, very comprehensive listing of cooking schools, cooking vacations, and recreational programs throughout the world.

Sinclair, Charles. *A Cook's Dictionary: International Food and Cooking Terms from A to Z*. London: Bloomsbury Reference, 2005. A veritable tome of international cooking terms and ingredients.

Thomson Peterson's. *Culinary Schools* (8th ed.) Lawrenceville, New Jersey: Peterson's, 2005. A listing of over 500 programs in the U.S. and abroad.

Treuille, Eric. *The Guide to Cookery Courses: Cooking & Wine Schools, Courses & Holidays Throughout the British Isles and Further Afield* (3rd ed.). London: Metro Publications, 2003. Two hundred pages dedicated to courses in the British Isles, Europe, with a smattering of U.S., Canadian, and Australian venues, as well as a listing of cookbook stores, cookshops, and gourmet magazines.

Zibart, Eve. *The Ethnic Food Lover's Companion: A Sourcebook for Understanding the Cuisines of the World*. Birmingham, Alabaman: Menasha Ridge Press, 2001. Comprehensive guide to world cooking.

Magazines

A La Carte (by La Cuisine: The Cook's Resource)
www.lacuisineus.com/alacarte.php

American Institute of Baking Research Department Technical Bulletin
http://www.aibonline.org/products/bulletins/technical/

Art Culinaire
www.getartc.com

Art of Eating
www.artofeating.com

Asian Foodbookery
P.O. Box 15947 Seattle WA 98115 (206) 523-3575

Asian Home Gourmet
Geyling PO Box 0900, Singapore 9138

Australian Gourmet Traveller
www.gourmet.ninemsn.com

Baking with the American Harvest
626 Santa Monica Ave., #526 Santa Monica CA 90401 (310)399-8680

BBC Good Food (U.K.)
www.bbcworldwide.com/magazines/goodfood/

Beard Bites
www.jamesbeard.org/beardbites/

Better Homes & Gardens
Better Homes & Gardens Eating Right, Living Well
www.bhg.com

Bon Appetit
ww.epicurious.com

Chef
www.chefmagazine.com

Chile Pepper
www.chilepepper.com

Chocolatier
www.chocolatiermagazine.com

Condé Nast Traveler
www.cntraveller.com

Cook's Illustrated
www.cooksillustrated.com

Cooking for Profit
www.cookingforprofit.com

Cooking Light
ww.cookinglight.com

Cuisine
www.cuisine.co.nz
Cuisine at Home
www.cuisineathome.com

Cuisine Magazine (New Zealand)
www.cuisine-mag.co.nz

Culinary Online
www.culinary-online.com

Culinary Online
www.culinary-online.com

Culinary Trends
www.culinarytrends.net

Delicious
www.deliciousmagazine.com/au
www.deliciousmagazine.co.uk

Donna Hay Magazine (Australia)
www.donnahay.com.au

Eating Well
www.eatingwell.com

Fancy Food & Culinary Products
www.fancyfoodmagazine.com

Fine Cooking
www.taunton.com

Food & Wine
www.foodandwine.com

Food and Travel (UK)
www.foodandtravel.com

Fork, Fingers & Chopsticks
www.fwfs.com

Gambero Rosso
www.gamberorosso.it

Gastronomica: The Journal of Food and Culture
http://www.gastronomica.org/

Global Gourmet
www.globalgourmet.com

Good Taste
www.goodtaste.com

Gourmet
www.epicurious.com/gourmet/

Gusto!
www.bendgusto.com

Italian Cooking and Living
www.italiancookingandliving.com/magazines/

Journal of Gastronomy
www.netphera.com/journal_of_gastronomy/
Magazine of La Cucina Italiana
www.piacere.com

Martha Stewart Living
www.marthastewart.com

Sainsbury's Magazine (UK)
http://www.sainsburysmagazine.co.uk/

Saveur
www.saveur.com

Slow (Italy)
www.slowfood.com

Square Meal, The Magazine (UK)
www.squaremeal.co.uk

Star Chefs: The Magazine for Culinary Insiders
www.starchefs.com

Sunset
www.sunset.com

Vogue Entertaining and Travel (Australia)
www.vogue.com.au/in_vogue/vogue_e_t/vogue_entertaining_travel

Waitrose Food Illustrated (UK)
www.wfi-online.com

Wine Country Living
www.winecountryliving.com

Index

Index of Contributors

Recipe Index

Acknowledgments

So many individuals have been kind to me when I have been on the road, many who remained nameless as they opened a door, a table, a generous heart and made the world seem a welcoming place: The woman on the bus to Manhattan who sensed my fearful innocence, took my hand and guided me to the passport office; the Indian gentleman who pulled me from flood waters in Bombay and the family who then cared for me; the woman at the train station in Milan who gave me lire coins when a vending machine ate mine; Ramli, my guide in Sarawak who quickly figured out I didn't want to eat at KFC or MacDonald's; all the French cabbies who insisted on correcting my grammar and everyone who has ever brought me a cup of tea. Cuisine may vary around the world but human kindness is the one ingredient we all need, and most savor. *Gracias, danke, mille grazie, merci beaucoup, terima kasih, vinaka, aabar, dyanyavaad, tukk, maherbani,* thank you and *mahalo* to all.

—Michele Anna Jordan

A huge debt of gratitude to my large and extended TT family, past and present, who have tutored me, tolerated me, and tasted everything I have ever made for them, especially James, Larry, Jen, Lisa, Tara, Krista, Tanya, and Raj. To my intern Emilia, whose sole job it was to help me get this one book out into the world, more appreciation than you can ever know. I'd also like to thank: The Oriental, Bangkok; The Boathouse in Phuket; The New Orleans Cooking Experience; Conrad Hao and the Taiwanese Government Information Office; Andrea Rademan and IFWTWA; Tea, for sharing her love of food and introducing me to the wonderful world of food blogs, and to the bloggers themselves who, along with my family and friends, have graciously taken on the task of testing the recipes in this book; and most deservedly to Jen, my travel companion and die-hard personal cheerleader, whose encouragement has led me down this path. To my family, for the collective culinary knowledge and wisdom of my grandparents, parents, godparents, siblings, and in-laws, thank you for sharing and providing the impetus for this book. To my long-suffering husband Jeff, who has tolerated my food forays into the world, and my children, Alex, Grant, and Gabe, who somewhat begrudgingly try everything I make, and have become (to my surprise) foodies themselves, I dedicate this book to you for your love, your support, and for actually making all things seem possible.

—Susan Brady

"In the Kitchen with Yuyo" by Augusto Andres published with permission from the author. Copyright © 2004 by Augusto Andres. This story originally appeared in *The Best Travelers' Tales 2004*, edited by James O'Reilly, Larry Habegger, and Sean O'Reilly.

"A World Without Latkes" by Robert Golling Jr. reprinted by permission of the author. Copyright © 1996 by Robert Golling Jr. This story originally appeared in *Travelers' Tales Food: A Taste of the Road*, edited by Richard Sterling.

"*Moqueca* Feast" by Avital Gad-Cykman published with permission from the author. Copyright © 2006 by Avital Gad-Cykman.

"Tastes of Generosity" by Judy Ware published with permission from the author. Copyright © 2006 by Judy Ware.

"Nawlins" by Sarah Pascarella published with permission from the author. Copyright © 2006 by Sarah Pascarella.

"Making the Small Tortilla" by Nancy Harless published with permission from the author. Copyright © 2006 by Nancy Harless.

"A Foodie Lession in Philo," by Lynell George reprinted from the September 11, 2005 issue of *The Los Angeles Times*. Copyright © 2005 by *The Los Angeles Times*. Reprinted by permission.

"Drowning the Snail" by Laura Florand published with permission from the author. Copyright © 2006 by Laura Florand.

"Tomatoes" by Mary Taylor Simeti excepted from *On Persephone's Island: A Sicilian Journal* by Mary Taylor Simeti. Copyright © 1986 by Mary Taylor Simeti. Reprinted by permission of Vintage Departures, a division of Random House, Inc.

"Mushrooming Before the Fall" by Deborah Garfinkle published with permission from the author. Copyright © 2006 by Deborah Garfinkle.

"Look Until Done" by Joan Haladay published with permission from the author. Copyright © 2006 by Joan Haladay.

"Mincing Garlic" by Michele Anna Jordan published with permission from the author. Copyright © 2006 by Michele Anna Jordan.

"Open House" by Catherine Watson originally appeared as "Into the Belly of Paris" in the March 11, 2001 issue of the *Minneapolis Star Tribune*. Copyright © 2001 by the *Minneapolis Star Tribune*. Reprinted by permission.

"Giuseppa's Secret Ingredient" by Catherine Ann Lombard published with permission from the author. Copyright © 2006 by Catherine Ann Lombard.

"Kitchen on Wheels" by Ann McColl Lindsay published with permission from the author. Copyright © 2006 by Ann McColl Lindsay.

"Basque Tortilla" by Melissa Kronenthal published with permission from the author. Copyright © 2006 by Melissa Kronenthal.

"Serendipity in Cyprus" by Wayne Milstead published with permission from the author. Copyright © 2006 by Wayne Milstead.

"Honor Thy Mother" by Rachel Newcomb published with permission from the author. Copyright © 2006 by Rachel Newcomb.

"Cooking with Jas" by Josh Flosi published with permission from the author. Copyright © 2006 by Josh Flosi.

"Flavor by the Spoonful" by Helen Gallagher published with permission from the author. Copyright © 2006 by Helen Gallagher.

"A Scandal in Senegal" by Tom Swenson published with permission from the author. Copyright © 2006 by Tom Swenson.

" A Taste of Ghana" by Lydia Polgreen reprinted from the February 1m, 2006 issue of *The New York Times*. Copyright © 2006 by The New York Times Company. Reprinted by permission.

"First, the Mustard Seeds" by Eileen Hodges Sonnad published with permission from the author. Copyright © 2006 by Eileen Hodges Sonnad.

"Japanese Salsa" by Laura Kline published with permission from the author. Copyright © 2006 by Laura Kline.

"Uzbek Cornmeal" by Ruby Long published with permission from the author. Copyright © 2006 by Ruby Long.

"Chef for a Day" by Bob Rice published with permission from the author. Copyright © 2006 by Bob Rice.

"Kimchi Cravings" by Jay Cooke published with permission from the author. Copyright © 2006 by Jay Cooke.

"Meat and Potatoes" by Jessica Jacobson published with permission from the author. Copyright © 2006 by Jessica Jacobson.

"Kaoru's Kitchen" by Tara Austen Weaver published with permission from the author. Copyright © 2006 by Tara Austen Weaver.

"Mama Rose's Coconut Bread" by Celeste Brash published with permission from the author. Copyright © 2005 by Celeste Brash. This story originally appeared in *30 Days in the South Pacific*, edited by James O'Reilly, Larry Habegger, and Sean O'Reilly.

"360 Days a Year" by Robert L. Strauss published with permission from the author. Copyright © 1999 by Robert L. Strauss. This story originally appeared in *The Advenure of Food*, edited by Richard Sterling.

"A Cooking School in Bangkok" by Kemp Miles Minifie reprinted from the November 1988 issue of *Gourmet*. Copyright © 1988 by *Gourmet*. Reprinted by permission of Conde Nast Publications, Inc.

"The Slaying of the Yabbies" by Lucy Friedland published with permission from the author. Copyright © 2006 by Lucy Friedland.

"Souvenir" by Cindy Wallach published with permission from the author. Copyright © 2006 by Cindy Wallach.

"Trin Diem Vy" by Richard Sterling published with permission from the author. Copyright © 2006 by Richard Sterling.

"Operation Kitchen" by William P. Pitts published with permission from the author. Copyright © 2006 by William P. Pitts.

"Pie on Ice" by Sarah Andrews published with permission from the author. Copyright © 2006 by Sarah Andrews.

Additional Acknowledgments (arranged alphabetically)

Selection from "*Banh Trung*: A Tet Tradition" by Michele Anna Jordan published with permission from the author. Copyright © 2006 by Michele Anna Jordan.

Selection from "Cooking the Lebanese Way" by Shelley Ann Wake published with permission from the author. Copyright © 2006 by Shelley Ann Wake.

Selection from "A Culinary Jam Session" by Mary Hughes published with permission from the author. Copyright © 2006 by Mary Hughes.

Selection from "Dream Come True" by Susan Brady published with permission from the author. Copyright © 2006 by Susan Brady.

Selection from "Extreme Camping" by Emilia Thiuri published with permission from the author. Copyright © 2006 by Emilia Thiuri.

Selection from "Feeding My Inner Wolf" by Carol Penn-Romine published with permission from the author. Copyright © 2006 by Carol Penn-Romine.

Selection from "Food of the Gods," by Deborah Fryer published with permission from the author. Copyright © 2001, 2005 by Deborah Fryer. This excerpt originally appeared in *Her Fork in the Road*, edited by Lisa Bach.

Selection from "Ghana: Fire and Water" by Penelope Wisner reprinted from Sallys-Place.com. Copyright © 2006 by Penelope Wisner. Reprinted by permission of the author.

Selection from *The Good Cook's Book of Mustard* by Michele Anna Jordan published with permission from the author. Copyright © by Michele Anna Jordan.

Selection from "The House on Bayou Road" by Susan Brady published with permission from the author. Copyright © 2006 by Susan Brady.

Selection from *How to Eat Around the World* by Richard Sterling copyright © 2005 by Richard Sterling. Reprinted by permission of Travelers' Tales, Inc.

Selection from "In a Sa Pa Kitchen" by Pamela Payne published with permission from the author. Copyright © 2006 by Pamela Payne.

Selection from "Kikuyu Hospitality" by Emilia Thiuri published with permission from the author. Copyright © 2006 by Emilia Thiuri.

Selection from "Life in a Chilean Kitchen" by Heidi Schmaltz published with permission of the author. Copyright © 2001 by Heidi Schmaltz. This excerpt originally appeared in *Her Fork in the Road*, edited by Lisa Bach.

Selection from "The Magic Elixir of Southeast Asia" by Michele Anna Jordan published with permission from the author. Copyright © 2006 by Michele Anna Jordan.

Selection from "Mandu Rolf-Bap" by Rolf Potts published with permission from the author. Copyright © 2006 by Rolf Potts.

Selection from "Meeting Alex" by Emilia Thiuri published with permission from the author. Copyright © 2006 by Emilia Thiuri.

Selection from *Mexico: The Beautiful Book*, recipes by Susanna Palazuelos, text by Marilyn Tausend copyright © 1996 by HarperCollins Publihsers, Inc. Reprinted by permission of HarperCollins Publishers, Inc.

Selection from "Mushroom Hunters" by Kay Sexton published with permission from the author. Copyright © 2006 by Kay Sexton.

Selection from "Oh, Hanukkah" by Lisa Bach published with permission from the author. Copyright © 2006 by Lisa Bach.

Selection from "The Old Way" by Susan Brady published with permission from the author. Copyright © 2006 by Susan Brady.

Selection from *On Food and Cooking: The Science and Lore of the Kitchen* by Harold McGee copyright © 1984, 2002 by Harold McGee. Reprinted by permission of Scribner, an imprint of Simon & Schuster, Inc.

Selection from *Postcards from Kitchens Abroad* by Diane Holuigue copyright © 1999 by Diane Holuigue. Reprinted by permission of New Holland Publishers, Australia.

Selection from "Priya's Wedding" by Emilia Thiuri published with permission from the author. Copyright © 2006 by Emilia Thiuri.

Selection from "Seven *Moles* of Oaxaca" by Susan Brady published with permission from the author. Copyright © 2006 by Susan Brady.

Selection from "Seville, Spain: Going *Tapas*," by Suzanne Dunning excerpted from TangoDiva.com. Copyright © Suzanne Dunning. Reprinted by permission of the author.

Selection from "The Spider Women of Skuon" by Rhymer Rigby excerpted from "Eating Tarantulas with the Spider Women of Skuon" at www.rhymer.net. Copyright © 2002 by Rhymer Rigby. Reprinted by permission of the author.

Selection from *The Story of Corn* by Betty Fussell copyright © 1992 by Betty Fussell. Published by Knopf, an imprint of Random House, Inc.

Selection from "The Ties That Bind" by Susan Brady published with permission from the author. Copyright © 2006 by Susan Brady.

Selection from "A Traveler's Pantry" by Jill Delehanty published with permission from the author. Copyright © 2006 by Jill Delehanty.

Selection from "Will You Be Having Pinstripes with Your Canard?" by Atticus Madison published with permission from the author. Copyright © 2006 by Atticus Madison.

About the Editors

When Michele Anna Jordan was offered a live sago worm at a farmers' market in Serian, Sarawak (one of two Malaysian states on the island of Borneo), she politely declined. It is the only food she has ever refused during cooking and eating adventures in dozens of countries on four continents. She ate durian in Kuala Lumpur and after her first bite of mangosteen bought a kilo and returned to her hotel, where she quickly devoured all of them. Jordan has written about food, cooking, culture and travel in newspapers, magazines, anthologies, and in sixteen cookbooks to date, including *California Home Cooking, The New Cook's Tour of Sonoma, Salt & Pepper*, and *The BLT Cookbook*. Her radio show "Mouthful" is available as a podcast at iTunes and Yahoo. Jordan teaches unique in-home cooking classes and is currently at work on several new books. See what she is up to at www.micheleannajordan.com.

Susan Brady has been cooking up a storm in the Travelers' Tales kitchen for the past fourteen years, preparing and plating almost 100 travel books. She has traveled from the shores of Southern Thailand to the chocolate shops of Belgium in her quest to taste the world's many cultures and is still hungry for more. A member of the International Food, Wine, and Travel Writers' Association, she is known as Mrs. B in the food blogging world (follow her culinary adventures at: www.eatingsuburbia.com). Susan and her busy stove reside in the suburbs outside of San Francisco, California.